The
Continual Burnt Offering

DAILY MEDITATIONS
ON THE
WORD OF GOD

First Edition — February, 1941 — 10,000

PRINTED BY

L. B. PRINTING CO.

19 W. 21st Street, New York City

The
Continual Burnt Offering

DAILY MEDITATIONS
ON THE
WORD OF GOD

By
H. A. IRONSIDE

Jubilee Edition

LOIZEAUX BROTHERS, BIBLE TRUTH DEPOT,
19 WEST 21ST STREET
NEW YORK CITY

1 9 4 1

To the Reader

1

IN Exodus 29: 42 we read of a "continual burnt offering" which was ever to be ascending to God from the brazen altar, where the people drew near to meet with the Lord as worshippers, to offer their praises and thanksgiving. Morning by morning and evening by evening a new burnt offering was placed on the altar that there might be no interruption in that which was intended to set forth the adoration of Israel to Him who had redeemed them.

There is no longer any material altar, nor need of any repetition of the sacrifice of the cross toward which all the oblations of old pointed, but we are exhorted to offer the sacrifice of praise continually, and this little book has been prepared with that end in view.

It is not intended to take the place of daily Bible reading, but rather to offer suggestive helps by focussing the attention on particular passages and offering simple comments designed to move the heart to a deeper sense of responsibility to God and devotion to our Lord Jesus Christ. The notes are mine, some new and others selected from my own books. The poems have been gathered from many sources. On Feb. 20, 1941, fifty years will have elapsed since this heart of mine was definitely won for Christ. That is why this is designated as "Jubilee edition."

H. A. IRONSIDE.

Chicago, 1941.

Why, Jubilee Edition?

✦

"Ye shall hallow the fiftieth year . . . it shall be a jubilee unto you" — Lev. 25 : 10.

✦

IT was on the night of Feb. 20, 1891, that I as a lad of fourteen entered into the knowledge of salvation through personal faith in Christ, whose love and grace have cared for me these fifty years since and brought me to this jubilee year.

H. A. IRONSIDE.

JANUARY 1

"In the beginning God created the heaven and the earth"—Gen. 1: 1.

WHAT a sublime introduction to the inspired Scriptures! We know not when this universe came into existence. Scientists differ by millions, and even billions, of years when they attempt to fix the age of the world. But go back as far as the human mind can think and we come right up against *God*. The universe is not the result of blind chance or of certain unexplained laws of nature. It is the product of a Master mind. A personal God brought it into existence. "He spake and it was done; He commanded, and it stood fast" (Ps. 33: 9). And this God has been revealed in Christ Jesus, and is the Father of all who believe in His Son. His power is unlimited, His wisdom is infinite, and all His resources are at the disposal of His saints as they cry to Him in faith.

> "The Maker of the universe
> As Man, for man was made a curse.
> The claims of Law which He had made,
> Unto the uttermost He paid.
>
> His holy fingers made the bough
> Which grew the thorns that crowned His brow.
> The nails that pierced His hands were mined
> In secret places He designed.
>
> He made the forest whence there sprung
> The tree on which His body hung.
> He died upon a cross of wood,
> Yet made the hill on which it stood.
>
> The sky that darkened o'er His head
> By Him above the earth was spread.
> The sun that hid from Him its face
> By His decree was poised in space.
>
> The spear which spilled His precious blood
> Was tempered in the fires of God.
> The grave in which His form was laid,
> Was hewn in rocks His hands had made,
>
> The throne on which He now appears
> Was His from everlasting years,
> But a new glory crowns His brow,
> And every knee to Him shall bow."

—F. W. Pitt.

"And God said, Let there be light: and there was light"—Gen. 1:3.

PLATO said, "The radiant light is the shadow of God." But David exclaims, "Thou clothest Thyself with light as with a garment." The declaration of the New Testament is, "God is light, and in Him is no darkness at all." It was His own brightness that, at His own command, illumined the darkness of that primeval earth. And the miracle of that first day of earth's recall from chaos and gloom pictures His present grace to the sin-darkened soul of men. For we are told that "God, who commanded the light to shine out of darkness, hath shined in our hearts to give the light of the knowledge of the glory of God in the face of Christ Jesus." He is the vessel to display that light throughout all the ages to come. Of the heavenly city it is written, "The glory of God did lighten it, and the Lamb is the light thereof." It was from His face that the light shone of old, and He is still the light of the world.

> "God in mercy sent His Son
>   To a world by sin undone;
> Jesus Christ was crucified—
>   'Twas for sinners Jesus died.
>
> Sin and death no more shall reign,
>   Jesus died and lives again!
> In the glory's highest height—
>   See Him, God's supreme delight.
>
> All who in His name believe,
>   Everlasting life receive;
> Lord of all is Jesus now,
>   Ev'ry knee to Him must bow.
>
> Oh, the glory of the grace
>   Shining in the Saviour's face,
> Telling sinners from above,
>   'God is light,' and 'God is love.' "

—H. K. Burlingham.

"Enoch walked with God . . . and begat sons and daughters"—Gen. 5: 22.

THE antediluvian patriarch, the seventh from Adam, who walked with God and prophesied of judgment to come and of the triumph of the Lord over all the forces of evil, as told so long afterwards by Jude (14, 15), was no recluse or ascetic. He was a family man, assuming all the responsibilities that are thereby implied. Yet in a difficult day he walked in fellowship with the Holy One as he sought to bring up his children in the fear of God and to keep them from the surrounding iniquity. In this he becomes an example for us. In order to walk with God it is not necessary to flee from the world to some monastic cell or to a convent's gloomy shelter. Whatever we may be called to do, however heavy the burden that may rest upon our shoulders, it is possible to walk with God and to enjoy His blessed companionship. All that is needed is a yielded will, and subjection of heart to Him who has saved us by His grace.

> "Who walks with God must take His way,
> Across far distances and gray,
> To goals that others do not see,
> Where others do not care to be.
>
> Who walks with God must have no fear
> When danger and defeat appear,
> Nor stop when every hope seems gone,
> For God, our God, moves ever on.
>
> Who walks with God must press ahead
> When sun or cloud is overhead,
> When all the waiting thousands cheer,
> Or when they only stop to sneer;
>
> When all the challenge leaves the hours
> And naught is left but jaded powers;
> But he will some day reach the dawn,
> For God, our God, moves ever on."

—Selected.

"And the Lord said unto Noah, Come thou and all thy house into the ark; for thee have I seen righteous before Me in this generation"—Gen. 7: 1.

IT is the desire of God to save the households of His people. Noah's family found a place in the ark because of their father's acceptance with God. Yet on their part there had to be obedience to the divine call. Invited by God, they entered the place of safety and so were "saved through water" from the judgment that overwhelmed the world of the ungodly.

It is still God's desire that the families of believers should share in the blessing vouchsafed to any individual member of the household. To the Philippian jailer the word came, "Believe on the Lord Jesus Christ, and thou shalt be saved and thy house." There was an evident response on the part of all the children, for we find him "rejoicing with all his house" in the knowledge of pardoning grace. So today the Christian parent is called to take hold of God in faith for all those linked with him by family ties, assured that it is the will of God to bring them into the ark, which is for us, Christ Himself.

"O happy home, where Thou art loved the dearest,
   Thou loving Friend and Saviour of our race,
And where among the guests there never cometh,
   One who can hold such high and honored place.

O happy home, where Thou art not forgotten
   When joy is overflowing, full and free;
O happy home, where every wounded spirit
   Is brought, Physician, Comforter, to Thee."

—Carl J. P. Spitta.
Trans. by Mrs. C. F. Alexander.

"He believed in the Lord; and He counted it to him for righteousness"—Gen. 15: 6.

IN three different New Testament books our attention is directed to this pivotal experience in the life of Abraham. In the simplicity of faith, he laid hold of the promise regarding the Seed through whom all the world was to be blessed. That Seed, as we are told in Galatians, was Christ. So, believing in Christ, the patriarch Abraham was justified. And in exactly the same way believers are justified today. To be justified is to be reckoned righteous. Justification is the sentence of the judge in favor of the prisoner. God justifies the ungodly—freeing them from every charge of guilt—when they put their trust in the Saviour He has provided, who was delivered up to death for our offences and was raised again for, or because of, our complete justification. When God imputes righteousness, He blots out forever the record of sin and gives the believer a completely new standing before His face. This is true of all who are accepted in the Beloved.

"A rock that stands forever,
　Is Christ my Righteousness;
And there I stand unfearing
　In everlasting bliss.
No earthly thing is needful
　To this my life from heaven,
And nought of love is worthy
　Save that which Christ has given."

—Paul Gerhardt.

"They went both of them together"—Gen. 22: 8.

THERE is a great mystery illustrated here: the mystery of the cross. Twice in this chapter we are told that Abraham, the father, and Isaac, the son, went both of them together to the place of sacrifice, the place where the only-begotten son (Heb. 11: 17) was to be offered up, though at the last, as one has well said, God spared that father's heart a pang He would not spare His own. So throughout all the ages it might be said of the Eternal Father and the Eternal Son, that they went both of them together. The cross was ever before God. Christ was delivered to death by the foreknowledge of God. Redemption was planned and provided for, long ere sin lifted up its ugly head to mar God's fair creation. All down the centuries the Father and the Son counseled together concerning the great redemption there to be wrought out.

> "Son of God, Thy Father's bosom
>   Ever was Thy dwelling-place,
>   His delight, in Him rejoicing,
>   One with Him in power and grace.
>
> Oh, what wondrous love and mercy!
>   Thou didst lay Thy glory by,
>   And for us didst come from heaven,
>   As the Lamb of God to die."

"For except we had lingered, surely now we had returned this second time"—Gen. 43: 10.

A FREE translation of these words of Judah's would be: "If we had not put it off, we would certainly have been back by now." He was referring to the contemplated second trip to Egypt, to get more corn, providing Benjamin was with them. Jacob could not bear the thought of permitting him to go, yet he and they knew it had to be. Procrastination only prolonged their exercises. When at last they acted as Joseph required of them, all went well. How often we lose much by putting off the inevitable! Many are risking the loss of their souls by waiting for a more convenient season. If you had not put it off, you might have been saved long ago. Or if already a Christian, you may be postponing obedience to some specific word of the Lord. If you had not put it off, what blessing might have been yours by now!

> "Life at best is very brief,
> Like the falling of a leaf,
> Like the binding of a sheaf,
>   Be in time.
> Fleeting days are telling fast,
> That the die will soon be cast,
> And the fatal line be passed,
>   Be in time.
>
> "Fairest flowers soon decay,
> Youth and beauty pass away,
> Oh, you have not long to stay,
>   Be in time.
> While God's Spirit bids you come,
> Sinner, do not longer roam,
> Lest you seal your hopeless doom,
>   Be in time."

—Anon.

"I have surely seen the affliction of My people . . .
and have heard their cry . . . for I know their sorrows"
—Exod. 3: 7.

GOD is no indifferent spectator of human suffering. He
feels for His people in all the sorrows and trials they
are called upon to endure. It is written, "In all their affliction He was afflicted and the angel of His presence saved
them." His great Father-heart enters into all the griefs
and wretchedness that we have to go through, and His ear
is ever open to our cry. We wrong our own souls when we
fail to turn to Him in our distress and restrain prayer before
Him.

"All thy griefs by Him are ordered,
    Needful is each one for thee;
All thy tears by Him are counted,
    One too much there cannot be;
And if whilst they fall so quickly
    Thou canst own His way is right,
Then each bitter tear of anguish
    Precious is in Jesus' sight.

"Far too well thy Saviour loves thee,
    To allow thy life to be
One long, calm, unbroken summer—
    One unruffled, stormless sea:
He would have thee fondly nestling
    Closer to His loving breast,
He would have that world seem brighter
    Where alone is perfect rest."

"When I see the blood, I will pass over you"
—Exod. 12: 13.

THIS was God's word to Israel and He could not deny Himself. All who were sheltered by the blood of the lamb, sprinkled on the door-posts and lintels of their houses, were as safe from judgment that night as God could make them. No angel of destruction could enter. The blood stood between the first-born and the condemnation of death, and so it is today for all who have taken their place in faith beneath the blood of the Lord Jesus Christ, God's Lamb, shed for the redemption of sinners. Judgment cannot reach them for it has fallen upon their Substitute already.

> "When God the way of life would teach,
>   And gather all His own,
> He put them safe beyond the reach
>   Of death, by blood alone.
> It is His Word, His precious word,
>   It stands forever true,
> When I the Lord shall see the blood
>   I will pass over you."

"Thou shalt not take the name of the Lord thy God in vain; for the Lord will not hold him guiltless that taketh His name in vain"—Exod. 20: 7.

GOD has said He "will be sanctified in them that come nigh" Him (Lev. 10: 3). "Holy and reverend is His name" (Ps. 111: 9). As we approach Him we should do so in reverence and godly fear (Heb. 12: 28). The name of God tells of what and who He is. It speaks of the divine character. Believers take His name upon them when they are identified with Him by profession of their faith in Him. The careless use of divine names and titles betrays a grossly irreverent state of mind, and is itself a grave sin against Him who is Creator of all men and Father of all who believe. We are called to "walk worthy of God" (1 Thess. 2: 12) because He is our Father and we are His children. Irreverence on the part of those who profess this high and holy calling is most deplorable, and is, in effect, to take the name of the Lord our God in vain.

Profanity is an abhorrent vice of which all decent people are ashamed, hence very few men are low enough to curse and swear in the presence of ladies or of persons of superior position and culture. But it is possible to profane the name of the Lord even though foul language is never used. To profess to love God and yet to dishonor Him by a godless and worldly life is to take that Holy Name in vain just as much as to be guilty of the irreverent use of holy expressions. In all our ways we are called upon to sanctify the Lord and thus to honor His Holy Name.

> "Holy, holy, holy, Lord God Almighty!
> Early in the morning our songs shall rise to Thee!
> Holy, holy, holy, merciful and mighty—
> God in three Persons, blessed Trinity."
>
> —R. Heber.

"Remember the sabbath day, to keep it holy"
—Exod. 20: 8.

THE Sabbath was given to Israel not only as a memorial of God's creation-rest, but as a reminder of their deliverance from the bondage of Egypt in order that they might enjoy the rest of Canaan (Deut. 5: 12-15). In giving them one day out of every seven for physical rest and spiritual upbuilding, God had their needs in view. His Sabbath was made for man. He designed it for His people's blessing. It is a sad commentary on the perversity of the human heart that many of them saw in this gracious provision a restriction upon their liberty, against which they rebelled, saying, "When will the . . . sabbath . . . be gone?" (Amos 8: 5), because of their desire to indulge in trade and the acquisition of wealth.

On the other hand, long ere our Lord appeared on earth, they had hedged the Sabbath about with so many of their own rules and regulations that what God intended to be a joy and a delight had become a heavy burden and an oppression of their spirits.

Similarly do men treat the Christian day of rest and worship, which for intelligent believers has displaced the Sabbath of the law. But how we would miss them were our Lord's Days taken from us and if we were forced to labor seven days a week with no respite for spiritual, cultural or physical upbuilding!

> "O day of rest and gladness,
>   O day of joy and light,
> O balm of care and sadness,
>   Most beautiful, most bright,
> On thee the high and lowly
>   Through ages joined in tune
> Sing, 'Holy, Holy, Holy!'
>   To the great God Triune.
>
> On thee at the creation
>   The light first had its birth;
> On thee, for our salvation,
>   Christ rose from depths of earth;
> On thee our Lord victorious,
>   The Spirit sent from heaven,
> And thus on thee most glorious
>   A triple light was given."

—C. Wordsworth.

"They shall eat those things wherewith the atonement was made, to consecrate and to sanctify them: but a stranger shall not eat thereof because they are holy"

—Exod. 29:33.

THE food of the priests was the offering of the Lord, In this they pictured believers, the priesthood of the new dispensation who, after having been justified through the redemption that is in Christ Jesus, now are to feed their souls upon Him who died for them and rose again. It is as we meditate upon what the Word reveals concerning our blessed Lord that we feast upon His body and drink His blood. The worldling cannot enter into this. It is only for God's anointed priests.

"God now brings thee to His dwelling,
Spreads for thee His feast divine,
Bids thee welcome, ever telling
What a portion there is thine."

JANUARY 13

"My presence shall go with thee and I will give thee rest"—Exod. 33: 14.

IT was God's promise to Israel after failure had come in, and, from their side, all covenant-blessing had been forfeited. But His love would not allow Him to forsake them, even as His grace demands that He never leave His people today. When distressed by a sense of unworthiness, how blessed to realize that He knew all we would ever be and do before He saved us at all, and His presence will go with us to the end and bring us into rest at last, for He has said, "I will never leave thee nor forsake," and we know that He is faithful that promised. He cannot deny Himself.

"How often I'd longed for a trustworthy friend,
  On whom in all seasons my heart might depend,
    Both my joy and my sorrow to share!
  But I met with so much disappointment and pain
  That I feared my seeking would prove to be vain,
    So I nearly gave o'er in despair.

"I was friendless and sad, my heart burdened with grief,
  And I knew not to whom I could look for relief,
    When I heard a voice, gentle and calm:—
'Oh, come unto Me, lay thy head on My breast,
  And I will refresh thee; in Me find thy rest,
    And I'll ever protect thee from harm.

"'I will soothe thee in sorrow, will comfort in pain;
  You never shall seek My assistance in vain;
    Then refuse not My offer of love.
  I will heighten thy joy; I will lessen thy woe;
  I will guide thee through life in the path thou should'st go,
    And will safely convey thee above.'"

"He shall offer it that he may be accepted"

Lev. 1: 3 (margin).

THE burnt offering typified Christ offering Himself without spot unto God for us, in ourselves so sinful and unworthy, but seen, by the Father, as complete in Him, "He hath made us accepted in the Beloved." So in faith we identify ourselves with the Offering, placing the hand of faith upon the head of Him who took our place, and in holy confidence we dare to believe that "as He is, so are we in this world." And so we bring to God our worship and thanksgiving all in the name of that worthy One who is the delight of the Father's heart and in whom we stand faultless in the presence of His glory.

"What great provision God has made
   In Jesus' death on Calvary!
   I hung with Him upon the tree,
And in His tomb I too was laid.

I rose with Him from out the grave—
   And how shall I who died to sin,
   Continue still to live therein,
The victor living as the slave?

At God's right hand He took His place,
   And while for saints my Saviour pleads,
   My heart for sinners intercedes
That they might know His saving grace.

Oh, what a name to me is given—
   A son of God, by second birth!
   I represent Him on the earth,
He represents me now in Heaven.

As Jesus dwells beyond the skies,
   I dwell within this world of strife;
   And as He lives within my life,
In Him I'm in the heavenlies!"

          —Barbara E. Cornet.

"The priest that offereth any man's burnt offering, even the priest shall have to himself the skin of the burnt offering which he hath offered"—Lev. 7: 8.

THE priest stood in the place of the Israelite who came to the altar with his burnt offering, all of which went up to God, being consumed in the fire of the altar. But the skin was given to the priest. He was to be dressed in the fleece of the offered victim. God, as it were, wrapped him up in the covering provided by the one who died. It is an Old Testament picture of the New Testament truth that all believers are made the righteousness of God in Christ.

> "Complete in Thee! No work of mine
> May take, O Lord, the place of Thine!
> Thy blood has pardon bought for me,
> And I am now complete in Thee."

—A. R. Wolfe.

"The life of the flesh is in the blood; and I have given it to you upon the altar to make an atonement for your souls; for it is the blood that maketh an atonement for the soul"—Lev. 17: 11.

YEAR after year as the blood was shed at the altar and carried into the Holiest God was telling out the story of redeeming grace. It is the precious blood of Christ poured forth at Calvary which alone has settled the sin question to the Divine satisfaction. By that mighty sacrifice iniquity has been put away and in the value of that blood the believer stands before God justified—cleared of every charge. Blood shed is life poured out, and it is through the life He gave up in death for us that we now live eternally.

"How often do I wonder
    That Christ should love me so;
But never can I answer
    Why He such love should show;
It passeth understanding,
    Out-reaching human thought,
That He, the Lord of glory,
    My soul with blood hath bought."

—E. G. K. Wesley.

"The seventh day is the sabbath of rest, an holy con-
vocation; ye shall do no work therein; it is the sabbath of
the Lord in all your dwellings"—Lev. 23: 3.

THE Sabbath of old and the Lord's Day now speak of
rest; the one of rest after labor, the other of rest before
service. People often ask, "Who changed the Sabbath?"
Properly speaking, the Sabbath has never been changed.
The Sabbath belongs to the old covenant, and is Israel's
Memorial Day. But Scripture tells us that after the death
and resurrection of Christ "the priesthood being changed,
there is made of necessity a change also of the law" (Heb.
7: 12). Under the new dispensation we see the first day
of the week taking the place of the seventh-day Sabbath,
and the Church has recognized this change from the beginning of the Christian era. We may safely say that the
guidance of the Holy Spirit led believers to give special
recognition to the memorial day of Christ's resurrection,
"This is the day which the Lord hath made; we will rejoice
and be glad in it" (Ps. 118: 24). This is the day of verses
22 and 23, when the rejected stone was made "head of the
corner," when God raised Christ from the dead.

"The day of resurrection!
    Earth tell it out abroad;
The Passover of gladness,
    The Passover of God.
From death to life eternal,
    From earth unto the sky,
Our Christ hath brought us over,
    With hymns of victory."

—John of Damascus,
Trans. by J. M. Neale.

"After that he is sold he may be redeemed again; one of his brethren may redeem him . . . or if he be able, he may redeem himself"—Lev. 25: 48, 49.

TO redeem ourselves was impossible. We were poor bankrupt sinners, sold under judgment. But One came from heaven to be a Kinsman-Redeemer, One who, though Lord of all, is not ashamed to call us brethren. He has redeemed us to God by His own most precious blood, having satisfied every claim that was against us and not only paid all our debt but provided for all our future.

> "My Redeemer! Oh, what beauties
> In that lowly name appear!
> None but Jesus in His glories
> Shall the honored title wear.
> My Redeemer!
> Oh, how sweet Thy name to bear!
>
> Sunk in ruin, sin and misery,
> Bound by Satan's captive chain,
> Guided by his artful treachery,
> Hurrying on to endless pain,
> My Redeemer!
> Thou didst my redemption gain!"

"The Lord bless thee, and keep thee; the Lord make His face shine upon thee, and be gracious unto thee; the Lord lift up His countenance upon thee, and give thee peace"—Num. 6: 24-26.

THIS was the blessing of the High Priest in Israel and it is, in a fuller sense, the blessing that is pronounced upon His people today by our Great High Priest, because of the finished work of the cross. The face of God now shines resplendent. Fulness of grace is extended to all who believe. The countenance of the Lord is lifted up upon us in happy approval, for peace has been made by the blood of the cross.

"Oh, the peace forever flowing
    From God's thoughts of His own Son!
Oh, the peace of simply knowing
    On the cross that all was done.

Peace with God, the blood in heaven
    Speaks of pardon now to me;
Peace with God, the Lord is risen,
    Righteousness now counts me free."

—A. P. Cecil.

"Caleb stilled the people before Moses, and said, Let us go up at once and possess it; for we are well able to overcome it"—Num. 13: 30.

THE name "Caleb" means *wholehearted*, and it was well suited to the character of the man who bore it. When the ten spies brought back their evil report of the land and made the heart of the people to melt, it was Caleb who quieted the troubled host by saying, "Let us go up at once, and possess it; for we are well able to overcome it" (Num. 13: 30). And when all the people murmured against Moses and Aaron and were on the verge of setting up a rebel captain to lead them back to Egypt, Caleb joined with Joshua in endeavoring to dissuade them from their evil purpose and to encourage them to go up in dependence upon God, and take possession of the inheritance He had promised them.

So when the rest were doomed to wander in the wilderness until all the men of that generation had passed away, these two faithful warriors were preserved alive as witnesses to the unchanging purpose and omnipotent power of the Lord of hosts (Num. 14: 1-30).

Forty-five years afterward we see this doughty old chieftain, at the age of eighty-five, claiming his portion, as promised by God, and entering into possession of Hebron and its surroundings. It is a marvelous picture of the energy of faith in one who was not of double heart, but wholly devoted to the Lord.

"True-hearted, whole-hearted, faithful, and loyal,
   Lord of our lives, by Thy grace we will be,
 Under the standard exalted and royal,
   Strong in Thy strength we would battle for Thee."
                                                —F. R. Havergal.

"When the dew fell upon the camp in the night, the manna fell upon it"—Num. 11: 9.

THE dew is a type of the refreshing influence of the Holy Spirit of God, "He shall be as the dew unto Israel." The manna speaks of Christ Himself, the Living Bread who came down from heaven to give His life a ransom for many. He came in the power of the Holy Spirit, taking the lowest place on earth. The manna lay upon the ground—so that every Israelite when he stepped out of his tent in the morning had to do one of two things: he must trample it beneath his feet or gather it up for his food. So Christ today is either spurned or received in faith as Saviour.

> "Nothing but Christ as on we tread,
>   The Gift unpriced, God's living Bread!
> With staff in hand, and feet well shod,
>   Nothing but Christ—the Christ of God."
>   —S. O'M. Cluff.

"And they came unto the brook of Eschol, and cut down from thence a branch with one cluster of grapes, and they bare it between two upon a staff; and they brought of the pomegranates, and of the figs"

—Num. 13: 23.

GOD permitted His people to see and taste, while still in the wilderness, of the fruits of the land to which they were bound. And so He does today. It is by the Holy Spirit that we who are journeying on to the rest which remains for the people of God, enjoy while here on earth an earnest of that which we shall delight in, in all its fulness, for eternity. In Rom. 8: 23 the apostle writes of "ourselves also, which have the firstfruits of the Spirit." Here are our Eshcol grapes and the pomegranates of Canaan. All that we enjoy of Christ now is by the Spirit. He delights to take of those things which concern our Risen Lord and reveal them unto us. May it be ours to appreciate and enjoy His gracious ministry.

"Our God is light: and though we go
    Across a trackless wild,
Our Jesus' footsteps ever show
    The path for ev'ry child.

At ev'ry step afresh we prove
    How sure our heavenly Guide,—
The faithful and forbearing love
    That never turns aside.

The manna and the springing well
    Suffice for ev'ry need;
And Eshcol's grapes the story tell
    Of where Thy path doth lead."

—Mary Bowley.

JANUARY 23

"Speak unto the children of Israel, and bid them that they make them fringes in the borders of their garments . . . and that they put upon the fringe of the borders a ribband of blue"—Num. 15: 38.

BLUE is the heavenly color. The ribband of blue on the border of the Israelite's garments was to remind the wearer that he belonged to the God of heaven and was responsible to act accordingly. So believers today are to walk as heavenly men and women in the midst of all the sin and corruption of this world. Our citizenship is in heaven. We represent another country. Here we are but strangers and pilgrims. The heavenly character should ever be manifested in all our words and ways.

> "Lord, since we sing as pilgrims,
>   Oh, give us pilgrims' ways,
> Low thoughts of self, befitting
>   Proclaimers of Thy praise.
> Oh, make us each more holy,
>   In spirit, pure and meek,
> More like to heavenly citizens,
>   As more of heaven we speak."

—M. Bowley.

"God is not a man that He should lie; neither the son of man that He should repent; hath He said and shall He not do it? or hath He spoken and shall He not make it good?"—Num. 23: 19.

FROM "the top of the rocks," Balaam saw further than he had ever seen before, and learned lessons to which he had previously been a stranger. Among these was the immutability of God's counsels. No power of man or of Satan can thwart His purpose. His Word shall stand forever! What comfort is this to the soul who trusts Him. He has promised eternal blessing to all who believe and He cannot go back on His solemn declaration. This is where faith rests: on the assured testimony of Him who cannot lie.

"The world may pass and perish—
  Thou, God, wilt not remove.
No hatred of all devils
  Can part me from Thy love:
No hungering nor thirsting,
  No poverty nor care,
No wrath of mighty princes
  Can reach my shelter there.

"No angel and no devil,
  No throne, no power, nor might;
No love, no tribulation,
  No danger, fear, nor fight;
No height, no depth, no creature
  That has been, nor can be,
Can drive me from Thy bosom,
  Can sever me from Thee."

—Paul Gerhardt.

"Thou shalt remember all the way which the Lord thy God led thee these forty years in the wilderness, to humble thee, and to prove thee, to know what was in thine heart, whether thou wouldest keep His commandments, or no"—Deut. 8:2.

ALL the wilderness experiences of God's redeemed ones are designed to bring them to an end of themselves and to cast them more implicitly upon Himself. If He suffers us to hunger it is that we may learn to appreciate the Bread from heaven. If He permits us to thirst it is that we may enjoy the more the clear crystal streams of grace flowing from the Smitten Rock. What memories all His ways will stir when safely home at last!

"All the way by which He led us,
All the grievings that He bore,
All the patient love that taught us,
We'll remember ever more;
And His rest will seem the sweeter,
As we think of weary ways,
And His light will shine the clearer,
As we muse o'er cloudy days."

"The Lord thy God will raise up unto thee a Prophet from the midst of thee, of thy brethren, like unto me; unto Him ye shall hearken"—Deut. 18: 15.

CHRIST JESUS is the Prophet, who, like unto Moses, is the Deliverer and Leader of His people, freeing from Satan's bondage and leading in triumph on to the rest that remains for the people of God. He who was with the Father from all eternity, became Man that He might qualify as the Mediator of our redemption. It was necessary that He partake of our nature apart from sin, that He might represent us before God and pay the penalty that we deserved. Now He is exalted as Prince and Saviour, and we are to heed His voice, following Him as we journey on to the Land of promise—to the inheritance laid up for us in heaven.

> "Great Prophet of our God,
>   Our tongues shall bless Thy name,
> Through whom the joyful news
>   Of free salvation came,
> The joyful news of sins forgiven,
> Of fears removed and peace with heaven."
>
> —I. Watts.

"When the host goeth forth against thine enemies, then keep thee from every wicked thing"—Deu. 23: 9.

GOD'S host of old was invincible so long as they walked in obedience to His Word. But sin tolerated rendered them weak and powerless against the enemy. We who wrestle not with flesh and blood but with wicked spirits in heavenly places, must deal unsparingly with every evil tendency in ourselves if we would triumph in the hour of conflict. Hidden sin, unjudged and unconfessed, will be our undoing when we attempt to meet the enemy. A bad conscience will nullify all our holy weapons and result in utter defeat. But if we deal unsparingly with the evil we can count on God to work in us and to fight for us.

> "Search out in me all hidden sin,
> And may Thy purity within
> So cleanse my life, that it may be
> A temple wholly fit for Thee.
>
> Oh, search my life, my will, my all,
> As now on Thee, my Lord, I call;
> Purge me from self, and sanctify
> My life, while Thee I glorify."

"The secret things belong unto the Lord our God; but those things which are revealed belong unto us and to our children forever, that we may do all the words of this law"—Deut. 29: 29.

MUCH that was secret in Moses' day has been revealed now. Jesus said, "I will utter things kept secret from the foundation of the world." All that has been revealed is for us, and should challenge our hearts to enter into and enjoy. There are still mysteries that we cannot solve and that God has not been pleased, as yet, to reveal, but some day all will be made plain. "In the days of the voice of the seventh angel, when he shall begin to sound, then shall the mystery of God be finished." Till then we are to appropriate in faith all that has been unfolded, as we study the Word in dependence on the Holy Spirit.

"O teach me, Lord, that I may teach
    The precious things Thou dost impart;
And wing my words, that they may reach
    The hidden depths of many a heart.

O give Thine own sweet rest to me,
    That I may speak with soothing power
A word in season, as from Thee,
    To weary ones in needful hour."

—F. R. Havergal.

"Yea, He loved the people; all His saints are in Thy hand; and they sat down at Thy feet; every one shall receive of Thy words"—Deut. 33: 3.

HERE God's saints are seen in three places. They are in His heart: "He loved the people!" How precious to dwell in the bosom of Infinite Love! What rest in the hour of strife and in the day of distress! They are also in His hand—the place of security, as our Lord tells us in John 10: 27-30, whence none can pluck them. Last of all, they are at His feet—the place of discipleship, learning His mind and will that they may walk in His ways. How abundant the provision which He has made for the comfort, security and instruction of all His redeemed ones!

"Low at Thy feet, Lord Jesus,
  This is the place for me;
There I have learned sweet lessons,
  Truth that has set me free.

Free from myself, Lord Jesus,
  Free from the ways of men,
Chains of thought that once bound me
  Never shall bind again.

None but Thyself, Lord Jesus,
  Conquered my wayward will;
But for Thy grace, my Saviour,
  I had been wayward still."

"And of Asher he said, Let Asher be blessed with children; let him be acceptable to his brethren, and let him dip his foot in oil"—Deut. 33: 24.

OIL is a well-known type of the Holy Spirit. He who dips his foot in oil will leave a mark behind him as he walks through this scene. It is walking in the Spirit that causes any life to count for God. Such an one will enjoy the fellowship of his brethren as they see Christ in his ways. And he will be blessed with children. It is the man who walks in the Spirit who is a successful soul-winner and knows the joy of seeing his children in the faith glorifying God on his behalf. Asher is the blessed or happy one. Happy indeed is he of whom these things are true.

"O Lord, whate'er my path may be,
  If only I may walk with Thee
  And talk with Thee along the way,
  I'll praise Thee for it ALL some day."

"Moses My servant is dead; now therefore arise, go over this Jordan, thou, and all this people, unto the land which I do give to them, even to the children of Israel. Every place that the sole of your foot shall tread upon, that have I given unto you, as I said unto Moses"

—Josh. 1: 2, 3.

THE book of Joshua is, in the Old Testament, what the Epistle to the Ephesians is in the New. It sets before us the inheritance of the people of God. Of old they were blessed with all temporal blessings in earthly places in the land of promise through Joshua. Today we are blessed "with all spiritual blessings in heavenly places in Christ." Joshua and Jesus are really the same names. Both mean "Jehovah, the Saviour." Joshua is from the Hebrew, Jesus from the Greek. This explains the seemingly strange statements in Acts 7: 45 and Hebrews 4: 8. The "Jesus" of those verses is, of course, really the Hebrew general, Joshua, who succeeded Moses as leader of Israel. He was distinguished for his faithfulness to God and to Moses, whose assistant he was (Num. 14: 6; 26: 65). He and Caleb were the two spies who encouraged the people to go up and take possession of the land when the ten brought back their evil report. By divine command Joshua was selected by Moses to be his successor (Deut. 34: 9), and was filled with the spirit of wisdom so as to enable him to lead the people into their inheritance. He was a valiant man of unimpeachable integrity, whose life and character challenged all to devotion to God and obedience to His Word.

"Oh for a faith that will not shrink,
  Tho' pressed by every foe;
That will not tremble on the brink
  Of any earthly woe.

Lord, give us such a faith as this,
  And then, whate'er may come,
We'll taste, e'en here, the hallowed bliss
  Of our eternal home."

—W. H. Bathurst.

"There shall be a space between you and it, about two thousand cubits by measure; come not near unto it, that ye may know the way by which ye must go: for ye have not passed this way heretofore"—Josh. 3:4.

THE ark going down into the Jordan pictured our blessed Saviour going into the dark waters of judgment for us. He had to go on alone, none could share with Him in the work of making expiation of iniquity. Just as the people of Israel waited until there was a space of two thousand cubits between them and the ark, and did not ·enter the river-bed till the floods were rolled back, so we, who had no part in the atonement, now obtain the benefit of that death which Jesus endured alone in order that we might be saved. We could only look on in awe-struck silence as He took our place and bore our penalty.

"Alone He bare the cross,
Alone its grief sustained,
His was the shame and loss,
And He the victory gained;
The mighty work was all His own,
Tho' we shall share His glorious throne."

—Swain.

"The manna ceased on the morrow after they had eaten of the old corn of the land"—Josh. 5: 12.

MANNA was food for the wilderness. It represented Christ come down from heaven to sustain the souls of His people as they pass through this scene of desolation. He took the lowly place with them and as they feed on Him they are enabled to make progress on the pilgrim road. But the old corn of the land speaks of the risen Christ. The corn of wheat fell into the ground in death. In resurrection He becomes the food of His people as they enter by faith into their heavenly inheritance. He sits now exalted on the Father's right hand, where faith beholds Him as the mighty Victor. Occupied with Him, His saints become like Him, and become strong in the Lord and the power of His might.

> "Rise, my soul! Behold, 'tis Jesus.
>   Jesus fills thy wondering eyes;
> See Him now in glory seated,
>   Where thy sins no more can rise.
> God now brings thee to His dwelling,
>   Spreads for thee His feast divine,
> Bids thee welcome, ever telling
>   What a portion there is thine."

—J. Denham Smith.

"Nevertheless my brethren that went up with me made the heart of the people melt: but I wholly followed the Lord my God"—Josh. 14: 8.

THE greatness of the character of Caleb is expressed in his name. He was not of double heart. Mixed motives had no place in his life. He had settled it years before that he was to be entirely the Lord's, and ever after he lived up to his name as the "whole-hearted." Undoubtedly, the cause of much of our failure today is that we are so lacking in this spirit of disinterested devotion to the will of God. Of old, the disciples were exhorted that with purpose of heart they should cleave to the Lord (Acts 11: 23). Jesus declared, "If . . . thine eye be single, thy whole body shall be full of light" (Matt. 6: 22). When we sanctify the Lord God in our hearts and give Him the place of supreme authority, all controversy is at an end, and the life is entirely under His control. This is the path of victory and blessing. No one can be successful in his Christian life who is endeavoring to have God and the world share his heart (1 John 2: 15).

> "All for Jesus, all for Jesus!
>   All my being's ransomed powers.
> All my thoughts and words and doings,
>   All my days and all my hours.
> Let my hands perform His bidding,
>   Let my feet run in His ways,
> Let my eyes see Jesus only,
>   Let my lips speak forth His praise."
>
> —Mary D. James.

"There failed not ought of any good thing which the Lord had spoken unto the house of Israel; all came to pass"—Josh. 21: 45.

WHAT a testimony to the faithfulness of God! He fulfilled His word to the letter, whether in grace or in government, as He brought His people through the wilderness and into the promised inheritance. As they looked back they could say, "All that God promised He has accomplished." So shall it be with those who now know Him as revealed in Christ Jesus. When we have ended our pilgrimage and from the vantage-point of our eternal home in the Father's house we survey the way we have come, we shall praise and adore Him who saved us and guided us to an assured habitation, whose Word has been our confidence through all the journey.

> "God, the Lord, shall never fail thee,
>   He thy cause will undertake;
> All the way His hand shall hold thee,
>   Faithful love can ne'er forsake.
>
> Rest then on His own sure promise,
>   For His word He cannot break;
> To green pastures, by still waters,
>   He will lead for His name's sake.
>
> Everlasting joy awaits thee,
>   When the earthly journey's o'er;
> Waiting for thee in the glory
>   There are pleasures evermore."

—F. Buckley.

"And they gave Hebron unto Caleb, as Moses said: and he expelled thence the three sons of Anak"
—Judges 1:20.

HEBRON means *fellowship* or *communion*. It speaks of that happy state which is the inheritance of the man of faith, who, by overcoming all difficulties, puts fellowship with God above every other good, and refuses to be kept out of its enjoyment by the hosts of evil—the world-rulers of this darkness, the wicked spirits in the heavenlies, who seek to hinder the believer from the present possession of the privileges which are his in Christ Jesus (see Eph. 6:12, in any critical translation). Of old the Anakim under the command of Arba had held this citadel and called it the city of Arba. But faith expelled the giants who defied the will of God and turned a scene of idolatrous rites and wicked revels into a place for communion with God. These powerful enemies typified the wicked spirits against which the believer is called to battle today. No foe can withstand him who dons the whole armor of God and defies them in the power of the Holy Spirit.

"Stand not in fear, thy adversaries counting,
   Dare every peril, save to disobey;
Thou shalt march on, all obstacles surmounting,
   For I, the Strong, will open up the way.

Wherefore go gladly to the task assigned thee,
   Having My promise, needing nothing more
Than just to know, where'er the future find thee,
   In all thy journeying I go before."

—Frank J. Exley, D.D.

"And Deborah, a prophetess, the wife of Lapidoth, she judged Israel at that time. And she dwelt under the palm tree of Deborah between Ramah and Beth-el in mount Ephraim: and the children of Israel came up to her for judgment"—Judges 4: 4, 5.

IN the book of Judges we have the story of Israel's repeated failures and God's marvelous intervention in grace, giving leader after leader to deliver His people from the deserved consequences of their own sins, when they turned to Him in repentance. He loved them too well to allow them to prosper in their rebellion against His word, but, on the other hand, He was ever ready to heed their cry when they humbled themselves before Him.

Ordinarily, it was some man of peculiar strength or ability who came to the front in the day of need and distress. But in chapters 4 and 5 we get the record of a woman-judge, Deborah, raised up in sovereign grace to do more than a man's part in giving victory to the oppressed people of God.

When we consider the times in which she lived, the story of this devoted and God-fearing woman seems all the more remarkable. Hers was a peculiar spiritual energy, coupled with sound common sense, which together made her 'the outstanding leader of her day. And through all her varied experiences she remained a modest and self-effacing woman, a wife and mother in Israel, exercising her divinely-given prerogatives in a manner at once wise and blameless. No trace of vanity, no arrogance or imperiousness are manifested in her behavior.

> " 'Lord, help me,'—so we pray,
> 'Help me my work to do;
> I am so ignorant and weak;
> Make me more wise and true.'
>
> " 'Lord, help me do Thy work,'
> We pray when wiser grown,
> When on the upward way
> Our feet have farther gone.
>
> " 'Lord, do Thy work through me,'
> So when all self we lose;
> His doing and His work, and we
> The tools His hand can use."

"Awake, awake, Deborah: awake, awake, utter a song: arise, Barak, and lead thy captivity captive, thou son of Abinoam"—Judges 5: 12.

A faithful woman, who knew God and dared to risk all upon His word, meant more to Israel in this time of crisis than all else beside. God ever delights to honor faith. He can be depended upon never to fail those who put their confidence in Him. We, today, are not, as Christians, called to conflict with the armies of flesh and blood. Our warfare is with the unseen Satanic hosts and the worldly spirit of the age, but it is still true that we conquer our foes as we resist them in the spirit of Deborah—faith in the living God. Among the overcomers there are many heroines as well as heroes who have had the courage to attack entrenched evil of all kinds with the courage of a Deborah. Many a faltering Barak, too, has been roused to valiant service by the encouragement of some devoted woman who knew the mind of God and was unafraid in the face of gravest danger.

"There must be thorns amid life's flowers, you know,
And you and I, wherever we may go,
Can find no bliss that is not mixed with pain,
No path without a cloud. It would be vain
For me to wish that not a single tear
Might dim the gladness that you hold so dear.
I am not wise enough to understand
All that is best for you. The Master's hand
Must sometimes touch life's saddest chords to reach
Its sweetest music, and His child to teach
To trust His love, till the long, weeping night
Is all forgotten in the morning light.
Trust, trust Him, then, and thus shall good or ill
Your trustful soul with present blessing fill.
Each loss is truest gain if, day by day,
He fills the place of all He takes away."

—Message, Ballarat.

"But the Spirit of the Lord came upon Gideon, and he blew a trumpet; and Abiezer was gathered after him"
—Judges 6: 34.

IT is literally, "the Spirit of the Lord clothed Himself with Gideon." His history exemplifies the importance of obedience to the Word of God. The man of faith dares to move at God's command even though, for the moment, the difficulties seem to be insurmountable, and the possibility of victory very remote. Gideon learned to know God in secret; therefore he ventured everything upon His Word in public.

The call of this young man came not when he was day-dreaming, but when he was busy at his accustomed tasks on the farm of his father. He was threshing wheat to hide it from the Midianites when the angel of the Lord appeared to him and gave him his commission to be the leader and deliverer of Israel. In "the irresistible might of weakness" Gideon accepted the trust, and began his work by destroying the image of Baal in his own community, for true service for God must begin at home.

"'Tis easy when the morning
    Appears at last to view
To praise thy strong Redeemer
    Who burst the bondage through,
But 'tis the praise at midnight
    That gives the foe alarm,
That glorifies thy Saviour,
    And bares His strong right arm.

A conqueror thou wouldst be,
    Yea, more than conqueror thou,
If thou wilt shout in triumph
    And claim the victory now;
The prison-doors will open,
    The dungeon gleam with light,
And sin-chained souls around thee
    Shall see Jehovah's might."

"And he divided the three hundred men into three companies, and he put a trumpet in every man's hand, with empty pitchers, and lamps within the pitchers. And he said unto them, Look on me, and do likewise: and, behold, when I come to the outside of the camp, it shall be that, as I do, so shall ye do"—Judges 7: 16, 17.

SURELY no other soldiers ever went to battle so strangely armed. Each man took an earthen pitcher, in which a torch was hidden. "We have this treasure in earthen vessels, that the excellency of the power may be of God, and not of us" (2 Cor. 4: 7). The lamp in the pitcher set forth divine power working in frail humanity. In the other hand each man held a trumpet, which was to be used only as indicated at the appointed time. (See 1 Cor. 14: 8.)

All was quiet in the Midianite camp, when in the middle of the night the sleeping host was awakened by the blare of three hundred trumpets followed by the crashing noise of the same number of earthen pitchers. On every side flashing torches were seen, which might well suggest that they were surrounded by a great host. Gideon's little force had been divided into three groups of a hundred each, under their respective captains, and all directly responsible to their ardent and patriotic chief. As the battle-cry rang out, the Midianites were terrified, not knowing what to expect next. The terror of the unknown, always worse than actuality, had gripped the foe and rendered them powerless for any concerted defensive or offensive action.

> "Be strong!
> We are not here to play, to dream, to drift,
> We have hard work to do, and loads to lift;
> Shun not the struggle; face it. 'Tis God's gift.
>
> Be strong!
> It matters not how deep intrenched the wrong,
> How hard the battle goes, the day, how long.
> Faint not, fight on! Tomorrow comes the song."
>
> —Maltbie D. Babcock.

"The Philistines took him and put out his eyes, and brought him down to Gaza, and bound him with fetters of brass; and he did grind in the prison-house"

—Judges 16: 21.

SAMSON'S sad failure because he did not judge himself before God and mortify the members of his body (as Paul exhorts the Colossians to do, Col. 3: 5) is intended to be a lesson to all who seek to serve the Lord. His life might have ended very differently if he had set the will of God above his own fleshly desires. Yielding to sensuality, he became a castaway. God allowed him to be set to one side. Blind and fettered, he became the servant of the very people from whom he might have delivered Israel had he walked with God. In darkness and bondage he learned his lesson, but it was too late for him to be given the place again of the deliverer of Israel.

> "Whatever dims thy sense of truth
>   Or stains thy purity,
> Though light as breath of summer air,
>   Count it as sin to thee."

"And Naomi had a kinsman of her husband's, a mighty man of wealth, of the family of Elimelech; and his name was Boaz. And Ruth the Moabitess said unto Naomi, Let me now go to the field, and glean ears of corn after him in whose sight I shall find grace. And she said unto her, Go, my daughter"—Ruth 2: 1, 2.

THERE is a charm about the inspired Hebrew idyl, the book of Ruth, that cannot but appeal to every one of literary taste, whether its divine inspiration be recognized or not. But when we receive and believe it as part of the God-breathed Word, we see added beauties which the natural mind cannot discern. It is, emphatically, an unfolding of the story of redemption. Through Boaz, the kinsman-redeemer (Lev. 25: 25), Ruth, the stranger, is brought into the family of God and recognized as one of the covenant people. The great-grandmother of King David, she has her place in the ancestral line of our Lord Jesus Christ (Matt. 1: 5, 6). By natural birth the Moabite was barred from the congregation of the Lord unto the tenth generation(Deut. 23: 3). By grace Ruth found an honored place among the mothers of Israel.

Jehovah had made special provision for "the poor and the stranger" (Lev. 19: 9, 10). By humbling herself in order to avail herself of that provision, Ruth attracted the notice of Boaz, and so this lovely Bible romance came to a happy conclusion.

"Grace, 'tis a charming sound,
　　Harmonious to the ear,
Heaven with the echo shall resound
　　And all the earth shall hear.

O let Thy grace inspire
　　My soul with strength divine;
May all my powers to Thee aspire
　　And all my days be Thine."

"And Hannah prayed, and said, My heart rejoiceth in the Lord, mine horn is exalted in the Lord; my mouth is enlarged over mine enemies; because I rejoice in Thy salvation"—1 Sam. 2: 1.

THE story of Hannah and her son Samuel is one of perennial freshness and beauty, and is designed of God to be an encouragement and to some degree an example to all mothers. From the primeval promise as to the Seed of the woman bruising the serpent's head, motherhood has ever been hallowed and safeguarded in the Word of God. Because the Eternal Son of God chose to come to earth as a little helpless babe, to all outward appearance dependent on a mother's care, all mothers have a peculiar place in the divine economy. Who can tell the far-reaching effects of a godly mother's prayers, counsel, and example? The most hardened men melt when reminded of a good mother, no matter how far they have strayed from her precepts.

Surely, if anyone on earth needs really to know God and to live for Him before others, it is the mother of children, whose eternal destiny depends so largely upon their early training. As we study the story of Hannah's yearning, her prayer, her promise, and her faithfulness, it should draw out all our hearts to that God who has said, "As one whom his mother comforteth, so will I comfort you" (Isa. 66: 13).

> "Hush, my dear, lie still, and slumber;
>   Holy angels guard thy bed,
> Heavenly blessings without number
>   Gently falling on thy head.
>
> How much better thou'rt attended
>   Than the Son of God could be,
> When from heaven He descended,
>   And became a child like thee!
>
> Mayest thou live to know and fear Him,
>   Trust and love Him all thy days;
> Then go dwell forever near Him,
>   See His face and sing His praise."
>
> —Isaac Watts.

"I have told him that I will judge his house for ever
for the iniquity which he knoweth; because his sons made
themselves vile, and he restrained them not"

—1 Sam. 3: 13.

IN Eli, the high priest in Hannah's day, we see a thoroughly good man, who, however, was prone to misjudge
others and yet was weak when it came to disciplining his
own family. The fact that in his last days he was "an old
man, and heavy," suggests that he was over-indulgent in
regard to his personal habits, the pleasures of the table
evidently having a strong appeal which he was not able to
resist. In chapters two and four, inclusive, we get enough
information concerning him to enable us to form a reasonably
accurate picture of his character. Coupled with real concern for the things of God was lack of ability to master his
appetites and to "command his children and his household
after him" (Gen. 18: 19) in such a way as to glorify God in
family life. Such men are often met with in Christian service, who possess many amiable qualities but are sadly lacking where they should be strong.

It is ever important to remember that the grace of God
does not set aside the divine government. There are responsibilities that flow from grace which cannot be ignored
with impunity. Antinomianism (lawlessness) and legality
are both opposed to grace. But a recognition of the divine
authority and careful subjection to the government of God
should flow from the knowledge of His unmerited favor.
Fatherly discipline is expected of all who head up Christian
households. Weakness here is a sign of low thoughts of the
holiness and righteousness which are becoming in all who
draw nigh to God.

> "Thy heavenly grace to each impart,
>   All evil far remove,
> And shed abroad in every heart
>   Thine everlasting love.
>
> Oh, still restore our wandering feet
>   And still direct our way;
> Till worlds shall fail, and faith shall greet
>   The dawn of endless day."

"And Samuel spake unto all the house of Israel, saying, If ye do return unto the Lord with all your hearts, then put away the strange gods and Ashtaroth from among you, and prepare your hearts unto the Lord, and serve Him only: and He will deliver you out of the hand of the Philistines"—1 Sam. 7: 3.

EVEN before the death of Eli it became evident that Samuel was his divinely-appointed successor as judge in Israel. And so, after the disconcerting experiences of the Philistines in connection with the ark of the covenant led them to send it back to the people whose glory it was, we find the young prophet coming immediately to the front, and through his ministry there was a revival of interest in the worship of Jehovah and a true return to God on the part of many. God works through human instruments and He always has the man ready when the hour of blessing strikes. The history of the great awakenings throughout the centuries, first in Israel and then in the Church of the new dispensation, is largely the story of the chosen servants prepared by God and subject to His will, who have been raised up to call an erring people to repentance and to bring them back to their only proper allegiance. Of these, Samuel stands out as one of the greatest of the whole army of the reformers.

"My Saviour, by His powerful word,
　　Hath turned my night to day;
And all those heavenly joys restored
　　Which I had sinned away.

Blest Lord, I wonder and adore,
　　Thy grace is all divine;
Oh, keep me, that I sin no more
　　Against such love as Thine.

Oh, speak that gracious word again,
　　And cheer my drooping heart;
No voice but Thine can soothe my pain,
　　And bid all fear depart."

"The Lord hath sought Him a man after His own heart, and the Lord hath commanded him to be captain over His people, because thou hast not kept that which the Lord commanded thee"—1 Sam. 13: 14.

IT was in his confident trust that David was a man after God's own heart (1 Sam. 13: 14). He was in himself a sinner like all others (Rom. 3: 23), but he repented bitterly of his failures, which brought him so much unhappiness, and which entailed grave dishonor upon the sacred name so dear to him. He rested at last upon "the sure mercies of David" (Isa. 55: 3), that is, the divine promises, and his songs of joyous confidence in the God of his salvation have become the models for all true praise and worship, and have been loved by both pious Jews and devout Christians throughout all the centuries since he sang them in Judea so long ago.

"Thou Holy One of God!
  The Father rests in Thee;
And in the savor of that blood
  That speaks to Him for me,
The curse is gone—through Thee I'm blest,
God rests in Thee—in Thee I rest.

The slave of sin and fear,
  Thy truth my bondage broke;
My willing spirit loves to bear
  Thy light and easy yoke;
The love that fills my grateful breast,
Makes duty joy, and labor rest.

Soon the bright, glorious day,
  The rest of God shall come!
Sorrow and sin shall pass away,
  And I shall reach my home!
Then, of the promised land possessed,
My soul shall know eternal rest!"

—J. G. Deck.

"And Samuel said, Hath the Lord as great delight in burnt offerings and sacrifices, as in obeying the voice of the Lord? Behold, to obey is better than sacrifice, and to hearken than the fat of rams. For rebellion is as the sin of witchcraft, and stubbornness is as iniquity and idolatry. Because thou hast rejected the word of the Lord, He hath also rejected thee from being king"

—1 Sam. 15: 22, 23.

SAUL'S life, or at least his official history, began well and gave promise of a most successful and brilliant career, but it ended in bitter disappointment. He has been rightly called "The Man after the Flesh." As such, he possessed many admirable traits and at the start he seemed to be an ideal king. But his goodness was like the morning cloud that soon passes away. It was only the attractiveness of nature. We would like to believe that when "the Lord gave him another heart," it means he was born again. But it seems rather to imply that he was given a new outlook on life, with new courage and new ambitions to fit him for the high office to which he was appointed. Apparently he never knew God in the true sense, as Samuel did before him, and as David did, who succeeded him. His life should be a solemn warning to those who would make a fair show in the flesh, emphasizing the importance of true repentance and genuine faith.

"Be this the purpose of my soul,
   My solemn, my determined choice,
To yield to Thy supreme control,
   And in Thy kind commands rejoice.
Oh, may I never faint or tire,
   Nor wandering leave Thy holy ways;
Father, accept my soul's desire,
   And give me strength to live Thy praise."

"And it came to pass, when he had made an end of speaking unto Saul, that the soul of Jonathan was knit with the soul of David, and Jonathan loved him as his own soul. . . . Then Jonathan and David made a covenant, because he loved him as his own soul"

—1 Sam. 17: 1, 3.

THE beautiful record of the friendship between Jonathan, the heir to the throne of Israel, and David, the outlawed hero whom the people revered, is one of the most interesting and affecting stories in all literature. The Greek tale of Damon and Pythias is perhaps its nearest counterpart in secular literature.

It illustrates in a remarkable way that heart devotion to Christ, "great David's greater Son," which should characterize every truly converted soul. David's victory over Goliath typifies Christ's triumph over "him that had the power of death, that is, the devil" (Heb. 2: 14, 15). It was this that won Jonathan's heart and caused him to love David as his own soul. *He* should have challenged the giant, but David took his place. Henceforth the youthful victor had the pre-eminence in the mind of the prince-royal, who "stripped himself" to honor the deliverer of Israel (1 Sam. 18: 1-4).

"Jesus, these eyes have never seen
    That radiant form of Thine;
The veil of sense hangs dark between
    Thy blessed face and mine.

I see Thee not, I hear Thee not,
    Yet art Thou oft with me;
And earth hath ne'er so dear a spot
    As where I meet with Thee.

Yet though I have not seen, and still
    Must rest in faith alone;
I love Thee, dearest Lord, and will,
    Unseen, but not unknown.

When death these mortal eyes shall seal,
    And still this throbbing heart,
The rending veil shall Thee reveal,
    All glorious as Thou art."

—Ray Palmer, D.D.

"Jonathan stripped himself of the robe that was upon him and gave it to David, and his garments, even to his sword, and to his bow and to his girdle"—1 Sam. 18: 4.

IT was as though he said, "What things were gain to me, these I counted loss for" David—the one chosen of God to deliver Israel. In this Jonathan portrays the attitude of soul which all should manifest toward our Lord Jesus Christ who has overcome, for us, him that had the power of death in order that He might deliver those who through fear of death were all their lifetime subject to bondage. Jonathan's actions said, "Nothing is too good for David, for him who took his life in his hand to set us free from the dread Philistine who had terrorized Israel for so long." Surely we who owe all to Him who has wrought so much greater a deliverance should withhold nothing from Christ, who has brought us into "this grace wherein we stand."

"I had broken the law, and was sentenced to die;
I knew I was guilty, had naught to reply,
    And my conscience tormented me sore;
When my Friend came in view, showed His hands and His side,
And told me that once in my stead He had died,
    That I might have life evermore.

Such, then, is my Friend. Oh, I wish I could sound
The praise of His name to earth's uttermost bound!
    I would sound it again and again!
Do you ask who it is that has stilled my complaints?
Oh, listen, ye sinners! Oh, praise Him, ye saints!
    It is JESUS, the SAVIOUR OF MEN!"

—R. H. T.

"And they two made a covenant before the Lord; and David abode in the wood and Jonathan went to his house"—1 Sam. 23: 18.

JONATHAN loved David and was devoted to him, but he never separated himself from the house of his ungodly father to throw in his lot entirely with the friend he esteemed so highly. This verse tells of the last time the two frends met. David continued in the place of rejection. Jonathan went back to his own house and was destined to die on Mount Gilboa when Saul was overthrown. His dream of association with David in the coming day when the kingdom would actually be his, was never fulfilled. The lesson for us is a salutary one. We are called to put the claims of Christ above all others—even above the closest natural ties. Our reward hereafter will answer to what we have suffered by identification with our rejected Lord now.

"No time for trifling in this life of mine;
    Not this the path the blessed Master trod,
But strenuous toil; each hour and power employed
    Always and all for God.

With ceaseless blessings from my Father's hand
    My earthly path is every moment strawed;
God ever thinks of me; should I not be
    Always and all for God?"

—A. B. Simpson.

"David encouraged himself in the Lord his God"
—1 Sam. 30: 6.

IT was a dark day in David's life, probably the most trying ordeal he had been called upon to pass through. Because of the disaster that had befallen the families of his devoted followers, even they questioned his wisdom and righteousness and threatened to stone him as though he were responsible for all that had taken place. Self-defence was useless. It would have been a waste of effort to explain. So he turned from man to God and found encouragement there. It is a great thing to put God between the soul and adverse circumstances. He never fails the one who confides in Him. David's confidence was soon rewarded and his men realized as never before that God was with him.

"One there is above all others,
    Well deserves the name of Friend;
His is love beyond a brother's:
    Costly, free and knows no end.

Which of all our friends to save us,
    Could or would have shed his blood?
But our Jesus died to have us
    Reconciled in Him to God.

Oh, for grace our hearts to soften!
    Teach us, Lord, at length to love;
We, alas! forget too often
    What a Friend we have above."

"Died Abner as a fool dieth?"—2 Sam. 3: 33.

IT was David who asked the question as he lamented the treachery of Joab in slaying Abner at the very time that the former captain of Saul's host had yielded allegiance to him whom God had made king in Saul's stead. And the answer to the question must be in the affirmative. Abner did die as a fool dieth. He had slain Asahel the brother of Joab, much against his own will, but in order to save his life. He was guilty of manslaughter. Joab was the avenger of blood. Hebron was a city of refuge. Abner was entitled to asylum there, but he left the place of safety to go out and discuss matters with Joab who treacherously slew him. Thus he died because he failed to avail himself of the protection that God had provided for him. Alas, how many there are who take the same foolish course! Christ is the only City of Refuge today. They who flee to Him find shelter from the Avenger. Apart from Him there is no safety.

"Hail, sovereign love, which first began
The scheme to rescue fallen man!
Hail, matchless, free, eternal grace,
Which gave my soul a Hiding Place!

Should sevenfold storms of thunder roll,
And shake this globe from pole to pole,
No thunderbolt shall daunt my face,
For Jesus is my Hiding Place."

"Now, O Lord God, the word that Thou hast spoken concerning Thy servant, and concerning his house, establish it forever, and do as Thou hast said"—2 Sam. 7: 25.

THIS is faith's response to the promises of God, "Do as Thou hast said." Nothing can turn aside that which God has planned. He worketh everything according to the counsel of His own will. When He gives quietness none can disturb. He never promises one thing and does another. His Word is unchangeable and His covenant is everlasting. Overwhelmed with the assurances of blessing not only for the then present but for a long time to come, David bows his head in the presence of God and puts his Amen to what He has covenanted. He who thus confides in the sure Word of the Lord will never be put to shame.

> "I know not by what methods rare,
> But this I know, God answers prayer.
> I know that He has given His Word,
> Which tells me prayer is always heard,
> And will be answered, soon or late;
> And so I pray, and calmly wait.
>
> I know not if the blessing sought,
> Will come in just the way I thought,
> But leave my prayers with Him alone,
> Whose will is wiser than my own,
> Assured that He will grant my quest,
> Or send some answer far more blest."

"And David said unto Nathan, I have sinned against the Lord. And Nathan said unto David, The Lord also hath put away thy sin; thou shalt not die. Howbeit, because by this deed thou hast given great occasion to the enemies of the Lord to blaspheme, the child also that is born unto thee shall surely die"

—2 Sam. 12:13, 14.

IN considering the subject of forgiveness of sins we need to remember that Scripture presents it in several different aspects. There is, first of all, the forgiveness which God gives to all who believe upon His Son (Acts 10:43; 13:38, 39). This is perfect and complete, and is never repeated. The basis of it is the work of the cross, the blood of Christ shed for our redemption (Eph. 1:7). He who comes to God as a sinner and puts his trust in the Lord Jesus passes from death unto life (John 5:24) and is henceforth a child of God, justified before His throne and accounted clear of every charge (Rom. 8:33, 34). His responsibility as a sinner having to do with the judgment of God is over for eternity. But now a new responsibility begins: that of a child having to do with his Father. If the child sins he loses fellowship and needs restorative forgiveness. This is granted when he comes to his Father in contrition, confessing his failure (1 John 1:9). There is a third and very important aspect of forgiveness which we may call governmental. In the government of God there are certain consequences of a temporal (and often a physical) character, which follow the commission of sin. These consequences go on for years, or God may in mercy remit them, if we walk humbly before Him. In David's case most serious governmental consequences followed long after Nathan assured the penitent king the Lord had put away his sin.

"My sins forgiven, my fears removed,
I know that Thou hast ever loved."

"I shall go to him but he shall not return to me"
—2 Sam. 12: 23.

DAVID'S confidence as to life after death and heavenly reunion shines out brightly here. He knew the child was with God. He knew that he, in spite of his sad failure, was also a child of God, and so he could look on in faith to a day when he would find the babe again and never be separated more. What consolation does this assurance afford in the time of bereavement! Our loved ones who have died in Christ are not lost to us. They are with Him in paradise. It is not according to God's plan that they should return to this earth life to communicate with us, but we know that when we too are absent from the body we shall be present with the Lord, and shall find again our loved ones gone before.

"And those dear loved of ours we miss so sorely,
    Do they not, too, all glad, expectant, wait?
Till down the steeps of light, athrob with glory,
    They'll throng—that shining host—from Heaven's gate!

We'll meet them in that Resurrection morning!
    We'll find each dear, familiar, longed-for face;
We'll know them e'en though radiant and transfigured;
    Once more we'll clasp our own—oh, gift of grace!"

—Mrs. Donald A. Day.

"For we must needs die and are as water spilt on the ground, which cannot be gathered up again; neither doth God respect any person: yet doth He devise means that His banished be not expelled from Him"

—2 Sam. 14: 14.

THE wise woman of Tekoah made her appeal to sentiment rather than to righteousness, therefore the return of Absalom was the prelude to a greater disaster than had yet befallen David. Many imagine that God acts as the king did, and brings back His banished without the settlement of the sin-question. But His holy nature forbids this. He has indeed devised means to recover the sinner, but it has been at the cost of the life of His own beloved Son, our Lord Jesus Christ. Through His expiatory work on the cross God can be just and the Justifier of him that believeth on Jesus.

"He laid on Him the sinner's guilt
  When came the appointed day,
And by that blood on Calvary spilt
  Takes all our sins away.
How glorious, blessed, and complete
  That finished work must be
When God with man delights to meet,
  There He has met with me."

"Thou art worth ten thousand of us"—2 Sam. 18: 3.

THIS was the estimate his devoted followers put upon David their king. To them his life meant so much that they would not have him adventure in battle lest they be bereft of his leadership and his shepherd-care. It was their love and regard for him that led to such care for his safety. In this David portrayed Him who is to His redeemed "the altogether lovely," the "fairest of ten thousand." His worth is beyond all comparison. All of the sons of earth together are not deserving of Him. And yet, in grace, He gave Himself for us. In order that sinners might be saved He sacrificed Himself. He, the infinite One, stooped to death to save poor lost sinners such as we.

"Hast thou heard Him, seen Him, known Him?
   Is not thine a raptured heart?
Chief among ten thousand own Him,
   Gladly choose the better part.

What has stript the seeming beauty
   From the idols of the earth?
Not the sense of right or duty,
   But the sight of peerless worth.

Not the crushing of those idols,
   With its bitter void and smart:
But the beaming of His beauty,
   The unveiling of His heart."

"And Mephibosheth said unto the king, Yea, let him take all, forasmuch as my lord the king is come again in peace unto his own house"—2 Sam. 19:30.

MEPHIBOSHETH was the lame son of Jonathan to whom David had shown the kindness of God for his father's sake (2 Sam. 9). When David fled from Absalom he was unable, because of his infirmity, to go with his benefactor and was lied about and his motives in remaining behind misrepresented by his servant Ziba to whom David gave all the property of Mephibosheth because of the deception. Returning at last in triumph Jonathan's son came to greet him and soon cleared himself of the charges of disloyalty. Sorry that he had mistrusted him, David gave instructions that Ziba and he should divide the land. In his answer Mephibosheth showed that David himself meant more to him than all his benefits. His heart was satisfied to have the king at home in peace. So Christ can satisfy every yearning of the heart, and all else counts as nought compared with Him.

"Take the world but give me Jesus,
Let me have His constant smile,
Then throughout my pilgrim journey
Faith shall cheer me all the while."

"He shall be as the light of the morning, when the sun riseth, even a morning without clouds; as the tender grass springing out of the earth by clear shining after rain"—2 Sam. 23: 4.

IN such language David, in his last words, portrayed the coming to reign of "a righteous ruler over men, a ruler in the fear of God," who is to spring from his house in due time and set up the kingdom which will never be destroyed. We are waiting still for His glorious advent. He came once in lowly grace to bring in redemption. He will come again to bring in the promised glory. What a relief it will be, after the long centuries of man's misrule when the Lord Jesus shall show in His own times who is that blessed and only Potentate, King of kings and Lord of lords!

> "Lamb of God, Thou soon in glory
>   Wilt to this sad world return,
> All Thy foes shall quake before Thee,
>   All that now despise Thee mourn.
> Then shall we at Thine appearing
>   With Thee in Thy kingdom reign;
> Thine the praise and Thine the glory,
>   Lamb of God for sinners slain."

—J. G. Deck.

"God said, Ask what I shall give thee"—1 Kings 3:5.

DOES He not know far better than we do what is good for us? Is it not, then, needless to come to Him with our requests? He who so reasons overlooks the fact that it is God Himself who bids us ask and who tells us, "Ye have not because ye ask not." It is clear from this scripture that He has blessings prepared for us which He loves to give, but which will be withheld until we request them. He would have us realize that we have to do with a living God. When we go to Him in prayer and ask Him to give what is on our hearts—of which others know nothing— and then He opens His hand and gives so freely and so generously, we have a positive demonstration that prayer is more than a formal religious exercise. We have reached the ear of God and He has answered in His love and wisdom.

> "My Father, this I ask of Thee;
> Knowing that Thou wilt grant the plea—
> For this, and only this, I pray,
> Strength for today—just for today.
>
> I do not ask a lifted load,
> Nor for a smooth and thornless road;
> Simply for strength enough to bear
> Life's daily burdens anywhere."
>
> —E. E. Rexford.

MARCH 1

"And upon the top of the pillars was lily work: so was the work of the pillars finished"—1 Kings 7: 22.

EVERYTHING in the temple, as in the tabernacle before it, spoke of Christ. "In His sanctuary every whit of it uttereth His glory" (Ps. 29: 9, literal rendering). The great pillars Jachim ("He shall establish") and Boaz ("In Him is strength") speak of His power and might. The lily work at the top speaks of the lowliness and beauty of His character. To those who overcome He says, "I will make him a pillar in the temple of My God" (Rev. 3: 12). His pillars must be strong in the Lord and the power of His might, but there must also be the beauty of holiness, the lowly grace which was seen in all perfection in Him. No experience is valueless which tends to reproduce Christ in us. No suffering is too great if it result in that lily-work which is so precious in the eyes of God. The lovely flowers of His grace give beauty to the sturdy pillar that tells of His power.

"In this, Thy temple, Lord, Thy lilies carve.
Upon the pillars of my soul engrave
Thy handiwork. Let me not save
One corner from the sharpness of Thy chisel,
That might make known to others Thou wast there
And marked it for Thyself. Let sorrow, care,
And pain leave only echoes of Thy beauty,
Fast in the pattern of my heart and face
Thy hammer hews. This would I, by Thy grace."

—Henrietta Runyon Wintrey.

"And the king answered the people roughly, and forsook the old men's counsel that they gave him; and spake to them after the counsel of the young men, saying, My father made your yoke heavy, and I will add to your yoke: my father also chastised you with whips, but I will chastise you with scorpions"—1 Kings 12: 13, 14.

ONE of Solomon's own proverbs, if taken to heart by his son, might have saved the entire situation: "A soft answer turneth away wrath: but grievous words stir up anger" (Prov. 15: 1). Another proverb might have given added guidance: "Only by pride cometh contention: but with the well advised is wisdom" (Prov. 13: 10). Rehoboam lost the greater part of his kingdom because of refusing the good advice of the elders and following the foolish counsel of the young men. Puffed up with pride, he met the reasonable demands of the people with "grievous words," instead of conciliatory speech, which might have bound their hearts to him and saved from much strife and bitterness. It is a lesson that we are all very slow to learn. We so readily forget that "the wrath of man worketh not the righteousness of God" (Jas. 1: 20). Many family, business, church, and national troubles might be avoided were this lesson taken to heart.

"So many hearts are breaking,
And many more are aching,
To hear the tender word.
　God, make me kind!
For I myself am learning
That my sad heart is yearning
For some sweet word to heal my hurt.
　O Lord, do make me kind.

God, make me kind!
So many hearts are needing
The balm to stop the bleeding
That my kind words can bring.
　God, make me kind!
For I myself am learning
The cure in some one's keeping
He should impart to my sick heart.
　O Lord, do make me kind."　　—Duncan McNeil.

MARCH 3

"And it came to pass, when Ahab saw Elijah, that Ahab said unto him, Art thou he that troubleth Israel? And he answered, I have not troubled Israel: but thou, and thy father's house, in that ye have forsaken the commandments of the Lord, and thou hast followed Baalim"—1 Kings 18: 17, 18.

HE who has the testimony of his own conscience that he is walking in accordance with the revealed will of God will be courageous in the hour of danger, when the enemies of the truth oppose with violence or deceitful pretense. There is a mere fleshly bravado which may exist where one is playing fast and loose with that which is of God. But holy boldness is another thing altogether and is the accompaniment of genuine piety and true loyalty to the Word of the Lord. It is this that we see exemplified in the life of Elijah, and in this we may well seek grace to emulate the devoted man of God who came to call the people back to the law they had forgotten.

"I bind unto myself today
    The power of God to hold and lead,
His eye to watch, His might to stay,
    His ear to hearken to my need,
The wisdom of my God to teach,
    His hand to guide, His shield to ward,
The Word of God to give me speech,
    The heavenly host to be my guard.

Christ be with me, Christ within me,
Christ behind me, Christ before me,
Christ beside me, Christ to win me,
Christ beneath me, Christ above me,
    Christ in quiet, Christ in danger,
Christ in hearts of all that love me,
    Christ in mouth of friend and stranger."

—St. Patrick of Ireland.

"He requested for himself that he might die; and said, It is enough; now, O Lord, take away my life; for I am not better than my fathers . . . And he said, I have been very jealous for the Lord God of hosts: for the children of Israel have forsaken Thy covenant, thrown down Thine altars, and slain Thy prophets with the sword; and I, even I only, am left; and they seek my life, to take it away"—1 Kings 19: 4, 10.

IT took real courage—the courage borne of the conviction that he was God's own messenger—for this sturdy Tishbite to rebuke so powerful and wicked a ruler as Ahab, and even more to declare beforehand what nature saw no evidence of, but which faith counted on God to perform (1 Kings 18: 41). Yet we see this bold man quail before the wrath of a proud, haughty, vixen-like Jezebel (1 Kings 19: 2, 3), whose threatening words so disturbed him that he preferred death to further conflict (1 Kings 19: 4). In this we may see how truly he was a man of like passions with ourselves: not some wonderful, mysterious, superhuman being, but a very human person indeed, whom God had taken up in grace and commissioned for a great work. His greatest weakness was in connection with his outstanding testimony: he was inclined to think of himself as almost Jehovah's sole representative on earth. When he said, "I only, am left (1 Kings 19: 14), God rebuked him by telling of seven thousand hidden ones in Israel who had not bowed the knee to Baal (chap. 19: 18). We need to learn the same lesson. However faithful or devoted we may imagine ourselves to be, God has many more than ourselves who are true to His Word and faithful in their stand against apostasy.

"Not that there be less to bear, not that there be more to share;
But for braver heart for bearing, but for freer heart for sharing—
 Here I pray.
Not that joy and peace enfold me, not that wealth and pleasure
  hold me;
But that I may dry a tear, speak a word of strength and cheer
  On the way."

"And as thy servant was busy here and there, he was gone"—1 Kings 20: 40.

THE parable of the missing man which the unnamed son of the prophet used in seeking to stir up the slothful spirit of the king of Israel has a similar lesson for us. We are exhorted to redeem the time, literally to buy up opportunities of testimony for witnessing for Christ; to be as alert for witnessing to the lost as bargain-hunters are to purchase goods to advantage. Yet how often we neglect to use the circumstances which are put in our way, where we may say a word for our Lord and endeavor to point the lost to Him. Our intentions are good, but we become so occupied with other matters, many of them trifling in the extreme, and ere we realize it, the man to whom we should have spoken is beyond our reach.

"Is it justice, is it kindness,
   Thus to leave them in their sin,
'Midst the ignorance and blindness,
   Not a ray of hope within?
None to tell them of the Saviour
   Who has died their souls to win.

Lord, increase our love, we pray Thee,
   Fields are ripe and servants few;
Help us gladly to obey Thee;
   Give us willing hearts and true,
That, responsive to Thy bidding,
   We may seek Thy will to do."

—H. Wilson.

"And Micaiah said, As the Lord liveth, what the Lord saith unto me that will I speak"—1 Kings 22: 14.

IT was nobly said. Micaiah's faithfulness stands out in vivid contrast to good king Jehoshaphat's temporizing with evil by his association with ungodly Ahab. When the prophet was urged to prophesy smooth things so as to curry favor with the wicked king of Israel he refused to compromise and to play fast and loose with God's truth. He was under orders as a soldier of the Lord and he felt he could only obey his Captain. As a steward of a divine revelation he must be found faithful. He got a prison for his pains, but Micaiah in jail made a greater figure in the sight of God than Jehoshaphat in the robes of Ahab!

"I do not ask for mighty words
    To leave the crowd impressed,
But grant my life may ring so true
    My neighbor shall be blessed.
I do not ask for influence
    To sway the multitude;
Give me a "word in season" for
    The soul in solitude.

I do not ask to win the great—
    God grant they may be saved!—
Give me the broken sinner, Lord,
    By Satan long enslaved.
Though words of wisdom and of power
    Rise easily to some,
Give me a simple message, Lord,
    That bids the sinner come."

—Barbara Cornet Ryberg.

"And it came to pass, as they still went on, and talked, that, behold, there appeared a chariot of fire, and horses of fire, and parted them both asunder; and Elijah went up by a whirlwind into heaven"—2 Kings 2:11.

IT was a glorious consummation to a noble life. Surely Elijah must have rejoiced in the hour of his ascension that his petulant prayer when he was under the juniper tree was not answered. He prayed to die, but God had something far better for him. He was the only man since Enoch who was carried up to heaven without passing through death. And so God is often better than our faith and deals with us according to the lovingkindness of His great heart rather than according to our poor thoughts and our ill deserts. He would have us learn to trust Him to do the best for us and to know that if He does not grant our exact requests it is because He has something better in store for us.

> "He was better to me than all my hopes,
>   He was better than all my fears;
> He made a bridge of my broken works,
>   And a rainbow of my tears.
> The billows that guarded my sea-girt path
>   But carried my Lord on their crest;
> When I dwell on the days of my wilderness march
>   I can lean on His love for the rest."
>
> —Anna Shipton.

"Now Naaman, captain of the host of the king of Syria, was a great man with his master, and honorable, . . . he was also a mighty man in valor, but he was a leper. And the Syrians had brought away captive a little maid; and she waited on Naaman's wife. And she said unto her mistress, Would God my lord were with the prophet that is in Samaria! for he would recover him of his leprosy"—2 Kings 5: 1-3.

THE blight of sin is set forth in a striking way in the disease of leprosy. In the case of Naaman we have human nature at its best in many respects. He was evidently a kindly, gracious man, though proud and sensitive, as his attitude toward the prophet's message indicates. A soldier of renown, he was honored by his sovereign and looked up to by the nation to which he belonged. He was blessed with an affectionate, solicitous wife, who sought his well-being. "But he was a leper." And this dreadful fact blighted everything else. So one may be admirable in many things and his circumstances generally be pleasing and satisfactory, but if he be a sinner, unsaved and uncleansed, all else counts as nought.

The little captive maid who waited upon Naaman's wife is a precious example of faithfulness under adverse circumstances. Torn away from her home and loved ones, instead of giving herself over to grief and despair, she maintains a bright testimony to the power of Israel's God and becomes the honored instrument of bringing her afflicted master into touch with the prophet of Jehovah, through whom he finds, not only healing for the body, but the knowledge of the one living and true God whom he will worship henceforth (ver. 17).

"Lord, Thou hast given to us a trust, a high and holy dispensation,
To tell the world, and tell we must, the story of Thy great salvation,

We all are debtors to our race, God hold us bound to one another;
The gifts and blessings of His grace were given us to give our
brother."

"Then they said one to another, We do not well: this day is a day of good tidings, and we hold our peace: if we tarry till the morning light, some mischief will come upon us: now therefore come, that we may go and tell the king's household"—2 Kings 7: 9.

THE four lepers who had found abundance in the deserted camp of the Syrians were conscience-stricken as they realized that, while they were feasting, others were dying of starvation. Acting on their best impulses then, they hurried back to tell the royal household that all might share in the bounteous provision God had made for them. The lesson is an important one for those of us who are now enjoying the riches of divine grace. Millions are still without the knowledge of Christ. How great is our guilt if we allow them to die in their sins, without doing all we can to acquaint them with the gospel of God, which alone can save all who put their trust in Christ. Let us go and tell. It is our bounden duty and we will be held responsible if we fail to respond.

"If He should come today
    And find I had not told
One soul about my Heavenly Friend
    Whose blessings all my way attend,
What would He say?

If He should come today
    Would I be glad—quite glad?
Remembering He had died for all
    And none, through me, had heard His call,
What would I say?"

—Grace E. Troy.

"And Hezekiah received the letter of the hand of the messengers, and read it: and Hezekiah went up into the house of the Lord, and spread it before the Lord"
—2 Kings 19: 14.

IT was a "letter of blasphemy" sent from the God-defying Syrian leaders, in order to terrify good King Hezekiah and impress him with the hopelessness of attempting to defend Jerusalem against the vast armies of the cruel enemy. But Hezekiah found his resource in prayer. He laid the letter before the Lord and counted on Him to act for His own' glory, and in a most wonderful way God intervened. Hezekiah knew to whom to turn in the hour of stress. God has said, "Call upon Me in the day of trouble. I will deliver thee and thou shalt glorify Me" (Ps. 50: 15). The promise was most blessedly fulfilled, as in every case where faith lays hold of the Lord and counts on Him to act for His own glory.

"God's delays are not denials,
　　He has heard your prayer;
He knows all about your trials,
　　Knows your every care.

God's delays are not denials,
　　Help is on the way.
He is watching o'er life's dials,
　　Bringing forth the day.

God's delays are not denials,
　　You will find Him true,
Working through the darkest trials,
　　What is best for you."

—Grace Troy.

"At that time Berodachbaladan, the son of Baladan, king of Babylon, sent letters and a present unto Hezekiah: for he had heard that Hezekiah had been sick. And Hezekiah hearkened unto them, and shewed them all the house of his precious things, the silver, and the gold, and the spices, and the precious ointment, and all the house of his armour, and all that was found in his treasures: there was nothing in his house, nor in all his dominion, that Hezekiah shewed them not"
—2 Kings 20: 12, 13.

YESTERDAY we saw Hezekiah spreading out the letter of blasphemy before the Lord. Today we see how sadly he failed and how differently he acted when there came a letter and a present from the idolatrous king of Babylon. Hezekiah was flattered by this attention and did not feel the need of taking it to God as he did in the other case. And so he erred grievously and Israel was destined to suffer terribly for the king's blunder. We need to be as much before God when the world patronizes us as when it openly disapproves. It is never safe to forget to pray.

"We bless Thee for Thy peace, O God!
　　Deep as the soundless sea,
Which falls like sunshine on the road
　　Of those who trust in Thee.

We ask not, Father, for repose
　　Which comes from outward rest,
If we may have through all life's woes
　　Thy peace within our breast.

That peace which suffers and is strong,
　　Trusts where it cannot see,
Deems not the trial way too long,
　　But leaves the end with Thee."

—Anon.

"And Jabez was more honourable than his brethren: and his mother called his name Jabez, saying, Because I bare him with sorrow. And Jabez called on the God of Israel, saying, Oh that Thou wouldest bless me indeed, and enlarge my coast, and that Thine hand might be with me, and that Thou wouldest keep me from evil, that it may not grieve me! And God granted him that which he requested"—1 Chron. 4: 9, 10.

IN the midst of what seems to many like a wilderness of forgotten names, how refreshing it is to come across the brief story of Jabez. His name means "Sorrowful," but through grace he was determined to rise above the sorrow that overshadowed his life and enter into the joy of fellowship with God. His prayer is fourfold. "Bless me indeed." That is, "Give me true happiness." This is only found as one prevails and walks with God. "Enlarge my coast." He was not content to go on only with what he had. He would enter into and enjoy more of the inheritance of the Lord. "That Thine hand may be with me!" He counted on God's protecting care. And lastly, he prayed, "Keep me from evil that it may not make me sorrowful." Sin is the only thing that can rob a child of God of his joy in the Lord.

"Do you know what happened on that day
When, burdened for souls, you tried to pray?
Did you think you failed to touch the Throne
When your lips were dumb, your prayer a groan?

Over the sea in a hot, dry land,
A sower sowed with faltering hand—
But, lo! in that hour refreshing came:
God's servant spoke with a tongue of flame!
And souls long steeped in a land of night
Passed from gloom to marvelous light;
Away from idols they turned to God,
Finding their peace in Jesus' blood.
'Twas your faith had moved God's mighty hand,
His blessings poured down in a desert land."

—Margaret D. Armstrong.

"And these are the singers, chief of the fathers of the Levites, who remaining in the chambers were free: for they were employed in that work day and night"
— 1 Chron. 9: 33.

IS singing work? It is certainly not labor in the sense of toilsome effort. But we read of the "service of song." And when our hearts are lifted up to God in praise and our lips intone thanksgivings to His Name, it is indeed a work in which He finds delight. He has said, "Whoso offereth praise glorifieth Me" (Ps. 50: 23). Of old the Levites, who were set apart for the special ministry of song, were "employed in that work day and night." It is no light thing to be appointed to lead the praises of God's people. It is a blessed and joyous service in which the heart must be continually occupied. Paul and Silas were true singing Levites, even in a prison cell with their feet fast in the stocks. It is God alone who giveth songs in the night.

"When shadowed in the darkness,
And pressed by every foe,
Then let your gladdest carols
And sweetest anthems flow;
The praise so sweet to Jesus,
The "sacrifice of praise,"
Is when no earthly sunshine
Pours forth its cheering rays.

'Tis then your song is wafted
All human heights above,
And mingles with the angels'
In realms of perfect love;
'Tis then the God of Glory
Makes Satan fear and flee,
And sends a mighty earthquake
To set His ransomed free."

"Howbeit I believed not their words, until I came, and mine eyes had seen it: and, behold, the one half of the greatness of thy wisdom was not told me: for thou exceedest the fame that I heard. Happy are thy men, and happy are these thy servants, which stand continually before thee, and hear thy wisdom"

—2 Chron. 9: 6, 7.

WHAT the Queen of Sheba said of King Solomon may well be applied to our blessed Lord Jesus Christ. None can realize His worth until they come to Him in faith and prove for themselves the wonders of His grace and the glory of His power. Then indeed the adoring heart admits with joy and gladness that His wisdom and goodness are far beyond all that has ever been proclaimed by the heralds of His gospel. Faith, we are told, comes by hearing (or, a report). He who hears the Word and believes the message is the recipient of life eternal and enters into fellowship with Him who is the Source of that life. Then the heart can say, "The half has not been told me."

"For Thou exceedest all the fame
Our ears have ever heard;
How happy they who love Thy Name
And trust Thy faithful Word."

"And Asa cried unto the Lord his God, and said, Lord, it is nothing with Thee to help, whether with many, or with them that have no power: help us, O Lord our God; for we rest on Thee, and in Thy name we go against this multitude. O Lord, Thou art God; let not man prevail against Thee"—2 Chron. 14: 11.

GOD'S power is omnipotent and He is prepared to back up the man of faith, no matter how difficult the circumstances that he may have to face. We today are not called to battle with flesh and blood, using carnal weapons, but our conflict is with Satanic hosts, who would seek to rob us of the enjoyment of our inheritance in Christ (Eph. 6: 12). But, for faith, the devil is already a defeated foe (Heb. 2: 14). As we meet the enemy in the power of the cross, victory is sure (Gal. 6: 14). He who wrought for Asa will undertake for us as we rely upon His faithfulness and walk in obedience to His Word. Asa's prayer is soul-stirring and indicates strong faith and high spirituality. He put God between him and the enemy. It was a case of divine power versus human assumption, the might of Jehovah against mere brute Satanic strength and artfulness.

"Thanks be to God for Jesus Christ, who turns
    Defeat to victory in every heart.
When battles rage and, crushed, the spirit yearns
    To "cease from man," God rends the clouds apart
And sets a banner in the troubled sky—
    It is the face of Jesus Christ, and He
Becomes the challenge that we conquer by;
    Nay, more than that: He IS the victory.

Thanks be to God for Jesus Christ; the One
    Who never lost a battle; who laid down
His life a ransom, and, when that was done,
    Arose unvanquished and put on the crown;
Who knows when foes oppress, when eyes grow dim,
When life is hard. Thanks be to God for HIM!"

—Helen Frazee-Bower.

"And the Lord was with Jehoshaphat, because he walked in the first ways of his father David, and sought not unto Baalim; but sought to the Lord God of his father, and walked in His commandments, and not after the doings of Israel. Therefore the Lord established the kingdom in his hand; and all Judah brought to Jehoshaphat presents; and he had riches and honor in abundance"—2 Chron. 17:2-5.

THE path of obedience is the path of blessing. This is the great lesson emphasized in the life of King Jehoshaphat. Disobedience always results in sorrow and disappointment. Yet how slowly we learn these things, simple and so often demonstrated as they are! What can be more foolish than to suppose that we, poor finite creatures of a day, are capable of ruling ourselves and finding lasting happiness in acting in accordance with our own unrestrained impulses, rather than by yielding ourselves unto God to do His will and be controlled and directed by Him as He has revealed His mind to us in His holy Word? It is His love for us that leads Him to give us suited instruction for a safe way through this scene. Our greatest wisdom is manifested in surrendering ourselves wholly to Him, in order that He may be glorified in and through us.

"His will be done," we say with sighs and trembling,
　　Expecting trial, bitter loss and tears;
And then how doth He answer us with blessings
　　In sweet rebuking of our faithless fears.

God's will is peace and plenty and the power
　　To be and have the best that He can give,
A mind to serve Him and a heart to love Him,
　　The faith to die with and the strength to live.

It means for us all good, all grace, all glory,
　　His kingdom coming and on earth begun,
Why should we fear to say: "His will—His righteou
　　His tender, loving, joyous will—be done?"

　　　　　　　　　　　　　　—Annie Johnson Flint.

"But when he was strong, his heart was lifted up to his destruction: for he trangressed against the Lord his God, and went into the temple of the Lord to burn incense upon the altar of incense"—2 Chron. 26: 16.

THERE is a very real danger in success even for those who are children of God. It is easy to become proud and to take credit to oneself instead of giving all the glory to Him through whom alone promotion comes (Ps. 75: 6, 7). King Uzziah, as he is called here, otherwise known as Azariah (2 Kings 14: 21; 15: 1-7), is a striking illustration of this truth. Like many others, he began well and ended badly. In his early years he was earnest and energetic in building up the kingdom of Judah and in furthering the observance of the law of the Lord. While under the helpful influence of "Zechariah, who had understanding in the visions of God" (2 Chron. 26: 5), he sought after God, and as long as he did so he prospered. "But when he was strong, his heart was lifted up to his destruction." In his old age he became a "castaway" (1 Cor. 9: 27). He was set to one side as unfit to be used of the Lord, while his son acted as regent in his place.

"There is a service God-inspired,
  A zeal that tireless grows,
Where self is crucified with Christ,
  And joy unceasing flows.
There is a being "right with God,"
  That yields to His commands
Unswerving, true fidelity,
  A loyalty that stands.

There is a meekness free from pride,
  That feels no anger rise
At slights, or hate, or ridicule,
  But counts the cross a prize.
There is a patience that endures
  Without a fret or care,
But joyful sings, "His will be done,
  My Lord's sweet grace I share."

"Now be ye not stiffnecked, as your fathers were, but yield yourselves unto the Lord, and enter into His sanctuary, which He hath sanctified for ever: and serve the Lord your God, that the fierceness of His wrath may turn away from you. For if ye turn again unto the Lord, your brethren and your children shall find compassion before them that lead them captive, so that they shall come again into this land: for the Lord your God is gracious and merciful, and will not turn away His face from you, if ye return unto Him"—2 Chron. 30: 8, 9.

GOD is always ready to grant revival and blessing when His people turn wholeheartedly to Him. He cannot pour out His Spirit upon a disobedient and gainsaying people. But He responds at once to those who humble themselves before Him, put away all known sin, and seek to yield implicit obedience to His Word. These were the characteristic features of the great awakening in the days of Hezekiah, and these things are written for our learning (Rom. 15: 4) that we, too, might seek the Lord in His own appointed way. It has been well said that we may have revival in any place, at any time, when willing to pay the price. There will always be blessing when the people of God return to obedience to the written Word. It is appalling how far the professing Church has drifted in many instances from that which God has revealed as His holy will, in the Bible. We need to come back to first principles, and instead of sitting in judgment on the Scriptures, give the Word of God the place of absolute authority in all things. Then we may be assured of the divine approval.

> "The dearest idol I have known,
>   Whate'er that idol be,
> Help me to tear it from its throne
>   And worship only Thee.
>
> So shall my walk be close with God,
>   Calm and serene my frame,
> So purer light shall mark the road
>   That leads me to the Lamb."
>
> —Cowper.

"For Ezra had prepared his heart to seek the law of the Lord, and to do it, and to teach in Israel statutes and judgments"—Ezra 7: 10.

THE order here is most instructive, particularly for any who desire to serve the Lord in ministering to others. Note the four things that characterized Ezra. First "he prepared his heart." We are told that "the preparation of the heart of man is from the Lord" (Prov. 16: 1). This is all-important. A prepared mind will never take the place of a prepared heart. In the second place, Ezra sought the law of the Lord. He endeavored to become acquainted with his Bible. Thirdly, he set himself to do according to what he found written therein. He was obedient to the Word. Then, lastly, he began to teach others the statutes and judgments of the Lord. To do and then to teach was what was exemplified in our Lord Himself (Acts 1: 1). We can only help others as we walk in obedience ourselves. It is the surrendered life that counts for God.

> "O grant, Lord Jesus, mine may be
> A life surrendered unto Thee.
> The vessel need not be of gold,
> Need not be strong, or wise, or bold,
> But, Lord, the vessel Thou shalt choose,
> It must be clean for Thee to use.
> So fill my heart till all shall see
> A living, reigning Christ, in me."

—Barbara E. Cornet.

"They which builded on the wall, and they that bare burdens, with those that laded, every one with one of his hands wrought in the work, and with the other hand held a weapon. For the builders, every one had his sword girded by his side, and so builded. And he that sounded the trumpet was by me"—Neh. 5: 17, 18.

THE story of the building up again of Jerusalem's ruined wall, as told in the book of Nehemiah, is most interesting and suggestive. A wall speaks of separation and also of security. God's children need to be walled in from the world if they would enjoy fellowship with their Lord and with one another. But the maintaining of this means activity in service and watchfulness against the enemy. Into all of our hands God puts the trowel for service and the sword for conflict. Then we need to be ever on the alert listening for the trumpet call that so we may act consistently for God and glorify Him as we take our places on the walls of Zion.

"The Saviour bids thee watch and pray
Through life's momentous hour,
And grants the Spirit's quickening ray
To those who seek His power."

"On that night could not the king sleep, and he commanded to bring the book of records of the chronicles; and they were read before the king"—Esther 6: 1.

THE king's insomnia may have seemed but an accidental occurrence on that night when Haman was plotting the destruction of Mordecai, the faithful Jew who would not bow to the enemy of his people and his God. But on that sleepless night, there hung the fate of a nation. It was God Himself who kept Ahasuerus from repose. He was working out His plan for the deliverance of His people and the wakeful king was but a cog in the machinery of the divine purpose. Thus, in ways too innumerable to mention does the Lord work out everything according to His own will. He is never indifferent to His people's needs. He will never disdain their cries for help, but in every hour of need He is on hand to bless.

"His purposes will ripen fast,
Unfolding every hour;
The bud may have a bitter taste,
But sweet will be the flower."
—Cowper.

"For Mordecai the Jew was next unto king Ahasuerus, and great among the Jews, and accepted of the multitude of his brethren, seeking the wealth of his people, and speaking peace to all his seed"—Esther 10: 3.

MORDECAI, the faithful Jew who withstood Haman the Agagite, whom he recognized as the enemy of God and His covenant people, became their benefactor when advanced to the position where he administered the affairs of the kingdom at the king's behest. In this he reminds us that God is now "speaking peace by Jesus Christ," who has overcome our great enemy. He has annulled him that had the power of death, even the devil, and delivered those who once trembled beneath the sentence of death, and given them that cloudless peace which can never again be disturbed.

> "A mind at perfect peace with God!
>   Oh, what a word is this!
> A sinner reconciled by blood,
>   This, this, indeed is peace.
>
> By nature and by practice far,
>   How very far from God,
> But now by grace brought nigh to Him,
>   Through faith in Jesus' blood."

—C. Paget.

"Then Job arose, and rent his mantle, and shaved his head, and fell down upon the ground, and worshipped, and said, Naked came I out of my mother's womb, and naked shall I return thither: the Lord gave, and the Lord hath taken away; blessed be the name of the Lord. In all this Job sinned not, nor charged God foolishly"
—Job 1: 20-22.

SUDDENLY bereft of nearly all that his heart held dearest, Job's confidence in God shines out most brilliantly. He made no foolish charge against his Creator, as though such testings were a denial of His love. He recognized that he had to do with One infinite in wisdom, as in grace, and he could glorify Him in the hour of trial. Bereavements often prove just where the heart is. If occupied with persons, however dear, rather than with the Lord Himself, there will be a break-down when human props are taken away. But where God fills the vision of the soul, the heart will rest in Him though all else may vanish.

"I cannot tell why life should thus be shorn,—
  Or heart thus emptied be:
Why stricken, broken, desolate, forlorn,
  Should be my life's decree:
Yet—through my blinding tears I fain would trace
The unchanged outline of Thy tender face."

—J. Danson Smith.

"I know that my Redeemer liveth, and that He shall stand at the latter day upon the earth: and though after my skin worms destroy this body, yet in my flesh shall I see God: whom I shall see for myself, and mine eyes shall behold, and not another; though my reins be consumed within me"—Job 19: 25-27.

THE poetical part of this book of Job begins with chapter 3 and goes on to chapter 42: 6. In this great drama we have Job in controversy with his three friends, who insist that God does not permit a righteous man to suffer, but that affliction is the portion of the wicked only; therefore Job's case implies that God is dealing with him because of some sin or sins, open or secret, which the patriarch cannot or will not acknowledge. When the friends fail to convince him of wickedness, Elihu appears "to speak on God's behalf" and shows that suffering is not necessarily punishment for sins actually committed, but may often be chastening or discipline in order to bring man to a deeper realization of his own impotence, as also to emphasize man's littleness and ignorance and to magnify the greatness and wisdom of God. This the Lord Himself enlarges upon when He speaks to Job out of the storm, with the result that the heart of the sufferer is bowed in reverence and repentance before Him.

During all the perplexing experiences, Job maintains his faith in God and has absolute assurance that some day all will be made clear. Meantime he can say, "Though He slay me, yet will I trust in Him," for he has a sure hope of resurrection when he shall, in his flesh, see God and all will be made plain.

> "I know that, though He may remove
> The friends on whom I lean,
> 'Tis that I thus may learn to love
> And trust the One unseen.
> And, when at last I see His face
> And know as I am known,
> I will not care how rough the road
> That led me to my home." —Grace Troy.

"Behold in this thou art not just: I will answer thee, that God is greater than man. Why dost thou strive against Him? for He giveth not account of any of His matters"—Job 33: 12, 13.

THOUGH God's ways with His people are often perplexing and baffling to human reason, we may be assured that He will justify Himself at last. If we never understand the reasons for many of His dealings with us here on earth, all will be clear when we stand eventually in His presence, in the full blaze of resurrection glory. Till then faith can afford to wait, knowing that infinite wisdom cannot err, and that all the sufferings of this present life will be repaid abundantly with bliss eternal. This was Job's confidence even when his distress was so deep that he seemed to be overwhelmed in a sea of trouble and false accusation.

"I know not why His hand is laid
   In chastening on my life,
Nor why it is my little world
   Is filled so full of strife.

I know not why, when faith looks up
   And seeks for rest from pain,
That o'er my sky fresh clouds arise
   And drench my path with rain.

I know not why my prayer so long
   By Him has been denied;
Nor why, while others' ships sail on,
   Mine should in port abide.

But I do know that God is love,
   That He my burden shares,
And though I may not understand,
   I know, for me, He cares."

—Grace Troy.

"I have heard of Thee by the hearing of the ear: but now mine eye seeth Thee. Wherefore I abhor myself, and repent in dust and ashes"—Job 42: 5, 6.

"YE have heard of the patience of Job," writes the Apostle James (Jas. 5: 11), "and have seen the end of the Lord; that the Lord is very pitiful, and of tender mercy." That "end" was to give to Job such a realization of the greatness, the majesty, the power, and the goodness of God, that it would produce in His servant such a sense of his own nothingness as to bring him to repentance (Job 42: 2-6). But it was the repentance of a saint, not of a sinner; for God's children need to see their own good-for-nothingness as truly as the unregenerate. No matter how careful our walk or how consistent our behavior, we are ever to say with Paul, "I know that in me (that is, in my flesh,) dwelleth no good thing" (Rom. 7: 18). Hence it is that when God would write a book on repentance, He searches the world over, not for the worst, but for the best man He can find, and then He shows how He brought that good man to an end of himself.

"Less, less of self each day
　And more, my God, of Thee;
Oh, keep me in Thy way,
　However rough it be.

Less of the flesh each day,
　Less of the world and sin;
More of Thy love, I pray,
　More of Thyself within.

Riper and riper now,
　Each hour let me become;
Less fond of things below,
　More fit for such a home.

More moulded to Thy will,
　Lord, let Thy servant be;
Higher and higher still—
　Nearer and nearer Thee."

"Blessed is the man that walketh not in the counsel of the ungodly, nor standeth in the way of sinners, nor sitteth in the seat of the scornful. But his delight is in the law of the Lord; and in His law doth he meditate day and night"—Ps. 1: 1, 2.

THIS blessed man is God's ideal of what man ought to be in this scene. It finds its perfect fulfilment in the holy behavior of our Lord Jesus Christ, who ever did the things that pleased the Father. We, in our measure, are called to walk as He walked (1 John 2: 6), according to the example He has left us (1 Pet. 2: 21). To do this we must be regenerated (Titus 3: 5). It is a life of holy separation from all evil that is in view. The blessed man is careful to avoid any participation with the ungodly so far as their attitude toward divine things is concerned. His piety does not consist in a negative attitude toward evil alone, but in the positive enjoyment of what is good. The Word of God is precious to him and is his spiritual food, assimilated by meditation (Jer. 15: 16).

Perennially fresh and ever fruitful, the blessed man is likened to a tree whose roots go down to the water streams, ever drawing up that which tends to growth and enrichment, so that he is a witness for God to all who know him, as they see how richly grace is working in his soul.

> "O Lord, when we the path retrace,
>   Which Thou on earth hast trod,
> To man Thy wondrous love and grace,
>   Thy faithfulness to God.
>
> We wonder at Thy lowly mind,
>   And fain would like Thee be,
> And all our rest and pleasure find
>   In learning, Lord, of Thee."

—J. G. Deck.

"The heavens declare the glory of God; and the firmament showeth His handiwork. . . . The law of the Lord is perfect, converting the soul: the testimony of the Lord is sure, making wise the simple"—Ps. 19: 1, 7.

IN this nineteenth Psalm we are called to consider the twofold testimony of creation and of the Word, or the Bible, as we call it. God has revealed His eternal power and deity in the wonders of the created universe (Rom. 1: 20). This testimony is so full and so wonderful, so compelling, if considered carefully, that men are without excuse if they reject it. In addition, however, He has revealed His love and His righteousness in the Scriptures, where we learn of His marvelous plan of redemption for lost mankind. It is this which, if received in faith, will produce the new birth (1 Pet. 1: 23-25).

The amazing mechanism of the universe declares there is a Master Mind behind it. It is designed to lead men to recognize the personality and omnipotence of God. Well has Young written, "An undevout astronomer is mad." The heavens are ever telling of their Creator's wisdom, and calling men to bow reverently before Him and to seek His face. But it is only in the Scriptures that we have the full revelation of His Fatherhood and His redemptive plan. We should never understand His grace apart from its manifestation in our Lord Jesus Christ, who is Himself the central theme of both Testaments. It is through this unveiling that we are enabled to draw nigh to God, knowing He is full of mercy and compassion, infinitely holy and righteous, yet ready to forgive all who trust His Son, who has made full expiation for all our sins.

"Heaven above is softer blue,
    Earth around is sweeter green!
Something lives in every hue
    Christless eyes have never seen:
Birds with gladder songs o'erflow,
    Flowers with deeper beauties shine,
Since I know, as now I know,
    I am His, and He is mine."   —Wade Robinson.

"The Lord is my Shepherd; I shall not want"
—Ps. 23: 1.

SOMEONE has said, "Psalm 23 is the best loved of all the Psalms and it is the one least believed!' Do we really believe it? We all love it; do we not? Its beautiful imagery, its wonderful idyllic poetry, its expressions of confidence in Jehovah, our Great Shepherd, appeal to every discriminating and Spirit-taught mind. But do we know the blessedness of resting upon its implied promises? When out of employment, laid aside by illness, or facing bereavement, are we able to say from the heart, "The Lord is my Shepherd; I shall not want?" Not want what? Another psalm answers, "They that seek the Lord shall not want any good thing" (Ps. 34: 10). And again, "There is no want to them that fear Him" (Ps. 34: 9). Why, then, should the child of God ever be troubled and distressed by thoughts of future ill? God is over all and He is undertaking for us.

Since the Lord is my Shepherd, I shall not want:

Rest—"He maketh me to lie down."
Refreshment—"He leadeth me beside the still waters."
Restoration—"He restoreth my soul."
Guidance—"He leadeth me in the paths of righteousness."
Confidence—"I will fear no evil."
Companionship—"Thou art with me."
Comfort—"Thy rod and thy staff they comfort me."
Provision—"Thou preparest a table."
Unction—"Thou anointest my head."
Satisfaction—"My cup runneth over."
Protection—"Goodness and mercy shall follow me."
A Home at last—"I will dwell in the house of the Lord for ever."

"I had fainted unless I had believed to see the good-ness of the Lord in the land of the living"—Ps. 27: 13.

THE first three words are italicized in our English ver-sion and do not represent any words in the original text. Actually, the sentence is, in a sense, unfinished. Or it may be considered as an exclamation, "Oh, if I had not believed to behold the goodness of the Lord in the land of the living!" Had David been without faith and spiritual insight, he could not, dare not, think what the sad results might have been when his enemies were seeking his de-struction and false witnesses were endeavoring to blight his life and ruin his testimony. But believing God, he triumphed over them all. Looking upon the promises of the Lord as certain of fulfilment, he was preserved from moral and spiritual shipwreck.

"Unless I had believed,
    I had fainted," long ago,
So buffeted by whelming seas,
    With treach'rous undertow;
I dare not think what might have been
    "Unless I had believed."

"Unless I had believed,"
    I could not have won the fight,
Too many and too fierce my foes
    To have withstood their might;
They would have torn me, limb from limb,
    "Unless I had believed."

Now that I have believed,
    Are my feet upon the Rock,
My soul established, strong, secure,
    To brave the earthquake shock;
What tragic loss, what black despair!—
    "Unless I had believed."

—T. O. Chisholm.

"The Lord will strengthen him upon the bed of languishing: Thou wilt make all his bed in his sickness"
—Ps. 41: 3.

SICKNESS is one of the many consequences of sin. Believers' bodies are as subject to illnesses as those of the unsaved, because we are still waiting for the redemption of the body (Rom. 8:23), which we shall receive at our Lord's return (Phil. 3: 20, 21). But we are encouraged to pray for physical health (Jas. 5: 16), and when granted, whether with or without means such as medicines, and so forth, we should recognize all as coming from God Himself.

When tempted to think that God has forgotten and that we have very little to praise Him for, let us consider how sinful and disobedient we have often been and how patiently He has borne with us. As we reflect on these things, we will have a new conception of His love and grace.

> "Oft have I sat in secret sighs
>   To feel my flesh decay;
> Then groaned aloud, with frightened eyes
>   To view the tottering clay.
>
> But I forbid my sorrows now,
>   Nor dares my flesh complain;
> Diseases bring their profit too—
>   The joy o'ercomes the pain."

—Isaac Watts.

"Give the King Thy judgments, O God, and Thy righteousness unto the King's son. He shall judge Thy people with righteousness, and Thy poor with judgment. The mountains shall bring peace to the people, and the little hills, by righteousness. . . . In His days shall the righteous flourish; and abundance of peace so long as the moon endureth. He shall have dominion also from sea to sea, and from the river unto the ends of the earth"
—Ps. 72: 1-3, 7, 8.

WAR is the result of the distrust and jealousies that prevail among the nations, and all of these are but expressions of the sinfulness of men's hearts. Until all this is curbed there can be no lasting peace for mankind. Men may try to bring about universal peace by treaties and covenants, but as long as sin rules in their hearts their efforts will only end in disappointment and heart-rending strife. Only when the Lord Jesus Christ asserts His power, at His second coming, will the kingdoms of this world become the kingdom of our Lord and His Christ (Rev. 11: 15). Then all the glorious predictions of the prophets will be literally fulfilled and wars will cease out of the earth, for everywhere men will own the authority of Him who alone can carry out the divine program. So long as He is rejected, there must be conflicts and misunderstandings among the nations, but when He comes to reign as King of kings and Lord of lords (Rev. 19: 16), God's will shall be done on earth as it is done in Heaven (Matt. 6: 10).

"Soon Thou shalt come in bright array,
   With all Thy saints in train—
To conquer earth, erect Thy throne,
   And o'er creation reign.

Lord, haste that bright expected day
   When earth shall cease to groan;
When all Thine own shall be with Thee,
   And Thou upon Thy throne.

Then streams of everlasting praise
   To Thy blest name shall flow—
From all the ransomed in the skies,
   And those on earth below."   —C. C. Crowston.

APRIL 2

"Thou didst cause judgment to be heard from heaven; the earth feared, and was still, when God arose to judgment, to save all the meek of the earth. Surely the wrath of man shall praise Thee: the remainder of wrath shalt Thou restrain"—Ps. 76: 8-10.

NOTHING perplexes the average believer in the justice of God more than the mystery of His long toleration of evil. But the man of faith can afford to wait in quietness and confidence (Isa. 30: 15), assured that He who is the righteous Judge of all men will never permit anything in this universe which will not prove at last to have been under His overruling hand and allowed for some good purpose. He will never have to apologize to any of His creatures for anything He ever does or which He permits to be done by Satan and those who are subject to the great Adversary. All things are so ordered or overruled that He will be glorified and man will be blessed when the mystery of God is finished (Rev. 10: 7) and the kingdoms of this world become the kingdoms of our God and of His Christ (Rev. 11: 15).

> "Thy calmness bends serene above
>   My restlessness to still,
> Around me flows Thy quickening life
>   To nerve my faltering will;
> Thy presence fills my solitude,
> Thy providence turns all to good.
>
> Embosomed deep in Thy great love,
>   Held in Thy law, I stand;
> Thy hand in all things I behold,
>   And all things in Thy hand;
> Thou leadest me by unsought ways,
> And turn'st my mourning into praise."
>
> —Samuel Longfellow.

"**O sing unto the Lord a new song: sing unto the Lord, all the earth. Sing unto the Lord, bless His name; show forth His salvation from day to day. Declare His glory among the heathen, His wonders among all people**"
—**Ps. 96: 1-3.**

THE book of Psalms is composed largely of poetical expressions of worship, but on reading these matchless hymns of praise we need to remember that redemption was not yet actually accomplished. The veil was unrent. God was hidden in the thick darkness (2 Chron. 6: 1). His people worshiped in an earthly sanctuary and their understanding of His truth was very limited compared to that full revelation now given in the New Testament, particularly in the Epistles, which open up the truth of Christ's finished work on the cross, the rent veil permitting God to come out to man and man to go in to God. Our place of worship is the heavenly sanctuary (Heb. 10: 19), where Christ sits exalted at the Father's right hand. We are called to worship in spirit and in truth (John 4: 24), as those whose citizenship is in heaven (Phil. 3: 20), and who are in the joyful consciousness that we have been accepted in the Beloved (Eph. 1: 6).

"The holiest we enter
    In perfect peace with God,
Through whom we found our centre
    In Jesus and His blood:
Though great may be our dullness
    In thought and word and deed,
We glory in the fullness
    Of Him that meets our need.

Much incense is ascending
    Before th' eternal throne;
God graciously is bending
    To hear each feeble groan;
To all our prayers and praises
    Christ adds His sweet perfume,
And Love the censer raises,
    These odors to consume."

—Mary Bowley.

"Oh that men would praise the Lord for His goodness, and for His wonderful works to the children of men"
—Ps. 107: 8, 15, 21, 31.

FOUR times in Psalm 107 we have these same words, calling for praise and thanksgiving. Elsewhere we read, "Praise is comely for the upright" (Ps. 33: 1), and again we are told, "Whoso offereth praise glorifieth Me" (Ps. 50: 23). Praise is the spontaneous outcome of a grateful heart who has experienced the saving grace of God and who recognizes His providential dealings and Fatherly care day by day. It is strange indeed that we should need to be urged to praise. But we are so prone to be forgetful of the source of our mercies and to rejoice in the gifts (which we so readily take for granted) rather than in the Giver Himself, who is worthy of our constant adoration. How often we pray for blessings and forget to give thanks when our cries are heard!

> "Our Father, we give thanks to Thee
>   That Thou hast given to us food
> And shelter, hast supplied our needs
>   And brought our hearts to joyous mood.
>
> Yet we do thank Thee more, that if
>   These temporal things should fail, and we
> Be hungry, naked, desolate,
>   We still could place our trust in Thee;
>
> And know that though the darkness come,
>   The dawning is not far away,
> And Thou whose mercy cannot cease
>   Will bring to us the light of day."
>
> —Clara Aiken Speor.

APRIL 5

"If I take the wings of the morning, and dwell in the uttermost parts of the sea; even there shall Thy hand lead me, and Thy right hand shall hold me"
—Ps. 139: 9, 10.

A REALIZATION of the omnipresence of God must be a source of wretchedness to the wicked, who would fain find a hiding-place where His holy eye cannot see them, but it occasions great joy and comfort to the tried believer, who knows that, through grace, God is his own loving Father and that His holy eye ever looks down in compassion upon His people as they face the trials and testings of this life. The personality of God means so much to the soul who trusts Him. No mere impersonal force or unsympathetic principle of nature can comfort the heart and meet the need of the one who yearns for fellowship with the living God (Ps. 42: 1, 2). He is the God of the spirits of all flesh (Num. 16: 22), the Father of spirits (Heb. 12: 9), who is the Creator of the ends of the earth (Isa. 40: 28), and the Sustainer of all who turn to Him (Ps. 55: 22). He is above all and through all and in us all (Eph. 4: 6), and nothing is hidden from His eyes (Ps. 11: 4), those eyes which run to and fro through the whole earth to take note of all who confide in Him and seek to do His will, that He may show Himself strong in their behalf (2 Chron. 16: 9).

"With Thee by faith I walk in crowds—alone,
Making to Thee my wants and wishes known:
Drawing from Thee my daily strength in prayer,
Finding Thine arm sustains me everywhere;
While, thro' the clouds of sin and woe, the light
Of coming glory shines more sweetly bright;
And this my daily boast—my aim—my end—
That my Redeemer is my God—my Friend!"

—C. H. I.

"The path of the just is as the shining light, that shineth more and more unto the perfect day. The way of the wicked is as darkness: they know not at what they stumble"—Prov. 4: 18, 19.

HOW marked is the difference between the way of the wicked and the path of the just! That of the latter leads ever onward and upward to that city which is enlightened by the glory of God, and from whose gates streams that glory which shines brighter and brighter unto the perfect day. Death is but the entrance of the saint into the presence of the Lord and the beginning of a richer, fuller life, "far better" (Phil. 1: 23) than anything known on earth. But how terrible the contrast when we consider the way of the lawless! Bent on enjoying the present moment, seeking ever some new thrill, they cast all caution to the winds and run in the path of iniquity.

Proverbs has been called "The Young Man's Book." It abounds in wholesome instruction, which, if implicitly followed, will insure a life of happiness and rectitude. It was not written to show the way of salvation, nor does it deal with prophecy or great spiritual doctrines. It is as truly applicable for this age of grace as for that of law, which preceded it.

"Child of My love, fear not the unknown morrow,
　　Dread not the new demand life makes of thee;
Thy ignorance doth hold no cause for sorrow
　　Since what thou knowest not is known to Me.

Thou canst not see today the hidden meaning
　　Of My command, but thou the light shall gain;
Walk on in faith, upon My promise leaning,
　　And as thou goest all shall be made plain.

One step thou seest—then go forward boldly,
　　One step is far enough for faith to see;
Take that, and thy next duty shall be told thee,
　　For step by step thy Lord is leading thee."

　　　　　　　　　　　　　　　—F. J. Exley.

"The Lord possessed me in the beginning of His way, before His works of old. I was set up from everlasting, from the beginning, or ever the earth was. . . . When He gave to the sea His decree, that the waters should not pass His commandment: when He appointed the foundations of the earth: then I was by Him, as one brought up with Him: and I was daily His delight, rejoicing always before Him; rejoicing in the habitable part of His earth; and My delights were with the sons of men"
—**Prov. 8: 22, 23, 29-31.**

IT is easy to see in Wisdom, as personified in Prov. 8, our blessed Lord Jesus, the eternal Wisdom and Word of God, who was one with the Father from all eternity, and participated with Him in the creation of the universe. How precious to read that His "delights were with the sons of men." He foresaw all that they would be guilty of, yet loved them still. Creation was in order to redemption: It is a mystery far too great for our poor minds to take in, but it tells of a love that is infinite and eternal.

> "Ere God had built the mountains,
>   Or raised the fruitful hills;
> Before He filled the fountains
>   That feed the running rills;
> In Thee, from everlasting,
>   The wonderful I Am
> Found pleasures never wasting,
>   And Wisdom is Thy name.
>
> And couldst Thou be delighted
>   With creatures such as we,
> Who, when we saw Thee, slighted
>   And nailed Thee to a tree?
> Unfathomable wonder!
>   And mystery divine!
> The voice that speaks in thunder
>   Says, 'Sinner, I am thine!' "

—Wm. Cowper.

"The backslider in heart shall be filled with his own ways: and a good man shall be satisfied from himself"
—Prov. 14: 14.

DISTRUST of self and full trust in God is the sure way to prevent backsliding. It is never safe to depend upon past experiences for future blessing, or to rely on one's own ability to stand in the hour of temptation. "He giveth more grace." We see this in the account of Peter's failure. Had his dependence been upon the Lord Himself, he would not have failed so miserably in the hour of stress. It is important to realize, however, that there is a vast difference between spiritual declension and apostasy. No matter how genuine one's Christianity may be, he is never beyond the possibility of failure or backsliding while in this scene, but no real believer will ever become an apostate, for that involves a definite turning away from the truth as to Christ and His redemptive work. The Spirit of God will reclaim the backslider, but there is no such promise for the recovery of the apostate.

The downward path is an easy and rapid one. Peter's boastfulness, when warned by the Lord Jesus of danger, was mistaken for true courage, but when courage was really needed he became a coward and denied all that once he had gloried in.

"Call Thy people back, O Lord,
  As in the early days,
When love was warm, and fresh, and bright
  When first we knew Thy grace;
When first Thy light broke through our night,
  And set our hearts ablaze.
    Lord, call us back!

Call us back to those sweet days
  When hearts were knit as one,
When prayer was as the breath of life;
  Ere we were so undone,
Ere souls were rife with endless strife;
  For Jesus' sake, Thy Son,
    Lord, call us back!"

—H. McDowell.

"Righteousness exalteth a nation, but sin is a reproach to any people"—Prov. 14: 34.

WHEN nations or communities of lesser size turn from the paths of rectitude and self-restraint to those of wickedness and careless self-indulgence, they are in the way of inevitable ruin. It was not the barbarians that destroyed the Roman Empire in the fourth century of our era. It was the voluptuousness and drunkenness of its citizens. Israel could never be vanquished by foes from the outside. It was always the enemies within that caused defeat and brought ruin and desolation. The nation or community that trains its youth to walk in righteousness and shun licentiousness, drunkenness, and other vicious types of behavior will become and remain strong and powerful. Where it is otherwise, its weakness will soon become manifest. It is as true of whole groups as of individuals, that whatsoever they sow will surely be reaped (Gal. 6: 7).

> "Lord, while for all mankind we pray,
>   Of every clime and coast,
> Oh, hear us for our native land,
>   The land we love the most.
>
> Unite us in the sacred love
>   Of knowledge, truth, and Thee,
> And let our hills and valleys shout
>   The songs of liberty.
>
> Lord of the nations, thus to Thee
>   Our country we commend;
> Be Thou her refuge and her boast,
>   Her everlasting Friend!"

"Where there is no vision the people perish"
—Prov. 29: 18.

WE need the revelation of coming glory in order to sustain us in our present conflict with sin and to lift us above discouragement as we often see the apparent thwarting of the will of God. But it is only apparent. Nothing can hinder the eventual carrying out of the divine program. The kingdoms of this world shall yet become the kingdom of our God and His Christ. At the present time we are called upon to suffer for righteousness' sake, to endure trial and persecution, to share in our Saviour's rejection. But as surely as there is a God in Heaven, so surely shall His kingdom come at last and the Crucified shall become King over all the earth. In that day "a King shall reign in righteousness" (Isa. 32: 1). "Righteousness shall be the girdle of His loins" (Isa. 11: 5). Then the law and the prophets shall all be fulfilled and the days of Heaven will be known on earth.

> "The storm-clouds o'er nations that thicken,
>   The woe that is followed by woe,
> But brighten His rainbow of praise—
>   Give this hope greater lustre and glow.
> The voices that echo His coming
>   Ring out o'er the sea and the land,
> The omens that gleam on earth's dial
>   Proclaim that my Lord is at hand.
>
> Then, come, blessed Lord! Call away
>   The blood-purchased Bride of Thy heart;
> No longer delay, but speak Thou the word
>   That bids her from earth to depart.
> Thy joy and her joy will then be complete,
>   While measureless ages roll by;
> She'll then see the infinite measure of love
>   That brought Thee from glory to die!"

—C. C. Crowston.

"**Vanity of vanities, saith the Preacher; Vanity of vanities, all is vanity. . . . All things are full of labor, man cannot utter it, the eye is not satisfied with seeing, nor the ear with hearing**"—Eccl. 1: 2, 8.

THE natural man finds himself caught as on a great whirling wheel, with no power to stay the controlling hand of what seems like a relentless fate. So he finds life to be all vanity and a pursuit after the wind. But the Spirit-taught believer looks up and sees an exalted Christ at God's right hand and knows that He is, in Himself, the Wisdom of God, and so can commit his life in confidence to His loving care, and can exclaim with gladness, "For me to live is Christ, and to die is gain."

"The great wheel of the world goes round,
    And nothing is at a stay;
The generations come and pass,
As shadows move upon the grass,
    More permanent than they.

But yet, though the wheel be high, look up:
    For a Form, and a Human Form,
Sitteth in peace above it still,
And guideth it with a perfect will,
    Through brightness and through storm.

And the wheel of the world is His chariot-wheel,
    For His triumph it moveth on;
And we catch from His glorious face to-day
The peace of its promise all the way,
    Till the goal of His rest be won."

—F. C. Jennings.

"I said in mine heart, Go to now, I will prove thee with mirth, therefore enjoy pleasure: and, behold, this also is vanity"—Eccl. 2: 1.

"I SAID in mine heart." This is one of the key expressions in the book of Ecclesiastes. It is the story of the effort of a man to find the supreme good, apart from divine revelation. He looks into his own heart, follows its dictates, and after trying all that earth has to offer finds all is vanity or emptiness. Worldly folly never satisfied anyone who sought it. Frivolity may captivate the senses for a moment, but it leaves regret behind. How many a devotee of pleasure has exclaimed at last, "Life is not worth living!" Solomon tried to find solace in the pleasures of the wine cup, though determined not to act the part of a fool and allow himself to become a drunkard. He would drink in moderation, hoping in this to find "what was good for the sons of men." His book tells how vain was the effort to find lasting enjoyment in self-indulgence of any kind. He had almost unlimited wealth, and he determined not to deny himself anything that his eyes desired or his heart craved. He gave himself, for a time, at least, wholly to the pursuit of self-gratification, hoping in this to find perfect happiness. But as he looked back upon wasted years and blighted hopes he realized that the selfish life is the empty life. All was emptiness and a pursuit of the wind. Nothing under the sun can satisfy a man made for eternity.

"To walk with God, O fellowship divine!
Man's highest state on earth—Lord, be it mine!
With Thee, may I a close communion hold;
To Thee, the deep recesses of my heart unfold:
Yes, tell Thee all—each weary care and grief
Into Thy bosom pour—till there I find relief.
O let me walk with Thee, Thou Mighty One;
Lean on Thine arm, and trust Thy love alone;
With Thee hold converse sweet where'er I go;
Thy smile of love my highest bliss below!"

—J. J. P.

"I know that, whatsoever God doeth, it shall be for ever: nothing can be put to it, nor anything taken from it: and God doeth it, that men should fear before Him"
—Eccl. 3: 14.

GOD'S Word to us, His children, is not "Yea" and "Nay," but Yea, in Christ Jesus. When He promises nothing can change His purpose. He "will not call back His words" (Isa. 31: 2). To the one who trusts Him He gives eternal life and He has declared that such shall never perish, neither shall they ever be plucked out of His hands. The believer is as secure as God Himself can make him. He is justified from all things, the recipient of a new nature and a life that can never be destroyed, and is set apart to God for eternity in all the value of the finished work of Christ.

"O changeless love that loveth me, though I forget!
Infinite love that saveth me, though snares beset!
Love that cut Satan's tangled chain and set me free;
   Love that drew love from sin's domain;
   Broke Satan's power, bade mercy reign;
     I'll trust in Thee.

And, since I must go forth to meet the night's chill blast,
Thy love's full mantle, soft and warm, around me cast;
Let not the darkness hide from me Thy shining face,
   Until the Morning Star I see;
   Until from earth aloft I flee
     To Thine embrace."

"There was a little city, and few men within it; and there came a great king against it, and besieged it, and built great bulwarks against it: now there was found in it a poor wise man, and he by his wisdom delivered the city; yet no man remembered that same poor man"
—Eccl. 9: 14, 15.

THE little city is Bunyan's Mansoul. The cruel adversary is Satan, the prince and god of this world. The poor wise man is our blessed Lord Jesus Christ, who by His death on Calvary has delivered those once in fear of death and so held all their lifetime in dreadful bondage. Strange that we should ever forget One who has wrought so mightily on our behalf! Surely He should ever be in remembrance as we consider how much we owe to His wisdom, power and grace!

"Oh, 'twas wondrous grace that brought Thee
    From the glory there on high,
And 'twas wondrous love that led Thee
    Thus to stoop, to bleed and die;
Thou wast e'en from everlasting,
    E'er the worlds were brought to light,
Ever dwelling with Thy Father,
    As His own supreme delight.

Now in life and resurrection
    Thou hast link'd us up with Thee,
Standing 'twixt the cross and glory,
    Gladly we remember Thee.
Death and judgment gone forever,
    Glory is our portion now,
And, in spirit there already,
    We before Thy face would bow."

—L. W.

"The labor of the foolish wearieth every one of them, because he knoweth not how to go to the city"
—Eccl. 10: 15.

ALL through the Word of God one glorious city is before the eyes of His saints. It is the city for which Abraham looked, which hath foundations, whose Builder and Maker is God. We see it pictured in all its magnificence in the closing chapters of the Apocalypse. The way to that city is Christ Himself. He says so plainly, "I am the Way. . . . No man cometh unto the Father but by Me." Yet men labor on in their folly, seeking another way because they will not heed the plain message of the gospel. We are warned that, "There is *a* way that seemeth right unto a man, but the end thereof are the ways of death." Not *a* way, but *the* Way will bring us safely home.

> "O God, through Christ the living Way,
>   My Father and my God,—
> So near, and I so far astray,
>   Brought nigh Thee by His blood.
>
> And now by love's own power led on,
>   I reach the inmost rest—
> The nameless rapture of a son
>   Upon the Father's breast."
>
> —G. T. S.

"Cast thy bread upon the waters: for thou shalt find it after many days"—Eccl. 11:1.

THE reference is to the Egyptian method of rice sowing —scattering the seed over the land when flooded by the waters of the Nile, counting on a bountiful harvest later on. So it is with the sower of the gospel seed. He is to be diligent in giving out the Word of Life under all circumstances, knowing that God will not let His Word return unto Him void, but will use it in the salvation of the lost and needy. Oft-times the results of faithful sowing will appear long years afterwards, but in many more cases it will not be until we stand at the judgment-seat of Christ that the harvest will be manifested.

> "Sow thy seed, be never weary,
>   Let no fears thy soul annoy,
> Be the prospect ne'er so dreary,
>   Thou shalt reap the fruits of joy.
>
> Lo, the scene of verdure brightening!
>   See the rising grain appear.
> Look again! The fields are whitening,
>   For the harvest-time is near."

"He brought me to the banqueting house, and His banner over me was love"—Cant. 2: 4.

THE Song of Solomon is the book of communion. It sets forth the nuptial joys of the Heavenly Bridegroom and the Bride of His heart as they commune together in the full recognition of mutual love and faithfulness. The bride, in this verse, is seen in the royal banquet-hall, delighting in the bountiful provision of her Kingly Bridegroom, with love's banner waving overhead. That banner is the standard of the cross. It tells of a love that was stronger than death, which the many waters could not quench. Beneath its folds the loved one enjoys fullest fellowship as she exclaims, "I am my Beloved's, and His desire is toward me."

> "Oh, I am my Beloved's,
>   And my Beloved's mine!
> He brings a poor vile sinner
>   Into His "house of wine"!
> I stand upon His merit,
>   I know no safer stand,
> Not e'en where glory dwelleth,
>   In Immanuel's land.
>
> The bride eyes not her garment,
>   But her dear bridegroom's face;
> I will not gaze at glory,
>   But on my King of Grace—
> Not at the crown He giveth,
>   But on His pierced hand:—
> The Lamb is all the glory
>   Of Immanuel's land."

—Mrs. Cousins.

"A garden inclosed is my sister, my spouse, a spring shut up, a fountain sealed"—Cant. 4: 12.

IT is a poor thing when the Lord does not have the *first* place in the heart. He is thoroughly exclusive. He wants the whole heart for Himself. When it is thus set apart for Him, He will keep the key and He will enter in and enjoy all the sweet flowers and fruit that His own Holy Spirit produces. When this is actually true there will be abundance for the blessing of others, for the living fountain will flow out beyond the walls of the garden to bring refreshment and blessing to a needy world outside. But the great thing is to be sure that He alone holds the key, and that His seal is upon the door which none else can break.

"Take my poor heart, and let it be
Forever closed to all but Thee;
Seal Thou my breast, and let me wear
The pledge of love forever there."

"We have a little sister, and she hath no breasts; what shall we do for our sister in the day when she shall be spoken for?"—Cant. 8: 8.

THE more we enjoy of Christ ourselves, the more we will be concerned about under-privileged ones all about us, and in the regions beyond, who should know of the same blessed Saviour who means so much to us. Oh, these little sisters of ours, and brothers too, who are still sitting in darkness, waiting for the light to reach them! How can we be indifferent to their need? Our Lord has bidden us carry the glad gospel story into all the world, that millions more may share with us the joy of knowing that love which is beyond all telling. These lost sheep in the wilderness need to be sought after and brought to the Good Shepherd who died for them as well as for us.

"Have ye looked for sheep in the desert,
  For those who have missed their way?
Have ye been in the wild waste places,
  Where the lost and wandering stray?
Have ye trodden the lonely highway,
  The foul and the darksome street?
It may be ye'd see in the gloaming
  The print of My wounded feet."

"Then said I, Woe is me! for I am undone; because I am a man of unclean lips, and I dwell in the midst of a people of unclean lips: for mine eyes have seen the King, the Lord of hosts. Then flew one of the seraphims unto me, having a live coal in his hand, which he had taken with the tongs from off the altar: and he laid it upon my mouth, and said, Lo, this hath touched thy lips; and thine iniquity is taken away, and thy sin purged"
—Isa. 6: 5-7.

IT is always of interest when one is privileged to get a personal and intimate account of the revelation of God to a human soul. In this chapter Isaiah lets us into the secret of his wonderful power and equipment for service. He takes us into the sanctuary, shows us how the Lord was revealed to him, and lets us know the circumstances of his call to the prophetic office. This was the real starting-point of his effective ministry. We know from chapter 1: 1, that he began to witness for God in the days of King Uzziah. As the events recorded in chapter 6 took place in the year that ruler died, we conclude that these experiences were subsequent to his earlier prophetic testimony. Many another servant of God has preached to others before learning to know the Lord himself in a definite way and before being brought into the full consciousness of cleansing and enduement for service. Yet we need not think of this as Isaiah's "second blessing." It was rather a part of God's dealing with him in order that he might be better prepared to give out the Word to others because of knowing the reality of having to do with God himself.

"Speak Thou Thy living Word to me,
That I Thy messenger may be,
Indwelt by love and power divine,
To preach that precious truth of Thine.

For Thy strength is in weakness shown,
So, standing in Thy power alone,
Which by Thy grace shall in me dwell,
The story of the cross I'll tell."
—Robert R. Pentecost.

"Therefore the Lord Himself shall give you a sign: Behold, a virgin shall conceive, and bear a son, and shall call His name Immanuel"—Isa. 7: 14.

THE virgin birth of Jesus is a revealed truth, the importance of which no one can properly appraise. Upon this fact hangs the whole plan of redemption. It tells us that God entered into human conditions, became Man without ceasing to be God, took our flesh and blood apart from sin, in order that He might by Himself effect purgation of sins by dying upon the cross. With the denial of the virgin birth goes the denial of the true vicarious atonement of Christ.

Had He been a member of Adam's fallen race He would have needed a Saviour for Himself. As the virgin-born Son of the Father He came into the world as "that Holy One" uncontaminated by sin in the flesh, though in its likeness, and so was able to qualify as our Kinsman-Redeemer.

"Though in the very form of God,
  With heavenly glory crowned,
Thou didst a servant's form assume,
  Beset with sorrow round.

Thou wouldst like wretched man be made
  In ev'ry thing but sin,
That we as like Thee might become
  As we unlike had been."

—Stennett.

"All we like sheep have gone astray; we have turned every one to his own way; and the Lord hath laid on Him the iniquity of us all"—Isa. 53: 6.

HERE we have the entire story of the Bible epitomized: man's ruin both by nature and practice; and God's marvelous and all-sufficient remedy. The verse begins with *all* and ends with *all*. An anxious soul was directed to this passage and found peace. Afterward he said, "I bent low down and went in at the first *all*. I stood up straight and came out at the last." The first is the acknowledgment of our deep need. The second shows how fully that need has been met in the cross of Christ. Happy to be numbered among those who have put in their claim and found salvation through the atoning work which there took place!

> "I was lost, but Jesus found me,
>   Found the sheep that went astray;
>   Threw His loving arms around me,
>   Brought me back into His way."

"Ho, every one that thirsteth, come ye to the waters, and he that hath no money; come ye, buy, and eat; yea, come, buy wine and milk without money and without price. Wherefore do ye spend money for that which is not bread? and your labor for that which satisfieth not? Hearken diligently unto Me, and eat ye that which is good, and let your soul delight itself in fatness"
—Isa. 55: 1, 2.

IF it were not for the truth set forth in chapter 53 of Isaiah, there would be no possibility of the gracious invitation of chapter 55. Throughout this entire section of Isaiah (chaps. 49 to 57) God is presenting His chosen Servant, our Lord Jesus Christ, as the Redeemer of Israel and of the world, whose rejection at His first coming was foreknown and plainly predicted, but who by His propitiatory work was to open up the way for guilty sinners to find peace with God and pardon for all their transgressions. Because of His work God can send forth the gracious invitation for all men everywhere to partake of His salvation. Isaiah has been called "the evangelical prophet" and he well deserves to be so designated. Nowhere else in the Old Testament is the Person and work of our Lord set forth so clearly and fully as in this wonderful book. Man is shown to be utterly bankrupt spiritually, destitute of righteousness, and with no claim upon God whatever. Yet Christ, Jehovah's sinless Servant, is presented as the great sin offering through whose infinite sacrifice all who come to Him in faith will be justified in His sight. His salvation is based upon righteousness. In the cross the sin question has been settled in a righteous way, and so God can now save all who come to Him in faith.

> "I ask thee for nothing—
>   Come just as thou art;
> Come sinful—come guilty—
>   Come give Me thine heart;
> The fountain is open,—
>   It is open to thee,
> Let thy Saviour not say,—
>   'Thou lovest not Me'."

"If thou turn away thy foot from the sabbath, from doing thy pleasure on My holy day; and call the sabbath a delight, the holy of the Lord, honorable; and shalt honor Him, not doing thine own ways, nor finding thine own pleasure, nor speaking thine own words: then shalt thou delight thyself in the Lord; and I will cause thee to ride upon the high places of the earth, and feed thee with the heritage of Jacob thy father: for the mouth of the Lord hath spoken it"—Isa. 58: 13, 14.

IT is of all importance to realize that men are more to God than forms and ceremonies, even of His own devising. "The sabbath was made for man, and not man for the sabbath" (Mark 2: 27). He who is "Lord . . . of the sabbath" is pleased when we use His holy day to bless and help those in trouble, and to relieve the afflicted, so far as we are able to do so. Truly to keep the first day of the week holy to the Lord is to use it for rest, worship, and ministry to others. To think only of relaxation, and to spend this day in pleasure-seeking, is to misuse it and to fail to enter into the purpose God has had in mind in preserving its privileges for us. "I get so weary with all the burdens of business throughout the week," said a Christian tradesman to me once, "that I must have rest and exercise on Sunday. So I use the Lord's Day afternoons visiting in the hospital and seeking to comfort and help the friendless." He returned to work on Monday refreshed and ready for another six days of toil.

Let us cherish our privileges and neither despise them, on the one hand, nor hedge them about with legal enactments, on the other, for which there is no Biblical authorization.

"O sacred day of peace and joy!
    Thy hours are ever dear to me.
Ne'er may a single thought destroy
    The holy calm I feel for thee.

Thy hours are precious unto me,
    For God has given them in His love,
To tell how calm, how blest shall be
    The sabbath rest of heaven above."

"A wonderful and horrible thing is committed in the land; the prophets prophesy falsely, and the priests bear rule by their means; and My people love to have it so: and what will ye do in the end thereof?"—Jer. 5: 30, 31.

THE false prophets in Jeremiah's day ridiculed predictions of coming judgment and prated of peace and safety when the Judge stood at the door (6: 14; 8: 11). It is the same today and will be until the vials of the wrath of God are actually being poured out upon the earth (1 Thess. 5: 3). Men prefer these soft-spoken teachers of error who prophesy smooth things (Isa. 30: 10), to the faithful men of God who declare unflinchingly the Word of the Lord without fear or favor. But in the day of Christ, when every hidden thing is brought to light, God's true servants will be recognized and rewarded, and the preachers of falsehood will be dealt with in judgment.

"Servant of Christ, stand fast amid the scorn
  Of men who little know or love thy Lord;
Turn not aside from toil; cease not to warn,
  Comfort and teach. Trust Him for thy reward:
A few more moments' suffering, and then
Cometh sweet rest from all thy heart's deep pain.

For grace pray much, for much thou needest grace;
  If men thy work deride,—what can they more?
Christ's weary foot thy path on earth doth trace;
  If thorns wound thee, they pierecced Him before;
Press on, look up, though clouds may gather round;
Thy place of service He makes hallowed ground."

—J. J. P.

"This is His name whereby He shall be called, THE LORD OUR RIGHTEOUSNESS"—Jer. 23: 6.

THIS is one of the great covenant names of God: "Jehovah Tsidkenu." It tells us that God has a righteousness for those who can pretend to none of their own. Christ Himself is made unto all who believe in Him, wisdom, righteousness, sanctification and redemption. In order that this might be, He, the sinless One, was "made sin for us that we might be made the righteousness of God in Him" (2 Cor. 5: 21): He is Himself the righteousness in which every redeemed one stands perfect and complete before God. Paul exclaims with rapture that it was his glory "to be found in Him, not having mine own righteousness which is by the law, but the righteousness which is of God by faith" (Phil. 3: 9).

"Jehovah Tsidkenu, my treasure and boast,
Jehovah Tsidkenu, I ne'er can be lost,
By Thee I shall conquer through flood or by field,
My cable, my anchor, my breast-plate and shield."

—R. M. McCheyne.

"I have not sent these prophets, yet they ran: I have not spoken to them, yet they prophesied. But if they had stood in My counsel, and had caused My people to hear My words, then they should have turned from their evil way, and from the evil of their doings"

—Jer. 23: 21, 22.

JEREMIAH is often called "The weeping prophet" because of his tenderness of heart and the grief that possessed him on account of the defection of his people (9: 1). But he could also be very stern when rebuking iniquity. In these things he manifested the same spirit that was seen in all perfection in our blessed Lord, whose tears and denunciations were in perfect keeping. False prophets have ever been the bane of those who are ready to accept almost anyone claiming to speak with divine authority, instead of testing him by what God has already revealed. It was true of old; it is just as true now (2 Pet. 2: 1-3). Therefore we need to try the spirits whether they be of God (1 John 4: 1), for Satan has his ministers who speak plausibly but are really seeking to mislead rather than to edify (2 Cor. 11: 14, 15). Justin Martyr wrote long ago: "Many spirits are abroad in the world and the credentials they display are splendid gifts of eloquence and ability. Christian, look carefully. Ask for the print of the nails."

" 'What think ye of Christ?' is the test
   To try both your state and your scheme;
You cannot be right in the rest,
   Unless you think rightly of Him:
As Jesus appears in your view—
   As He is beloved or not,
So God is disposed to you,
   And mercy or wrath is your lot.

Some take Him a creature to be—
   A man, or an angel at most;
But they have not feelings like me,
   Nor know themselves wretched and lost.
So guilty, so helpless am I,
   I durst not confide in His blood,
Nor on His protection rely,
   Unless I were sure He is God."   —John Newton.

"Behold, the days come, saith the Lord, that I will make a new covenant with the house of Israel, and with the house of Judah: not according to the covenant that I made with their fathers, in the day that I took them by the hand to bring them out of the land of Egypt; which My covenant they brake, although I was a husband unto them, saith the Lord: but this shall be the covenant that I will make with the house of Israel; After those days, saith the Lord, I will put my law in their inward parts, and write it in their hearts; and will be their God, and they shall be My people"—Jer. 31: 31-33.

THE new covenant is the covenant of grace. The legal covenant demanded of man what the unrenewed person could not give—perfect righteousness—implicit obedience to the holy law of God as a ground of blessing. It is epitomized in the words, "Which if a man do, he shall live in them" (Lev. 18: 5). But it contained the solemn warning, "Cursed be he that confirmeth not all the words of this law to do them" (Deut. 27: 26). Because all were disobedient all found it to be a ministration of death and condemnation (2 Cor. 3: 7, 9). If it could have given life to dead sinners, it would then have produced righteousness, as Paul tells us in Galatians 3: 21.

But God used the law to show men their need of His grace because of their own utter sinfulness and their helpless condition. This grace is revealed in the new covenant.

"As debtors to mercy alone,
    Of heavenly mercy we sing;
Nor fear to draw near to the throne,
    Our person and off'rings to bring:
The wrath of a sin-hating God
    With us can have nothing to do;
The Saviour's obedience and blood
    Hide all our transgressions from view.

The work which His goodness began,
    The arm of His strength will complete;
His promise is Yea and Amen,
    And never was forfeited yet:
Things future, nor things that are now,
    Nor all things below nor above,
Can make Him His purpose forego,
    Or sever our souls from His love."

—Toplady.

"Is it nothing to you, all ye that pass by? Behold, and see if there be any sorrow like unto My sorrow, which is done unto Me, wherewith the Lord hath afflicted Me in the day of His fierce anger"—Lam. 1: 12.

WHILE these words, primarily, express the grief of God's afflicted people of Judah when the judgments of the Lord fell upon them, yet they may most suitably be used to express the sorrow of our blessed Lord when He, the true Israel, stood in the place of His people, and bore as our representative the wrath of God against sin, on the cross in those dark hours when the sun was blotted from view and His holy soul was made an offering for sin. Never was there sorrow like His. None other ever endured that which He passed through when all the waves and billows of wrath rolled over His soul. How our hearts should adore Him for such matchless grace as He there exhibited on our behalf!

"Is it nothing to you, all ye that pass by,
Beholding the Saviour uplifted on high,
Maltreated by men and forsaken by God,
Oh, why is He nailed to that cross of wood?"

"The Lord was as an enemy: He hath swallowed up Israel, He hath swallowed up all her palaces: He hath destroyed his strong holds, and hath increased in the daughters of Judah mourning and lamentation"

—Lam. 2: 5.

THE Lord was *as* an enemy. He was never really an enemy of His people. But He had declared, "You only have I known of all the inhabitants of the earth, therefore will I punish you for all your iniquities" (Amos 3:2). He chastens those whom He loves that they may be conformed to His holiness. But though He may use the rod there is always goodness behind it, directing every blow. It is in mercy that He afflicts. Faith recognizes this, and so can bow the head before Him and exclaim, "It is the Lord; let Him do what seemeth Him good;" assured that "He doth not afflict willingly, nor grieve the children of men" (Lam. 3:33). When the purpose of the chastening is accomplished, He will lift the rod and grant that governmental forgiveness in which He delights

"He chose this path for thee,
Though well He knew sharp thorns would tear thy feet,
Knew how the brambles would obstruct the way,
Knew all the hidden dangers thou wouldst meet,
Knew how thy faith would falter day by day,
And still the whisper echoed, 'Yes, I see
This path is best for thee'."

"He saith unto me, Son of man, I send thee to the children of Israel, to a rebellious nation that hath rebelled against Me: they and their fathers have transgressed against Me, even unto this very day. For they are impudent children and stiffhearted. I do send thee unto them; and thou shalt say unto them, Thus saith the Lord God. And they, whether they will hear, or whether they will forbear, (for they are a rebellious house,) yet shall know that there hath been a prophet among them"—Ezek. 2: 3-5.

THE servant of God is responsible to the Lord Himself. Having received his commission, he is to go forth in the name of the One who sends him, declaring the message committed to him. The results must be left with God. Whether men hear or whether they forbear, he who proclaims the Word faithfully has delivered his soul. The apostle Paul entered into this when he spoke of being a sweet savor of Christ unto God both in them that are saved and in them that perish (2 Cor. 2: 15). God is honored when His truth is preached, no matter what attitude the hearers take toward it, and that Word will not return void, but will accomplish the divine purpose (Isa. 55: 11).

"Be not men's servant: think what costly price
    Was paid that thou mayest His own bondsman be,
Whose service perfect freedom is. Let this
    Hold fast thy heart. His claim is great to thee:
None should thy soul enthrall, to whom 'tis given
To serve on earth, with liberty of heaven.

Be wise, be watchful. Wily men surround
    Thy path. Be careful, for they seek with care
To trip thee up. See that no plea is found
    In thee thy Master to reproach. The snare
They set for thee will then themselves inclose,
And God His righteous judgment thus disclose."

—J. J. P.

MAY 2

"The word of the Lord came unto me, saying, Son of man, What is the vine tree more than any tree, or than a branch which is among the trees of the forest? Shall wood be taken thereof to do any work? or will men take a pin of it to hang any vessel thereon? Behold, it is cast into the fire for fuel; the fire devoureth both the ends of it, and the midst of it is burned. Is it meet for any work?"—Ezek. 15: 1-4.

GOD is the God of truth. He loves reality and detests pretence. The Lord Jesus when on earth, as God manifest in the flesh, took this same attitude. While filled with love for lost sinners and tenderly compassionate toward any who desired to know the truth, He sternly denounced hypocrisy and self-righteousness, pronouncing severe judgments on those who thus attempted to cover up their real condition before God. Where there is divine life in the soul there will be fruit for Him outwardly. No amount of profession can make up for the lack of this evidence of genuine repentance and the regenerating grace of God. Character produced by the work of the Holy Spirit within will result in behavior that is in keeping therewith. The Lord is glorified when those who profess to belong to the household of faith bear the precious fruit which proclaims the genuineness of that which they say has been wrought in their souls. A professor who does not bear fruit is like a vine that does not produce grapes. It is practically useless. Believers are intended to be lights in a dark world, attracting others to Christ.

In order to meet these responsibilities one must be born from above, for the natural man cannot live on a spiritual plane. He has no understanding of the things of God (1 Cor. 2: 14). Therefore it is by their fruits that the servants of God are known. Service and fruit spring from the divine life implanted in the new birth.

> "I would not work my soul to save;
> That work my Lord hath done;
> But I would work like any slave
> For love to God's dear Son."

"When I say unto the wicked, O wicked man, thou shalt surely die; if thou dost not speak to warn the wicked from his way, that wicked man shall die in his iniquity; but his blood will I require at thine hand. Nevertheless, if thou warn the wicked of his way to turn from it; if he do not turn from his way, he shall die in his iniquity; but thou hast delivered thy soul"

—Ezek. 33: 8, 9.

WILLIAM BOOTH, the first General of the Salvation Army, called Ezekiel 33 "the duty chapter," and was constantly pressing its importance on his officers and soldiers. Every one who professes to be a follower of Christ may well lay it to heart. On the other hand, it is quite necessary that we understand the dispensational place of such a passage as this. It is not the unfolding of the gospel, but the setting forth of the principles of the divine government. In other words, it has to do with this life and man's responsibility to walk before God in righteousness here on earth. It has no bearing whatever upon the question of eternal salvation. It is not by turning from sin and walking in righteousness that we are justified before God. Nor does the believer forfeit life eternal who in the hour of temptation forgets the responsibilities resting upon him and turns into the bypath of disobedience. Such conduct will bring him under the disciplinary government of God, of which physical death is the last stroke. But this does not touch the matter of his redemption by the precious blood of Christ. It is because people are in covenant relationship with God that He chastens those who err (Heb. 12: 6). The two principles of grace and government run side by side and should never be confused, but carefully distinguished.

"Some have gone forth with the story so old,
  Reaping a harvest more precious than gold;
Are you, too, faithfully doing your share,
  Helping together by gifts and by prayer?"

—Grace Troy.

"Daniel purposed in his heart that he would not defile himself with the portion of the king's meat nor the wine which he drank"—Dan. 1:8.

DANIEL and his three friends, and Paul the apostle, are striking examples of men who would not risk the ruin of their testimony by self-indulgence or pandering to "fleshly lusts, which war against the soul" (1 Pet. 2:11). Christians cannot afford to be careless as to these matters. The body is the Lord's. It is the temple in which the Holy Spirit dwells. To defile it by any form of unclean living is to dishonor God and to render one powerless in the hour of stress.

In the world we hear much today of efficiency experts. Men realize that if a workman, a clerk, a professional man, or an executive, is to be at his best, he must eschew many things that others indulge in who think only of momentary pleasure and sensual gratification. The man to be trusted is the man who rules himself and holds all his appetites in subjection. In spiritual things the same rule applies. He who purposeth in his heart that he will not "defile himself," but yields to the control of the Holy Spirit, is the one who will be most used of God on earth, and some day will "stand before the King" to be rewarded in the day of manifestation.

> "There is a purity of heart,
>   A cleanness of desire,
> Wrought by the Holy Comforter
>   With sanctifying fire.
> There is a glory that awaits
>   Each blood-washed soul on high,
> When Christ returns to take His Bride
>   With Him beyond the sky."

> —Anon.

"He will deliver us out of thine hand, O king. But if not, be it known unto thee, O king, that we will not serve thy gods"—Dan. 3: 17, 18.

THERE is something very fine about the confidence expressed by these three young Hebrews. It was not necessary for God to deliver them from the furnace, if it were not His will. They could trust Him anyway. If He did not quench the flame He would give grace to endure, and they knew that in another world all would be appraised at its true value. It is a great lesson we all need to learn.

"A scoffing world is looking on,
    The furnace glows with furious heat;
The test is real, the foe is near,
    Waiting to witness my retreat.

Hosts of evil gather round me,
    The Son of God seems lost to view.
Oh, for faith to meet the crisis;
    Oh, for the courage to go through!

What, this sudden sweet empow'ring?
    Whence, this strange, exultant cry?
If my God comes not, I'll trust Him,
    Though to trust Him means to die!"

—Margaret Denison Armstrong.

"The kingdom and dominion, and the greatness of the kingdom under the whole heaven, shall be given to the people of the saints of the Most High, whose kingdom is an everlasting kingdom, and all dominions shall serve and obey Him"—Dan. 7: 27.

TWICE in the book of Daniel God has given great prophetic outlines of the course of world empire, culminating in the setting aside of all earthly dominions and the setting up of the long-looked-for kingdom of God in this scene, the kingdom of the Son of Man which will be as the days of heaven upon earth. This will be at the second advent of our Lord Jesus Christ when He will descend from heaven with all His saints to put down iniquity and establish righteousness throughout all the world. For this all creation sighs, and to this all instructed believers look forward. Then those who have suffered with Christ in the hour of His rejection shall reign with Him in the day of His glory.

> "Jesus shall reign where'er the sun
> Does his successive journeys run;
> His kingdom stretch from shore to shore,
> Till moons shall wax and wane no more."
>
> —I. Watts.

"Then said he unto me, Fear not, Daniel: for from the first day that thou didst set thine heart to understand and to chasten thyself before thy God, thy words were heard, and I am come for thy words"—Dan. 10: 12.

A GREAT mystery is unfolded here in regard to prayer. Daniel had been praying "three full weeks" about a certain matter, and when, finally, the answer came, he was told that at the beginning of his supplication God had heard, but an angel from heaven had been twenty-one days fighting his way through the evil hosts of Satan in order to reach him. The prince of the kingdom of Persia referred to in verse 13 was one of these wicked spirits evidently seeking to hinder God's plan. This should throw light on many delayed answers. God has not been indifferent, but a conflict is going on in the heavenlies (Eph. 6: 12), because of which there seems to be delay, but God's purpose is sure, and His plan will be carried out.

> "Unanswered yet?—The prayer your lips have pleaded
> In agony of soul these many years?
> Doth faith begin to fail, is hope departing,
> And think you all in vain those falling tears?
> Say not the Father hath not heard your prayer,
> You shall have your desire sometime, somewhere."

> —Mrs. Ophelia G. Adams.

"I will betroth thee unto Me for ever; yea, I will betroth thee unto Me in righteousness, and in judgment, and in lovingkindness, and in mercies. I will even betroth thee unto Me in faithfulness: and thou shalt know the Lord"—Hos. 2: 19, 20.

HOSEA is in some respects the tenderest of all the prophets, unless we except Jeremiah, who was a man of very similar spirit.

But the latter was unmarried, whereas Hosea had a very sad matrimonial experience, which was designed of God to set forth Israel's relationship to Himself and their unfaithfulness to the covenant He had made with them. Hosea's wife proved untrue to all her vows and became a poor characterless slave. Yet the prophet sought her out, redeemed her, and took her to himself in forgiving love, only to have his heart broken by her continued waywardness. It sets forth most graphically, not only Jehovah's unchanging love for Israel, His earthly people, but it pictures vividly His grace toward the individual soul. He is Redeemer, Restorer, and unfailing Friend, whose loving-kindness exceeds our worst offences and whose forgiveness is extended to every repentant sinner, no matter how dark and shameful the record may be.

"Loved with everlasting love,
　　Led by grace that love to know;
Spirit, breathing from above,
　　Thou hast taught me it is so!
Oh, this full and perfect peace!
　　Oh, this transport all Divine!
In a love which cannot cease,
　　I am His and He is mine."

—W. Robinson.

"Come, and let us return unto the Lord: for He hath torn, and He will heal us: He hath smitten, and He will bind us up. After two days will He revive us: in the third day He will raise us up, and we shall live in His sight. Then shall we know, if we follow on to know the Lord: His going forth is prepared as the morning; and He shall come unto us as the rain, as the latter and former rain unto the earth"—Hos. 6: 1-3.

IT is a great thing to realize that human sin and failure do not alter the love of God toward those who have offended Him so grievously. He loves us, not on account of anything meritorious that He sees in us, but simply because of what He is in Himself. "God is love" (1 John 4: 8, 16). This is not what He does, but what He is. It is His very nature. And loving us, He has Himself provided a way for our forgiveness in the first place, when we come to Him as needy sinners, and our restoration, when we fail, even after we have known His grace in this initial sense. We wrong Him if we doubt His love or if we give in to despair when our awakened consciences accuse us of base ingratitude and colossal iniquity in having offended against so holy a God and so loving a Saviour.

"God of the shadows, lead me through the gloaming,
    Arch the long road with fretted vaults of green;
Send but a gleam to tell me I am homing,
    Let not Thy face be seen.

Fold well Thy cloak of gentlest pity round me,
    Keep Thy bright secrets till the morning break;
Why should I seek Thee, Lord, when Thou hast found me,
    And know'st the way I take?"

"Therefore also now, saith the Lord, turn ye even to Me with all your heart, and with fasting, and with weeping, and with mourning: and rend your heart, and not your garments, and turn unto the Lord your God: for He is gracious and merciful, slow to anger, and of great kindness, and repenteth Him of the evil"—Joel 2: 12, 13.

THE only times that the Lord is spoken of as repenting, in connection with His own children, are when He turns from judgment to mercy, from chastening to restoring grace. He delights in manifesting the loving-kindness of His heart to His erring ones when they come to Him in self-judgment and contrition of soul, confessing their backslidings. Then His love can flow out freely and He can and will be a Father unto them who thus take the place before Him where they can appropriate His forgiving grace. A broken heart over sin, He will never despise.

"In a time of deep dejection
    Jesus journeyed by,
Saw my heart was dull and empty,
    Gently asked me 'Why?'

Then I told Him all the story
    Of my bitter woe,
How my hopes and joys had perished
    Many years ago.

And the tears were softly dropping
    As I told Him all,
Yet He did not chide my weeping,
    Though He saw them fall.

But when I had told the story,
    Lovingly He came,
Filled, Himself, the vacant chambers,
    Blessed be His name!

Now no more my heart is vacant,
    Nevermore can be;
Filled with Jesus, 'Jesus only,'
    For eternity!"

"Then answered Amos, and said to Amaziah, I was no prophet, neither was I a prophet's son; but I was an herdman, and a gatherer of sycomore fruit; and the Lord took me as I followed the flock, and the Lord said unto me, Go, prophesy unto My people Israel"

—Amos 7: 14, 15.

AMOS was divinely called. He had no thought of becoming or being recognized as a prophet, as some men today select the "ministry" as a profession. He would have been content to pursue his humble avocation as a small farmer, or possibly a mere farmer's hand, or assistant, if such had been the mind of God for him. But as he followed the flock, his soul was in communion with Jehovah. As he gathered wild figs his heart meditated on the great issues of the soul's relationship to God and the importance of obedience to His Word. From this humble service he was divinely called to proclaim the truth of God to the people.

Sad and solemn are the dirge-like measures of the prophet's lamentation over the fallen nation that he loved so well, and from which he could not dissociate himself. They had broken down utterly in their professed fidelity to God as was manifested in their unrighteous behavior and their contempt for the poor. The prophet calls them to face these things in the presence of God and to turn from sin to justice—to consider the cause of the needy and the under-privileged and to recognize their responsibility to hold all that they have as stewards of the Most High, to be dispensed in accordance with His Word. Surely all that has a voice for us today!

"His lamp am I, to shine where He shall say,
And lamps are not for sunny rooms,
Nor for the light of day.
And as sometimes a flame we find,
Clear, shining through the night,
So bright we do not see the lamp,
But only see the light;
So may I shine—His light the flame—
That men may glorify His name."

—Annie Johnson Flint.

"Upon mount Zion shall be deliverance, **and there shall be holiness; and the house of Jacob shall possess their possessions**"—Obadiah, ver. 17.

IT is a great thing to "possess our possessions." Some day this will be true of restored Israel, when they shall be once more in their own land and they will enjoy the inheritance God gave them so long ago, but which they have been bereft of throughout the years of their departure from God. What a lesson is there in this for those of us who through grace have been blessed with all spiritual blessings in the heavenlies in Christ! God cannot give us more than He has given. Yet how feebly do we apprehend the extent of our inheritance and how little of our possessions do we actually enjoy. Oh, for faith to plant our feet on God's promises and possess all that is ours in Christ!

"Things that once were wild alarms
    Cannot now disturb my rest;
Closed in everlasting arms,
    Pillowed on the loving breast.
Oh to lie forever here,
    Doubt and care and self resign,
While He whispers in my ear—
    I am His, and He is mine.

His for ever, only His;
    Who the Lord and me shall part?
Ah, with what a rest of bliss
    Christ can fill the loving heart!
Heaven and earth may fade and flee,
    First-born light in gloom decline;
But, while God and I shall be,
    I am His, and He is mine."

—Wade Robinson.

"God saw their works, that they turned from their evil way; and God repented of the evil, that He had said that He would do unto them; and He did it not"

—Jonah 3: 10.

THE Book of Jonah has a unique place in the Old Testament. It is primarily the book of the divine sovereignty. The confession of the pagan mariners, "Thou, O Lord, hast done as it pleased Thee" (1:14), is emphasized throughout. We are told that "the Lord sent out a great wind into the sea" (ver. 4); "the Lord had prepared a great fish" (ver. 17); "the Lord spake unto the fish" (2:10); "the Lord God prepared a gourd" (4:6); "God prepared a worm" (ver. 7), and "God prepared a vehement east wind" (ver. 8). It is the Sovereign of the Universe who worketh all things according to His own will (Eph. 1:11). This answers every question that foolish, unbelieving skeptics might raise regarding the strange experiences recorded.

God's love and grace transcend all national boundaries. His heart goes out to all the world. He would have all men repent and come to the knowledge of the truth, that judgment may be averted. He has no pleasure in the death of the wicked (Ezek. 18:23). He delights in mercy (Micah 7:18). Judgment is His strange work (Isa. 28:21). It is a great pity when His servants fail to recognize this and are more concerned about their own ease and reputation than about the needs of men to whom they are commissioned to go as God's messengers.

> "Sovereign grace, o'er sin abounding,
> Ransomed souls the tidings tell;
> 'Tis a deep that knows no sounding;
> Who its length and breadth can tell?
> On its glories
> Let my soul forever dwell."

"Truly I am full of power by the Spirit of the Lord, and of judgment, and of might, to declare unto Jacob his transgression, and to Israel his sin. Hear this, I pray you, ye heads of the house of Jacob, and princes of the house of Israel, that abhor judgment, and pervert all equity"—Micah 3: 8, 9.

THE ministry of the prophets was always corrective. They were sent by God to call His people back to the path of obedience. While prediction of things to come was included in their messages, this by no means exhausted their content. They were men who spoke for God in days of declension. They had, therefore, an authority which no servant of God has today, so far as any civil community is concerned. Israel was a theocracy. God was their acknowledged King. The prophets were His messengers to His own covenant people. The ministers of Christ today are a gift to the Church from the ascended Lord (Eph. 4:7-14). They are given for the perfecting of the saints, not for the regulating of the world. On the other hand, they are called to proclaim, fearlessly, those principles of righteousness upon which Christ's kingdom is to be set up, in order that men may see their true condition before God and turn to Him in repentance.

"A little while to sow in tears and weakness
    The precious seed along the vernal plain,
Till into life the tender blade expanding
    Fresh promise gives of summer's ripening grain.

A little while of patient, earnest labor,
    For His dear sake, our best and truest Friend;
A little while to wait for His appearing,
    And then the joy that nevermore shall end.

A little while to bear the cross for Jesus
    And meet the foes that once He overcame;
To stand unmoved, the sword of truth uplifting,
    And through its power to conquer in His name."

—Fanny Crosby.

"But in the last days it shall come to pass, that the mountain of the house of the Lord shall be established in the top of the mountains, and it shall be exalted above the hills; and people shall flow unto it. And many nations shall come, and say, Come, and let us go up to the mountain of the Lord, and to the house of the God of Jacob; and He will teach us of His ways, and we will walk in His paths: for the law shall go forth of Zion, and the word of the Lord from Jerusalem"—Micah 4: 1, 2.

TO MICAH, as to all the seers of the old Testament, the era of universal peace was still in the future and was linked up with the coming and reign of the Branch of Jehovah (Isa. 4: 2), who was destined to be born in Bethlehem (Mic. 5:2), but would be rejected when He came the first time and presented Himself as the appointed Ruler of Israel. Because of this, the earthly people were to pass through a long period of affliction, which will come to an end only when the promised Redeemer shall appear the second time to bring in the long-predicted Kingdom of peace founded upon righteousness.

Until our Lord's return there can never be settled peace among the nations in spite of all man's best and well-meant efforts, for He has declared that until the end of this age there will be wars and rumors of wars, nation rising against nation, and kingdom against kingdom (Matt. 24: 6, 7). In Ezekiel 21: 27 God says, "I will overturn, overturn, overturn, it: and it shall be no more, until He come whose right it is; and I will give it Him." This refers, as the context shows, to the first dominion which God has promised to Israel as His representative people on the earth. The Jew is, therefore, the key to the prophetic plan.

"Our God shall come, the silence shall be broken,
    Which long has reigned o'er this sin-stricken world;
The saints of every name and tongue shall gather
    Beneath His banner which shall be unfurled.
Our God shall come, to scatter all oppressors,
    For He the righteous Judge shall fill the throne;
No longer shall the tyrant have dominion,
    No longer shall the helpless captive groan."   —H. Bunn.

"The Lord is slow to anger, and great in power, and will not at all acquit the wicked: the Lord hath His way in the whirlwind and in the storm, and the clouds are the dust of His feet"—Nahum 1: 3.

THE prophecy of Nahum was directed against the godless and luxurious city of Nineveh. It is a very dark picture of sin and judgment. But this verse shines out like a bright star in a clouded sky. How precious to the soul to know that in all the strife and discord of earth the Lord hath His way. He has not vacated His throne as the Moral Governor of the Universe. He controls all the elements, and He causes man's wrath to praise Him. The very clouds that darken the heavens are the dust of His feet. He is just above them. His heart is ever towards His people, and He is working all things for the good of those who love Him. Soon He will be manifested and all troubles will cease.

World chaos reigns! bold lawlessness runs faster!
    And Earth's dark night with deeper darkness grows!
In many lands unparalleled disaster,—
        Wars, famines, earthquakes, floods,—'mongst many woes.

The darkness deepens!—yes, but Dawn is nearer!
    The Lord from Heaven may soon be on His way;
The "Blessed Hope" in these dark days grows dearer,—
        Our Saviour Christ will come,—"perhaps today"!

                                        —J. Danson Smith.

"Art Thou not from everlasting, O Lord my God, mine Holy One? We shall not die. O Lord, Thou hast ordained them for judgment; and, O mighty God, Thou hast established them for correction. Thou art of purer eyes than to behold evil, and canst not look on iniquity: wherefore lookest Thou upon them that deal treacherously, and holdest Thy tongue when the wicked devoureth the man that is more righteous than he?"
—Hab. 1: 12, 13.

IN the first four verses of his prophecy Habakkuk complains of the iniquity and violence which were so manifest. Jehovah's answer is given in verses 5 to 11. He has seen it all, and judgment is soon to fall. He is about to raise up the Chaldeans for the chastening of His people. In the remaining verses of the chapter the prophet protests against the use of so wicked a nation to punish Judah. He is perplexed that the Holy One should sanction such a procedure. For the moment there is no answer from God, so Habakkuk takes his stand upon the watchtower, waiting until the enigma may be solved. At last the answer comes—"The just shall live by faith." The righteous man has to trust God, assured that He will make all plain at last.

Then the voice of God speaks in majesty, showing that He does not approve of the wicked, but though He will use an evil nation as a rod, when He has accomplished His purpose it too shall be dealt with, and God will be glorified.

This moves the prophet's heart to prayer and subdues his distressed spirit, as set forth in chapter 3, wherein he pours out his soul in supplication for his people and expresses the most blessed resignation to the will of God.

"I know not, but God knows;
  Oh, blessed rest from fear!
All my unfolding days
  To Him are plain and clear.
Each anxious, puzzled "Why?"
  From doubt or dread that grows,
Finds answer in this thought:
  I know not, but He knows."
—Annie Johnson Flint.

"O Lord, revive Thy work in the midst of the years, in the midst of the years make known; in wrath remember mercy"—Hab. 3: 2.

GOD is always ready to visit His people in blessing and grant revival and spiritual refreshment when they judge their sins in His presence and cry to Him for the deliverance they need. Oh, that we today might be stirred to realize the great need of the whole Church of God, so that there would be a mighty cry of entreaty going up to the throne, accompanied by an honest purging ourselves from all known sin, and a true returning to the place of obedience to His Word! Who can say what blessed results might yet be vouchsafed to His people, and what the glorious effects might be upon a godless world outside?

"Revive Thy work, O Lord!
    Thy mighty arm make bare;
Speak with the voice that wakes the dead,
    And make Thy people hear.

Revive Thy work, O Lord!
    Disturb this sleep of death;
Quicken the smould'ring embers now
    By Thine almighty breath.

Revive Thy work, O Lord!
    Create soul-thirst for Thee;
But hung'ring for the bread of life,
    Oh, may our spirits be!

Revive Thy work, O Lord!
    Exalt Thy precious name;
And, by the Holy Ghost, our love
    For Thee and Thine inflame."

—A. Midlane.

"I will also leave in the midst of thee an afflicted and poor people, and they shall trust in the name of the Lord"—Zeph. 3: 12.

IT is the troubled and distressed who find their relief in God. Ofttimes temporal prosperity proves to be a hindrance to spirituality. It need not be so but we are so constituted that when all goes well in this scene and we have abundance of the good things of life we are apt to forget the Giver and be more occupied with His gifts than with Himself. In our afflictions and needy circumstances, if we turn to Him we learn how marvelously He can satisfy our hearts and lift us above the trials of the way.

"Think it not strange about the fiery trial,
　Which nigh consumes with seven-fold heated flame;
Count it not strange, as though some strange thing happened:
　Have not God's noblest ones endured the same?

Think it not strange that trial upon trial
　In quick succession follows, fierce and strong:
Trials most tragic, things which seem disaster,
　When cries the soul, 'How long, O Lord, how long?'

Think it not strange, partaker of Christ's sufferings;
　Tested and tried, thou art exalted sure:
Not to consume are these 'strange' things permitted,
　But to enrich, if we will but endure.

Think it not strange! Rejoice, rejoice the rather!
　Forward thy gaze until shall glory be;
Then, oh, the joy, the wonder, and the rapture,
　When thou shalt find His glory shared with thee."

　　　　　　　　　　　　　　　—J. Danson Smith.

"Now therefore thus saith the Lord of hosts; Consider your ways. Ye have sown much, and bring in little; ye eat, but ye have not enough; ye drink, but ye are not filled with drink; ye clothe you, but there is none warm; and he that earneth wages, earneth wages to put it into a bag with holes"—Haggai 1: 5, 6.

THERE are two key expressions in the little Book of Haggai that give us the purpose of this prophecy: "Consider your ways," and "Be strong." There are six books of the Old Testament that are intimately linked together—three historical, Ezra, Nehemiah, and Esther, and three prophetic, Haggai, Zechariah, and Malachi. These give us the story of God's dealings with the people of Judah after the Babylonian dominion was overthrown and the Medo-Persian empire, which was favorable to the Jews in the main, had succeeded to world sovereignty. In Ezra and Nehemiah we have the history of the returning remnant, and the three prophets throw light upon their moral and spiritual state. Haggai sought to encourage the people to go on with their God-appointed program, the rebuilding of the Temple, which had been hindered because of the opposition of the mixed races (the Samaritans, as they were afterward known) who were dwelling in the land of Palestine. He sought to exercise the consciences of the remnant, and called upon them to face their low spiritual condition before God and get right with Him. His searching ministry proved so effective that the people were stirred to "arise and build." Then he sounded out the note of encouragement, "Be strong."

> "So many a life is one long fever!
>   A fever of anxious suspense and care;
> A fever of fretting, a fever of getting,
>   A fever of hurrying here and there.
>
> Ah, what if in winning the praise of others
>   We miss at the last the King's 'Well done'—
> If our self-sought tasks in the Master's vineyard
>   Yield 'nothing but leaves' at the set of sun!"
>
> —Edith G. Cherry.

"**Rejoice greatly, O daughter of Zion; shout, O daughter of Jerusalem: behold, thy King cometh unto thee: He is just, and having salvation; lowly, and riding upon an ass, and upon a colt the foal of an ass**"—Zech. 9: 9.

OUR Lord's entry into Jerusalem at the beginning of His last week of public ministry had been foretold long before and was in exact accord with this prophetic Word. The joyous cries of the multitude who welcomed Him were also prophesied beforehand by David in Ps. 118: 25, 26. Thus there were two distinct scriptures fulfilled on this momentous occasion. Then when Jesus cleansed the Temple (for the second time), He referred to and quoted Isaiah 56: 7 as His authority for acting as He did. All this is in keeping with the character of Matthew's Gospel, which, as we have seen, is designed throughout to link the Old Testament promises and predictions with their New Testament counterparts. It might be said that everything Jesus did, and all He taught, was in exact accord with that which had been foretold by the voice of inspiration throughout the ages. In this, as in all else, we see the perfection of the Word of God. Prophecy is the seal of its divinely unique character. No other book is thus accredited. The Bible is in fact the only book of prophecy in the world. The so-called sacred literature of the great religions is without this mark and is puerile in the extreme when contrasted with the revelation given in the Holy Scriptures.

"Adorable Saviour! By faith I descry
The long-looked-for day of redemption draws nigh,
When the shame and contempt and the grief shall give place
To the holy rejoicings—the triumphs of grace!
Till we from this terrible desert are caught,
My heart would rejoice in this comforting thought,—
It may be tomorrow, or even tonight,
The fulness of glory will burst on my sight!"

"I will pour upon the house of David, and upon the inhabitants of Jerusalem, the spirit of grace and of supplications: and they shall look upon Me whom they have pierced, and they shall mourn for Him, as one mourneth for his only son, and shall be in bitterness for Him, as one that is in bitterness for his firstborn"—Zech. 12: 10.

IN these words Zechariah depicts the repentance of the people of Judah when at our Lord's return they recognize Him as their own Messiah whom their fathers rejected, but who comes again in power and glory for their deliverance and to fulfil all the glad promises of glory and blessing. The wounds in His hands and feet and side will abide for Eternity and will tell out the story of a love that was stronger than death. It is ours to see Him now by faith bearing these marks of His passion as He appears for us in the presence of God.

"Soon Thou wilt come—oh, blest anticipation!—
  And we shall gaze unhindered on Thy face;
Our longing hope shall have its glad fruition,
  And in those wounds we shall love's story trace.

Oh, cloudless morn of heavenly light and gladness,
  When God Himself shall wipe all tears away!
There shall be no more death and no more sadness,
  No trace of sin through God's eternal day."

—J. W. H. Nichols.

"Bring ye all the tithes into the storehouse, that there may be meat in Mine house, and prove Me now herewith, saith the Lord of hosts, if I will not open you the windows of heaven, and pour you out a blessing, that there shall not be room enough to receive it"—Mal. 3:10.

TITHING was in force before Moses (Gen. 14:20; Heb. 7:9). It was incorporated into the law of Sinai (Lev. 27:30). Under grace it is not mentioned, but proportionate giving is enjoined. The believer now is not to be less particular in honoring God with his substance than a Jew under law. "The righteousness of the law might be fulfilled in us, who walk not after the flesh, but after the Spirit" (Rom. 8:4). If I were a Jew under law, the tithe would be absolutely obligatory and the least I could give. Shall I as a believer, under grace, do less than if I were under law?

We rob God when we use what should be devoted to Him and to His work, for our own pleasure. Are we so faithful in setting aside the Lord's portion that we can have His approval in this regard?

The New Testament precept is, "On the first day of the week let every one of you lay by him in store, as God hath prospered him" (1 Cor. 16:2).

"We give Thee but Thine own,
      Whate'er the gift may be;
All that we have, is Thine alone,
      A trust, dear Lord, from Thee."

"Unto you that fear My name shall the Sun of Righteousness arise with healing in His wings; and ye shall go forth, and grow up as calves of the stall"—Mal. 4:2.

THE Old Testament closes with the prophecy of the day of the Lord and the coming of the Sun of Righteousness. The New Testament ends with the promise of the Morning Star. Both refer to our Lord Jesus, but the two aspects of His second advent are thus presented. He will return for His Bride, the Church, as the Morning Star. He will be manifested for the deliverance of Israel and the blessing of the world as the glorious Sun of Righteousness. The darker the night becomes the nearer must be the hour of the fulfilment of His pledge to come again. This blessed event is the hope of the Church, the hope of Israel and the hope of the world.

"The dark stream of evil is flowing apace,
  And man is still walking a stranger to grace,
  While daring rebellion is on the increase,
  Which mar not my joy, which disturb not my peace,
  For my heart is engaged with its own happy song;
  The Lord who has loved me will come before long;
  It may be tomorrow, or even tonight,
  That I shall behold Him in unclouded light!"

"While he thought on these things, behold, the angel of the Lord appeared unto him in a dream, saying, Joseph, thou son of David, fear not to take unto thee Mary thy wife: for that which is conceived in her is of the Holy Ghost. And she shall bring forth a Son, and thou shalt call His name JESUS: for He shall save His people from their sins"—Matt. 1: 20, 21.

WHAT could be more wonderful than that God came down to earth as a baby! Could anything tell out more perfectly His deep yearning over mankind and His earnest desire to have men love and trust Him? Almost everybody, even the most depraved, loves a baby.

No one need fear a baby, and the Babe of Bethlehem was the perfect manifestation of the heart of God, who would have all men know that He became incarnate, not to condemn, but to save.

By becoming a little child Himself, our Lord has changed the thoughts of untold millions as to the value and preciousness of the little ones. Christianity makes more of the children than any pagan religious system ever did. It rebukes the horrible crime of infanticide, which was accepted as a matter of course even among the cultured Greeks and the highly civilized Romans.

"I believe the Holy Jesus was the Son of God on earth;
That Mary was His mother and a virgin at His birth;
That the Holy Ghost begat Him as the Angel Gabriel said.
God in the Gospel of His Son, confirms the record made.

I believe the blessed Saviour came down from Heaven for me,
Endured the cross, despised the shame, from sin to set me free;
He died, was buried, rose again, and did to Heaven ascend.
I believe the good old Gospel from beginning to the end."

"Now when Jesus was born in Bethlehem of Judea in the days of Herod the king, behold, there came wise men from the east to Jerusalem, saying, Where is He that is born King of the Jews? for we have seen His star in the east, and are come to worship Him"—Matt. 2: 1, 2.

IT is all-important that we realize that nothing will take the place of personal faith in and subjection to the Lord Jesus Christ. Acquaintance with Scripture that does not control our lives will only add to our condemnation, rather than prove a means of salvation. Herod and the scribes knew what the prophets had predicted concerning the coming of the Messiah, but they had no room for Him in their hearts. On the other hand, His birth meant so much to the wise men that they took a long journey to seek for Him and to pour out their treasures at His feet. His star not only showed the way to Christ, but it was the cause of their deep rejoicing, for they recognized it as the messenger of God leading them to Him whom they received in faith as earth's rightful King and whom they worshipped with adoring love. To "keep Christmas" while refusing heart-allegiance to the One who was born to reveal the Father and to make propitiation for sins is but a sham and a mockery.

"To Him this day our prayers arise,
Each soul its tribute pays:
The precious myrrh of sacrifice,
The incense sweet of praise,
The glowing gold of sacred love
That knows no stain of fear,
These gifts we bring to Christ above
To-day and all the year."

"I indeed baptize you with water unto repentance: but He that cometh after me is mightier than I, whose shoes I am not worthy to bear: He shall baptize you with the Holy Ghost, and with fire: whose fan is in His hand, and He will throughly purge His floor, and gather His wheat into the garner; but He will burn up the chaff with unquenchable fire"—Matt. 3: 11, 12.

NOTHING could emphasize our Lord's deity more than John's declaration regarding Him and this twofold baptism. Imagine a creature baptizing in the Holy Spirit. Only One who is Himself divine could do this. And on Pentecost Peter unhesitatingly declares it was He who sent the Spirit (Acts 2: 33). He it is who will consign the impenitent to the fire of everlasting punishment (Matt. 25: 41). This is not to be confounded with the cleansing efficacy of the Holy Spirit, nor with the tongues "like as of fire" which appeared at Pentecost. "He will burn up the chaff with unquenchable fire" is placed in direct contrast with gathering the "wheat into the garner" (Matt. 3:12).

By the Spirit-baptism believers are now united in one Body and empowered for service.

> "The Holy Ghost is here,
>   Where saints in prayer agree;
> As Jesus' parting gift—is near
>   Each pleading company.
>
> Not far away is He,
>   To be by prayer brought nigh,
> But here in present majesty,
>   As in His courts on high.
>
> He dwells within our soul,
>   An ever-welcome guest;
> He reigns with absolute control,
>   As monarch in the breast.
>
> Our bodies are His shrine,
>   And He th' in-dwelling Lord;
> All hail, Thou Comforter divine,
>   Be evermore adored!"

—Chas. H. Spurgeon.

"Then was Jesus led up of the Spirit into the wilderness to be tempted of the devil"—Matt. 4: 1.

AS WE consider the solemn and important subject of our Lord's temptation, we need to remember that He is God and Man in one Person. While as truly Man as if He had never been God, He is yet as truly God as if He had never become Man, and therefore we must not think of Him as merely man on probation, as Adam was in the garden of Eden.

The testing of Jesus in the wilderness was not to see whether He would sin, but to prove that He was absolutely the sinless One and therefore the fit Substitute for those who were both sinners by nature and in practice.

When the question is asked (innocently enough, perhaps), "Could Jesus have sinned?" we need to consider ere answering in the affirmative what would have happened if He had sinned. He was not two persons, but one. He was the Son of the Father with two natures, the human and the divine. These natures could never be separated after He became incarnate. One nature could not act in opposition to the other; therefore the thought of sin in connection with Him is utterly abhorrent. He could say, "The prince of this world cometh, and hath nothing in Me" (John 14: 30). There was no traitor lurking within. From the moment of His birth he was "that Holy Thing" (Luke 1: 35). The temptation proved Him to be all that God the Father said He was: His beloved Son, in whom He had found all His delight (Matt. 3: 17).

> "Faithful amidst unfaithfulness,
>   'Mid darkness only light,
> Thou didst Thy Father's name confess,
>   And in His will delight;
>
> Unmoved by Satan's subtle wiles,
>   Or suff'ring, shame, and loss,
> Thy path, uncheered by earthly smiles,
>   Led only to the cross."
>
> —J. G. Deck.

"Jesus, walking by the Sea of Galilee, saw two brethren, Simon called Peter, and Andrew his brother, casting a net into the sea: for they were fishers. And He saith unto them, Follow Me, and I will make you fishers of men"—Matt. 4: 18, 19.

IT is a great thing to be called of God to sacrificial service on behalf of a lost world; a tremendous event in the history of a soul when the voice of Christ is heard saying, "Follow Me, and I will make you ———." All are not fitted for the same tasks; all cannot work in the same way. But each one who yields himself to the Lord Jesus for definite service will find that He enables, trains, and directs, so that the life thus surrendered will be used to His glory and to the winning of the lost and the blessing of the saved. "Fishers of men" is an apt figure. It requires much wisdom and great patience to become an effective agent in the business of "taking men alive," but he who is willing to learn at the Master's feet and is quick to obey His commands will indeed be "made" whatever He would have one be.

"Some have gone forth far from loved ones and home,
Leaving their all for His service alone;
Counting the gain of this world only dross,
Seeking no glory save that of His cross.

Some have gone forth into darkness so dense,
Darkness that crushes, a darkness intense;
There in far lands where their Lord is not known;
Gladly to work for His glory alone.

Some have gone forth, but so many remain
Safely at home—other honors to gain;
Millions of lost ones who never have heard,
Few—oh, so few—to go forth with His Word!"

—Grace Troy.

"Blessed are the peacemakers: for they shall be called the children of God. Blessed are they which are persecuted for righteousness' sake: for theirs is the kingdom of heaven. Blessed are ye, when men shall revile you, and persecute you, and shall say all manner of evil against you falsely, for My sake"—Matt. 5: 9-11.

THE sermon on the mount must not be taken as the proclamation of the gospel of the grace of God whereby needy sinners are saved. It is rather the announcement of the foundation principles of the Kingdom of God, principles utterly diverse from those on which earthly dominions are established. It gives us the law of love prevailing in all departments of life. Manifestly this can never be fully accepted and acted upon by an unregenerate world. But when people are born again they can see and enter into the kingdom of God even now, while the King Himself is rejected. To these the will of God is paramount, and they find in what seems to unsaved men an utterly impracticable standard of living, the ideal manner of life for those who are content to be identified with Christ in His rejection.

Just as it is a mistake to try to force these principles on the world of unsaved men and women, so it is as great a blunder to insist that they have no binding authority over the consciences of Christians today. Surely not; for in us is fulfilled all the righteous requirements of the law as we "walk not after the flesh, but after the Spirit" (Rom. 8:4).

"He giveth more grace when the burdens grow greater,
   He sendeth more strength when the labors increase;
To added affliction He addeth His mercy,
   To multiplied trials, His multiplied peace.
When we have exhausted our store of endurance,
   When our strength has failed ere the day is half done,
When we reach the end of our hoarded resources,
   Our Father's full giving is only begun.
His love has no limit, His grace has no measure,
   His power no boundary known unto men;
For out of His infinite riches in Jesus
   He giveth and giveth and giveth again."

—A. J. Flint.

"Ye have heard that it was said by them of old time, Thou shalt not kill: and whosoever shall kill shall be in danger of the judgment: but I say unto you, That whosoever is angry with his brother without a cause shall be in danger of the judgment: and whosoever shall say to his brother, Raca, shall be in danger of the council: but whosoever shall say, Thou fool, shall be in danger of hell fire"—Matt. 5: 21, 22.

GOD has said, "All souls are Mine." He alone has the right to say when life on earth shall end for any of its inhabitants. He has delegated certain powers to governments in order that evildoers may be dealt with righteously and as a warning to others (Gen. 9: 5, 6; Rom. 13: 4). But no one is authorized to take the law into his own hands and to slay his neighbor because of real or fancied offences. Back of the murderer's hand is the malicious mind and the wicked heart. So our Lord Jesus shows us that he who despises his neighbor, he who hates his brother, is a potential murderer and therefore under condemnation of the moral law. This is emphasized in Exodus 20: 13 and 1 John 3: 15. When the grace of God controls the inward being, hatred and all phases of ill-will disappear, and love, that doeth no ill to his neighbor, is manifested. Therefore in this, as in all else, love is the fulfilling of the law.

"Oh, that when Christians meet and part,
These words were graved on every heart—
  They're dear to God!
However willful and unwise,
We'll look on them with loving eyes—
  They're dear to God!

When tempted to give pain for pain,
How would this thought our words restrain,
  They're dear to God!
When truth compels us to contend,
What love with all our strife should blend!
  They're dear to God!

"Again, ye have heard that it hath been said by them of old time, Thou shalt not forswear thyself, but shall perform unto the Lord thine oaths: but I say unto you, Swear not at all; neither by heaven; for it is God's throne: nor by the earth; for it is His footstool: neither by Jerusalem; for it is the city of the great King"

—Matt. 5: 33-35.

YOUTHS often seem to regard profanity as an accomplishment of which to be proud. On the contrary, it is always a sign of weakness, and betrays a corrupt and wicked heart. No one admires a swearer. But all right-thinking people recognize the nobility of character that enables one to keep his lips clean and whose speech is wholesome and refined. Our Lord distinctly forbids the use of such expletives as "Heavens," "Jerusalem," and other terms. These do not add to the strength of one's language, but rather weaken it, and are utterly unbecoming in the lips of a believer on Christ.

"That name I just heard is delightfully sweet!
Jesus is Christ! and Him you must meet;
Now He is meeting poor sinners in grace,
He knocks at your heart. Oh, give Him a place!
He hears you blaspheme; but oh, if you knew
How much He loves sinners, how much He loves you,
You would fall at His feet and adoringly sing,
Jesus! my Saviour! my Lord! and my King!
'Twas for this that He died on Calvary's tree,
That sinners, the chief, might from judgment be free;
He's now up in glory—a Man on God's throne,
But He's coming again— it may be quite soon.
He left us this message, while He is above,
A message of mercy—a message of love:
Tell sinners I love them—tell Adam's whole race,
That this is the day of My patience and grace,
Yea, more—go, beseech—beseech them for Me,
Beseech by My blood, by My death on the tree,
It cleanses from sin and fits them to be
At once and forever in glory with Me."　　—J. H. Wilson.

"Therefore take no thought, saying, What shall we eat? or, What shall we drink? or, Wherewithal shall we be clothed? (For after all these things do the Gentiles seek:) for your heavenly Father knoweth that ye have need of all these things. But seek ye first the kingdom of God, and His righteousness; and all these things shall be added unto you. Take therefore no thought for the morrow: for the morrow shall take thought for the things of itself. Sufficient unto the day is the evil thereof"
—Matt. 6: 21-24.

THE Bible does not treat lightly of human need, but it shows the transcendent importance of attending to spiritual things. Christians are encouraged to thrift and prudence in handling their temporal affairs. The ideal believer is not the monkish recluse who seeks to be relieved of all responsibility for either his own or other people's comfort and well-being. But the Word of God always insists on the supreme importance of the welfare of the inner man. To put eternal things first means to get the very best out of this life as well as peace of heart in regard to the next one.

God makes Himself responsible to care for and sustain all those who, having been born of His Spirit, recognize Him as Father and seek to do His will as obedient children. This is to put His kingdom first—to live in subjection to His revealed truth. As we thus "trust and obey" we may be sure that He will faithfully perform that which He has promised, supplying our need, sustaining our hearts, and enabling us to live above carking care and anxiety (1 Pet. 5: 6, 7).

> "Oh, it is sweet to trust Him,
>   Knowing He loves and cares!
> Meeting life's burdens bravely,
>   Since in them all He shares.
> So on Faith's pillow resting,
>   Now I will go to sleep;
> Through night and day my Father
>   Safely His child will keep."

—E. L. Y.

"He healed all that were sick that it might be fulfilled which was spoken by Esaias, the prophet, saying, Himself took our infirmities and bare our sicknesses"
—Matt. 8: 16, 17.

THE very fact that disease was so prevalent in Israel was proof of the people's departure from God (Exod. 15: 26). Each different sickness has a spiritual significance and the healing of each case illustrates Christ's power over sin in all its forms, whether direct Satanic control (Mark 1: 24-26), the burning fever of sin as typified by the illness of Peter's wife's mother, the dreadful uncleanness of it as pictured by leprosy, or its helplessness as illustrated by the case of the palsied man (Matt. 9: 2-8). No matter in what form our sin may manifest itself, the great Physician can give complete deliverance.

Jesus is today the healing Christ. But He is far more concerned with giving spiritual health to sin-sick souls than healing people of fevers or cleansing leprous sores. These were of old the signs of His Messiahship. Now He is exalted to God's right hand as a Prince and a Saviour. All, no matter what their spiritual ailments, may find deliverance through faith in Him.

"The worst of all diseases
    Is light compared with sin;
On every part it seizes,
    But rages most within.
'Tis dropsy, palsy, fever
    And madness, all combined,
And none but a believer
    The least relief can find."

"He spake many things unto them in parables, saying, Behold, a sower went forth to sow"—Matt. 13: 3.

THIS parable of the Sower and the Seed should be both a warning and an encouragement to all who endeavor to labor in the gospel: a warning against the folly of taking at face value every profession of faith in Christ, but an encouragement when many who profess prove unreal, as we remember that even when the divine-human Preacher was the Sower of the gospel seed there were many who heard in vain and who never brought forth fruit unto perfection. It is our business to sow under all circumstances (Eccles. 11: 6), knowing that the seed is incorruptible (1 Pet. 1: 23) and that, though many give but momentary thought to the message, it will accomplish the purpose of God (Isa. 55: 11) and that all who hear in faith will be saved (John 5: 24).

The Word tests as well as saves. Where the heart is occupied with other things—such as the cares of this world or the deceitfulness of riches—there will be little appreciation of that message which speaks of another scene altogether and of riches that can never pass away. Where possible, the preacher is to break up the fallow ground and sow not among thorns (Jer. 4: 3). On the other hand, he is to be instant in season and out of season (2 Tim. 4: 2) even though this involves some seed falling upon hard, unprepared hearts, only to be devoured by the birds of the air, fit pictures of Satan and his demon host, who are ever on the alert to hinder the gospel.

> "We plough the fields and scatter
>   The good seed o'er the land,
> But it is fed and watered
>   By God's almighty hand;
> He sends the snow in winter,
>   The warmth to swell the grain,
> The breezes and the sunshine,
>   The soft, refreshing rain."

—M. Claudius.

"He answered and said unto them, Because it is given unto you to know the mysteries of the kingdom of heaven, but to them it is not given. For whosoever hath, to him shall be given, and he shall have more abundance: but whosoever hath not, from him shall be taken away even that he hath"—Matt. 13: 11, 12.

THE Gospel of Matthew is pre-eminently the Gospel of the Kingdom of Heaven. The "kingdom of heaven" is not Heaven itself, as many erroneously suppose, but the term refers to Heaven's rule established on this earth (Dan. 4: 17, 34). There is a very definite sense in which this has always been true, for God has never relinquished His authority as the Moral Governor of the Universe, but all Scripture looks forward to a time when this kingdom will be manifested visibly everywhere upon earth (Dan. 7: 27). When our Lord came in the fulness of time and presented Himself as the promised King, He was rejected, and He has gone back into Heaven "to receive for Himself a kingdom, and to return" (Luke 19: 12). In the meantime, the principles of His kingdom, as set forth in this Gospel of Matthew, are pervading the world, and as a result millions of men acknowledge Him as earth's rightful King and the Lord of their lives. Thus His kingdom is set up in "mystery." The King is absent, but His authority is owned by many. Some who outwardly acknowledge Him are unreal professors, and so in the present day there are good and bad found in the sphere of the kingdom of Heaven. This will be rectified when He returns (Matt. 13: 41, 42).

> "I walk with Thee and all is light
> At morn, at eve, at wakeful night;
>   The way I do not ask to see,
>   Thy presence is enough for me;
> Thou art my Guide, and fears take flight.
>
> O Saviour, Source of rest, of might,
> In vain the powers of evil fight,
>   When at Thy side, from sin set free,
>   I walk with Thee."

"Another parable spake He unto them: The kingdom of heaven is like unto leaven, which a woman took, and hid in three measures of meal, till the whole was leavened"—Matt. 13: 33.

OF old there was to be no leaven in the sacrifices or in the meal offering (Lev. 2:11; 6:17), and all leaven was to be put out of the Israelite's home at the time of the passover (Exod. 12:15; 13:7). This is explained for us in 1 Corinthians 5:6-8 as representing malice and wickedness. The disciples were warned against the leaven of the Pharisees, which is hypocrisy and self-righteousness, and the leaven of the Sadducees, which is false doctrine (Matt. 16:6, 11, 12), also of the leaven of Herod, which is worldliness and political corruption (Mark 8:15). The Corinthians were warned against the leaven of immorality, which, if unchecked, would leaven the whole Church (1 Cor. 5: 6), and the Galatians were warned in the same way against the leaven of legality (Gal. 5:9). Nowhere is the gospel likened to leaven, and certainly it is not to be "hidden," but openly declared.

The woman here represents the false Church who corrupts the truth of God. It is our responsibility to set forth that truth in the Spirit's power.

"Men tear the old faith into fragments,
　And build, on the truth they deny,
Strange towers of fancy and fable,
　And deem they can mount to the sky.
Away with 'New Thought' and 'New Knowledge'
　That voice the old lies of the past;
That only perplex and bewilder,
　To leave us in doubt at the last.

To Thee, the Life-Bringer, Life-Giver,—
　To Thee, the one Truth, the one Way,
The one Light that lightens our darkness,
　The one God who hears when we pray;
Who looseth the chains of the captives,
　And setteth the prisoners free;
O Jesus, Thou Son of the Father,
　To whom shall we go, but to Thee?"
　　　　　　　　　　　—Annie Johnson Flint.

JUNE 7

"The field is the world"—Matt. 13: 38.

IT is important to remember that, in accord with the plan of God, Jesus Christ came primarily to seek the lost sheep of the house of Israel. He was their Messiah, their Kinsman-Redeemer (Lev. 25: 48). While His heart went out to all mankind, His special message was to them first. Upon their rejection of allegiance to His authority (John 19: 15), He commanded His disciples to carry His gospel to all men everywhere (Matt. 28: 19, 20).

But while His earthly testimony was to Israel, His heart was concerned about all. It was because "God so loved the world" that He sent His only begotten Son into this scene (John 3: 16); therefore we need not be surprised to see His grace overleaping national bounds and going out even to sinners of the Gentiles, who were "strangers from the covenants of promise," who were without God and, so far as any knowledge of His Word was concerned, were without hope in the world (Eph. 2: 12). Grace recognizes no national or racial barriers, but sees in all men of all nations sinners for whom Christ died and who may be transformed into saints by the mighty life-giving power of the Holy Spirit.

> "Have ye carried the living water
>   To the parched and weary soul?
> Have ye said to the sick and wounded,
>   'Christ Jesus makes thee whole?'
> Have ye told My fainting children
>   Of the strength of the Father's hand?
> Have ye guided the tottering footsteps
>   To the shore of the 'golden land?'"

"And Simon Peter answered and said, Thou art the Christ, the Son of the living God. And Jesus answered and said unto him, Blessed art thou, Simon Bar-jona: for flesh and blood hath not revealed it unto thee, but My Father which is in heaven. And I say also unto thee, That thou art Peter, and upon this rock I will build My Church; and the gates of hell shall not prevail against it"
—Matt. 16: 16-18.

THE truth embodied in Peter's great confession, "Thou art the Christ, the Son of the living God," is the rock of our salvation. Upon this the Church is builded. Apart from a divine Saviour there would be no Church of God in the world. It is noticeable that Jesus Himself elicited this confession by direct questioning. He knew well both the attitude of men in general regarding His true character and also that which His disciples knew Him to be. But He would have them put themselves on record, and so Peter was led to speak for them all. It meant much to the Lord Jesus to discern the working of grace in their souls, and their growth in spiritual intelligence. On the other hand, it grieved Him deeply when they failed to enter into the truth concerning the work of redemption as readily as they had grasped something of the glory of His Person. Hence His severe rebuke when Peter would have turned Him aside, had it been possible, from the death of the cross. The blunder of Peter as to this might well give us to pause, as we realize how untrustworthy are the views of even the best of men unless they are the recipients of divine revelation. How good that God has given us His Word, thus revealing wondrous mysteries kept secret from the world's foundation!

> "If asked what of Jesus I think,
>   Though still my best thoughts are but poor,
> I say, He's my meat and my drink,
>   My life and my strength and my store;
> My Shepherd, my trust and my Friend,
>   My Saviour from sin and from thrall;
> My Hope from beginning to end,
>   My Portion, my Lord and my All."   —J. Newton.

"Then Jesus answered and said, O faithless and perverse generation, how long shall I be with you? How long shall I suffer you? Bring him hither to Me. And Jesus rebuked the devil; and he departed out of him: and the child was cured from that very hour"

—Matt. 17: 17, 18.

HE who is the delight of the Father's heart finds His greatest joy in manifesting the riches of His grace to needy sinners. While His condition on the mount was one of indescribable glory, His heart was the same as when He walked among men in lowliness and compassion. And so it is still. He abides for eternity "the same Jesus." To Him we may bring our dear ones for whose welfare we are concerned, assured that His interest in them is deeper and tenderer than ours ever can be. Fulness of grace resides in Him, for the benefit of all who come to Him in their need and distress. When at last He returns to reign and "every eye shall see Him" (Rev. 1: 7), He will be the very same as when He ministered so lovingly to those who sought His favor in the days of His flesh. It is the privilege of every parent to bring the children to Him, and claim, in faith, the saving power of the blood of Him who is the true Paschal Lamb.

"Beneath the blood-stained lintel I with my children stand;
A messenger of evil is passing through the land.
There is no other refuge from the destroyer's face;
Beneath the blood-stained lintel shall be our hiding-place.

The Lamb of God has suffered, our sins and griefs He bore;
By faith the blood is sprinkled above our dwelling's door.
The foe who seeks to enter doth fear that sacred sign;
To-night the blood-stained lintel shall shelter me and mine."

"And Jesus called a little child unto Him, and set him in the midst of them"—Matt. 18: 2.

THE child in the midst. When God became incarnate He chose to appear on earth as a baby. The sweetest, purest creature that we know in this scene is an artless, little child. And this is the chosen symbol of the representative of our Lord Jesus Christ. The Lord Jesus declared, "Verily I say unto you, Except ye be converted, and become as little children, ye shall not enter into the kingdom of heaven" (Matt. 18: 3). Who then can ever enter? Who can go back to the comparative innocence and purity of a little child? But note what really happened. The Lord Jesus *called* a little child. In trustful confidence he came to the Saviour, who took him in His arms and set him in the midst. Now note the analogy. He calls. We heed His voice, and so become converted and find a place in His kingdom. The law of that kingdom is love. Its subjects are to manifest the meekness and gentleness of Christ, hence not to seek great things for themselves (Jer. 45: 5), nor to sit in judgment on their fellow-servants (Matt. 7: 1, 2). Each one is to act as before the Lord, endeavoring in his measure to do the will of God and to glorify Him, while seeking to co-operate in the fullest way with all true service in which others may be engaged (Phil. 1: 27).

> "Oh, let the reaping of the after-years
>   Be of the sowing of your patient love
>   And many prayers.
>   Look up for strength;
>   The God who placed that child within your care
>   Wil give you all you need to teach of heaven
>   And guide it there."

"Verily I say unto you, Except ye be converted and become as little children, ye shall not enter into the kingdom of heaven. Whosoever therefore shall humble himself as this little child, the same is greatest in the kingdom of heaven"—Matt. 18: 3, 4.

NONE can be too young for the kingdom of Heaven. The children should be taught to come to Jesus as soon as they are able consciously to respond to His love and grace. As for those who are taken away from this scene ere they reach years of accountability, we can rely upon the precious words of chapter 18: 10, 14. The Good Shepherd has died for these lambs and will not permit one of them to be lost. Christian parents should bring their babes to Him from the very beginning of their lives and should count on Him to bless them by drawing their hearts to Himself, assured that the faith of a child is as real as that of a more mature person. In fact, the one is the model for the other.

A tremendous responsibility, moreover, rests upon those who are older to guide the feet of the young, both by precept and example.

"How oft a little one has found the road,
  The narrow pathway to that blest abode:
  Through faith in Christ has read its title clear,
  While learned men remain in doubt and fear!
  A little child! The Lord oft uses such
  The stoutest heart to break, or bend, or touch;
  Then by His Spirit bids the conflict cease,
  And once for ever enter into peace."

"Then his lord, after that he had called him, said unto him, O thou wicked servant, I forgave thee all that debt, because thou desiredst me: shouldest not thou also have had compassion on thy fellowservant, even as I had pity on thee? And his lord was wroth, and delivered him to the tormentors, till he should pay all that was due unto him. So likewise shall My heavenly Father do also unto you, if ye from your hearts forgive not every one his brother their trespasses"—Matt. 18: 32-35.

IF we fail to distinguish the various aspects of forgiveness as set forth in the Word of God, we are likely to be in great confusion of mind because of God's disciplinary dealings with us after our conversion to Christ. When He saves us He forgives us fully and eternally, and will never, as Judge, remember our sins again (Heb. 10: 17). But as His children, we are to confess our sins whenever we fail, and He gives restorative forgiveness (1 John 1: 9). Certain governmental results, however, may follow these failures, which are not to be construed as indicating that God has not pardoned, but He would teach us by discipline the heinousness of sin in His sight (2 Sam. 13, 14). Forgiven ourselves, we are to forgive our brethren who sin against us (Col. 3: 13). Members of the Church who offend against God's righteous principles are to be disciplined, but forgiven when they give evidence of repentance (Matt. 18: 17; 1 Cor. 5: 13; 2 Cor. 2: 7).

"Not far from New York, in a cemetery lone,
  Close guarding its grave, stands a simple headstone,
  And all the inscription is one word alone—
     "Forgiven."

It shews not the date of the silent one's birth.
  Reveals not his frailties, nor lies of his worth,
  But speaks out the tale from his few feet of earth—
     "Forgiven."

And when from the heavens the Lord shall descend,
  This stranger shall rise, and to glory ascend,
  Well known and befriended, to sing without end—
     "Forgiven."

"The kingdom of God shall be taken from you, and given to a nation bringing forth the fruits thereof"

—Matt. 21: 43.

ISRAEL after the flesh was to be put aside. The kingdom for which they had waited so long was to be lost to them forever. A new and elect nation, a regenerated Israel, shall possess the kingdom eventually. Meantime the grace of God is going out to the Gentiles.

It is a terribly dangerous thing to trifle with the mercy of God. Little did the Jewish leaders realize that they were sealing their own doom in rejecting Jesus, the One sent of God to bring them into fullness of blessing if they had received Him. They lost their opportunity because they were blinded by self-interest and so they failed to recognize their Messiah when He came in exact accord with the Scriptures of the prophets which they professed to reverence. Mere knowledge of the letter of the Word saves no one. It is those who believe in the Christ of whom the Book of God speaks who are made wise unto salvation (2 Tim. 3: 15). To reject Him is fatal.

"What will you do without Him,
　　When He has shut the door,
And you are left outside, because
　　You would not come before?
When it is no use knocking,
　　No use to stand and wait,
For the word of doom tolls thro' your heart,
　　That terrible 'Too late!' "

—F. R. Havergal.

"The kingdom of heaven is like unto a certain king, which made a marriage for his son, and sent forth his servants to call them that were bidden to the wedding: and they would not come"—Matt. 22: 2, 3.

IN preparing the gospel feast, God has made abundant provision that all men may be saved and enjoy the bounty of His redemptive grace. But to man has been given the power of choice, and it is his prerogative to accept or reject the invitation so freely extended to "whosoever will." No excuse that man can make is really valid. He owes it to himself to heed the call and to take his place at the King's table, where he may enjoy the rich repast so freely spread. He owes it, too, to God Himself to esteem at its proper value the privilege extended to him. He who seeks an excuse for rejecting the divine offer of mercy is doing despite to the Spirit of grace and trampling the blood of the covenant beneath his feet as though it were of little worth (Heb. 10:28, 29). Since God the Father has given His Son that all men might live through Him (1 John 4:9), and since the Holy Spirit has come from Heaven to bear witness (John 16:8) to the truth of the gospel, it behooves every man to accept with alacrity and gratitude the salvation so graciously offered. This is the lesson of the Great Supper.

> "All things are ready: come!"
>   "Yet there is room!"
> Christ every thing hath done:
>   "Yet there is room!"
> The work is now complete;
> Before the mercy-seat
> A Saviour you will meet:
>   "Yet there is room!"
>
> God's house is filling fast,
>   "Yet there is room!"
> Some guest will be the last,
>   "Yet there is room!"
> Yes! soon salvation's day
> To you will pass away,
> Then Grace no more will say—
>   "Yet there is room!"

"After a long time the lord of those servants cometh and reckoneth with them"—Matt. 25: 19.

IT was when the master returned that he took account of his servants. And it will be at the return of our Lord Jesus that He will summon His servants to stand before His judgment-seat, not to be condemned for their sins, for that judgment is past (John 5: 24), but to render an account of their service. Both for Israel and the Church rewards are to be given out at His coming. See Isaiah 62: 11 and Revelation 22: 12.

The wicked and slothful servant does not represent a child of God, because he is cast into the outer darkness. He has nothing for which he can be rewarded. It is otherwise with those who are regenerated. Of them it is written that in that day, "shall every man have praise of God" (1 Cor. 4: 5). This refers, of course, not to every man as such, but to every one of those who appear at the judgment-seat of Christ, where only believers will stand.

If we use whatever gifts we have, no matter how small and insignificant they may seem, in dependence on God, we shall find our capacity for service increasing constantly. We are told to covet earnestly the best gifts (1 Cor. 12: 31), and to use them in love.

"Go on, go on; there's all eternity to rest in,
    And far too few are on the active service list.
No labor for the Lord is risky to invest in;
    But nothing will make up, should His 'Well done' be missed."

"But Jesus called them unto Him, and said, Ye know that the princes of the Gentiles exercise dominion over them, and they that are great exercise authority upon them. But it shall not be so among you: but whosoever will be great among you, let him be your minister; and whosoever will be chief among you, let him be your servant: even as the Son of Man came not to be ministered unto, but to minister, and to give His life a ransom for many"—Matt. 20: 25-28.

OUR Lord Jesus Christ has given to mankind a new ideal. He has shown us that the truly great man is the one who seeks not his own good, but the blessing of others. Even here on earth the unselfish life is the most satisfactory one. To Baruch of old the message came, "Seekest thou great things for thyself? Seek them not" (Jer. 45: 5). This runs contrary to the pride and self-assertion of the natural man. "Men will praise thee, when thou doest well to thyself" (Ps. 49: 18). But after all is said and done, the truth abides that "for men to search their own glory is not glory" (Prov. 25: 27). Our Lord, who, because of His very nature, had every right to assert Himself and seek recognition and honor from the men whom He created, chose to take the place of servant of all. He humbled Himself to become Man, but that was not enough. As Man, He took the servant's place and at last gave Himself up to death for us in the sacrifice of the cross, that He might redeem us to God. He has glorified and exemplified the dignity of service and self-abnegation in such a way as to give an altogether new standard of greatness.

> "O teach us more of Thy blest ways,
>   Thou holy Lamb of God!
> And fix and root us in Thy grace,
>   As those redeemed by blood.
>
> O tell us often of Thy love,
>   Of all Thy grief and pain,
> And let our hearts with joy confess
>   That thence comes all our gain."

—Hutton.

"And as they were eating, Jesus took bread, and blessed it, and brake it, and gave it to the disciples, and said, Take, eat; this is My body. And He took the cup, and gave thanks, and gave it to them, saying, Drink ye all of it; for this is My blood of the new testament, which is shed for many for the remission of sins"

—Matt. 26: 26-28.

THE Lord's Supper in the Christian Church takes the place of the Passover among the Jews. The two are intimately linked together, for it was after the celebration of the paschal feast that Jesus offered His disciples the bread and wine and tenderly requested them to partake of them as setting forth His body about to be offered on the cross and His blood so soon to be shed for the remission of sins. Nearly two millenniums have elapsed since that solemn night, during which untold millions of grateful believers have partaken of these memorials in remembrance of Him who loved them even unto death.

The communion (1 Cor. 10: 16) is not in any sense a sacrifice. It commemorates the one perfect sacrifice offered by our Lord once for all when He gave Himself for us on Calvary. Neither should it be celebrated with any thought of its having saving value or increasing merit. It is the reminder that when we were utterly lost and helpless, Christ died for us to redeem us to God. It is true that the sacrifice of praise (Heb. 13: 15) should ever accompany it as we contemplate the great cost at which we were saved, and rejoice that He who endured such grief and shame for us is now alive forevermore, never again to have to submit to the pain of death. We call Him to mind as the Author and Finisher of faith, who for the joy that was set before Him, endured the cross, despising the shame, and now sits at the right hand of the throne of God.

> "Around the table of His grace,
> Spread with this feast of love,
> We meditate in perfect peace
> On our High Priest above:
> With praise and gratitude we trace
> The wonders of His love."

"Then saith He unto them, My soul is exceeding sorrowful, even unto death: tarry ye here, and watch with Me.   And He went a little farther, and fell on His face, and prayed, saying, O My Father, if it be possible, let this cup pass from Me: nevertheless not as I will, but as Thou wilt"—Matt. 26: 38, 39.

THE utter resignation of Jesus to the Father's will shines out in all these closing experiences, but particularly in that of Gethsemane.   While the horror of becoming the great sin offering, being made sin for us, overwhelmed His human soul and spirit, yet He was perfectly subject to the divine will, and had no thought of turning aside.   There are depths here that our minds can never fathom, but all is perfection on His part.   If He could have contemplated all that was involved in the sacrifice of the cross with equanimity, He would not have been the perfect Man that He was.   But knowing it all and realizing there was no other way by which He could become the captain of our salvation (Heb. 2: 10), He faced the ordeal unflinchingly in order that God might be glorified, and sinful men saved.

It was not in Gethsemane, but on Calvary, that the sin question was settled and expiation made for iniquity.   But the agony in the garden was a fitting prelude to the darkness of the cross.   In order to make an adequate propitiation for our sins, it was necessary that the Substitute be a man, but more than man; otherwise His sacrifice could not have been of sufficient value to be a ransom for all.   He must be a man on whom death and judgment had no claim; therefore one who had been tested and proved to be absolutely sinless—one who had never violated God's holy law in thought or word or deed.   But this very sinlessness of Jesus explains the suffering He endured in the contemplation of being made sin on our behalf.

"Hark! what sounds of bitter weeping,
From yon lonesome garden sweep!
'Tis the Lord His vigil keeping,
Whilst His followers sink in sleep.
Ah, my soul, He lov-ed thee,
Yes, He gave Himself for me." —J. J. Hopkins.

"Now from the sixth hour there was darkness over all the land unto the ninth hour. And about the ninth hour Jesus cried with a loud voice, saying, Eli, Eli, lama sabachthani? that is to say, My God, My God, why hast Thou forsaken Me?"—Matt. 27: 45, 46.

CHRIST crucified, says the Apostle Paul, is the power of God and the wisdom of God (1 Cor. 1: 23, 24). This is the very foundation of the Christian faith. "Christ died": that is history. "For our sins": that is doctrinal truth (1 Cor. 15: 3)—the great fact upon which our salvation rests. It is all-important to see that it was not simply the physical sufferings of Jesus that atoned for sin. It was what He endured in His inmost being in those hours of darkness when He was made sin for us. What He suffered at the hand of man was an expression of Satanic malignancy and showed up the sinfulness of mankind as nothing else could. What He endured at the hand of God made expiation for iniquity and told out the divine love and justice in the fullest possible manner. In the work of the cross the sin-question has been dealt with so completely and so satisfactorily that the floodgates of mercy have been opened wide and all who now believe the gospel may be saved eternally.

"His be the Victor's name,
  Who fought the fight alone;
Triumphant saints no honor claim,
  His conquest was their own.

By weakness and defeat
  He won the meed and crown,
Trod all our foes beneath His feet
  By being trodden down.

Bless, bless the Conqueror slain,
  Slain in His victory;
Who lived, who died, who lives again—
  For thee, His Church, for thee!"

—W. Gandy.

"And the angel answered and said unto the women, Fear not ye: for I know that ye seek Jesus, which was crucified. He is not here: for He is risen, as He said. Come, see the place where the Lord lay"—Matt. 28: 5, 6.

THE empty tomb of Jesus is the silent yet effectual witness to the fact of His resurrection. Had it been possible to find His body, His disciples would have received it and given it careful burial again. And if His enemies could have produced it, they would have displayed it in fiendish glee as a positive proof that His prediction that He would rise again the third day had been utterly falsified. But neither friend nor foe could locate it, for God had raised His Son from the dead in token of His perfect satisfaction in the work of the cross. The tomb was empty on that first Lord's Day morning, not because the disciples had come by night and stolen the body while the soldiers slept (an unheard-of proceeding), nor yet because the chief priests and their emissaries had dared to break the Roman seal upon the stone that covered the entrance to that rock-hewn grave, but because Jesus had fulfilled His words when He declared that if they destroyed the temple of His body, He would raise it again in three days. The resurrection is attributed to the Father (Heb. 13: 20), to the Son (John 2: 19-21; 10: 17, 18), and to the Holy Spirit (Rom. 8: 11). The entire Trinity had part in that glorious event, the supreme miracle of the ages, when He who died for our sins rose again for our justification. Joseph of Arimathea little thought of the honor that was to be his, when preparing the new tomb which was to be the dwelling-place for a few hours of the dead body of Him who is now alive forevermore.

"The Lord is risen; the Red Sea's judgment flood
Is passed, in Him who bought us with His blood.
The Lord is risen: we stand beyond the doom
Of all our sin, through Jesus' empty tomb."

—W. P. Mackay.

"Jesus came and spake unto them, saying, All power is given unto Me in heaven and in earth. Go ye therefore, and teach all nations, baptizing them in the name of the Father, and of the Son, and of the Holy Ghost: teaching them to observe all things whatsoever I have commanded you: and, lo, I am with you alway, even unto the end of the world. Amen"—Matt. 28: 19, 20.

THE great commission to evangelize the world is not given as a whole in any one of the Gospels, but we need to take all related passages in the three Synoptics and in Acts 1 to get it in its entirety. There are different aspects of the commission which are emphasized in each place. Then, in addition, we have the Lord's command to the eleven as given in John 20. These all agree in this: that it is our responsibility to carry the message of grace to all men everywhere, while we wait for our Lord to return, according to His promise. Matthew puts the emphasis on the kingdom—calling all men to become disciples of the Lord Jesus and proclaim their allegiance by baptism into the name of the Holy Trinity. Mark stresses the importance of faith on the part of those who carry the message, which was to be authenticated by "signs following." Luke, both in the Gospel and the Acts, links the subjective with the objective—repentance on the part of the sinner, forgiveness on the part of God. John dwells on the authority of the risen Christ who commissions His servants to proclaim remission of sins to all who believe, and retention of sins to those who spurn the message.

But all alike declare the urgency and the importance of carrying the witness-testimony, the proclamation of the gospel, into all the nations of the world in the shortest possible time.

"I hear the footfalls of God's mighty hosts
　Whom He is sending all the earth abroad;
Like them let me be busy for His cause,
　　Always and all for God.

Full soon will come to us the harvest-time,
The reaping of the seed that here we strawed;
Oh, then we'll not regret earth's spring,
　　Always and all for God!"
　　　　　　　　　　　—A. B. Simpson.

"**John did baptize in the wilderness, and preach the baptism of repentance for the remission of sins. . . . Jesus came from Nazareth of Galilee, and was baptized of John in Jordan**"—Mark 1: 4, 9.

JOHN'S baptism was unto repentance. He announced the near approach of the kingdom of God and called upon the people of Israel to get right with God that they might be ready to receive and enter into it. Those who justified God confessed their sins and were baptized (Luke 7: 29). Jesus had no sins to confess; He had nothing of which to repent, yet He came to John for baptism, much to the desert preacher's surprise (Matt. 3: 13, 14). But Jesus reassured him. He submitted to baptism as the divinely appointed way of declaring His interest in and identification with the godly remnant in Israel, who were waiting for His coming. His baptism was a pledge to fulfil every righteous demand of the throne of God on behalf of those who owned their guilt and took the place of repentance before Him. They were like debtors giving their notes to a creditor—acknowledging a debt they could not pay. He, by His baptism, endorsed all their notes and made Himself responsible to pay all they owed. On the cross He settled for all when He endured the baptism of judgment in our place.

"Lord Jesus, we remember
    The travail of Thy soul,
When in Thy love's deep pity
    The waves did o'er Thee roll.
Baptized in death's dark waters,
    For us, Thou Lord of glory,
    For us, Thou Lord of glory,
        Wast numbered with the dead."

—J. G. Deck.

"They came unto Him, bringing one sick of the palsy which was borne of four . . . when Jesus saw their faith, He said unto the sick of the palsy, Son, thy sins be forgiven thee"—Mark 2: 3, 5.

THE great outstanding purpose of our Lord's ministry as the Servant of Jehovah was to bring people into right relationship with God. What availed it if the sick were healed of physical ailments but continued on in their sins, unrepentant and unbelieving? The palsied physical condition of the man who was saved and healed pictures the real state of men generally—"without strength" (Rom. 5: 6), and therefore unable to deliver themselves from the dire results of their sins. But Jesus came not to help men save themselves, but to deliver them Himself from their lost estate. It is not when we have done our best that His grace comes in to make up full weight, as it were. But when we realize that we are utterly helpless and look to Him alone for salvation, He does for us what no one else could do.

It is all of grace through faith, that the glory might be His alone. The faith of the four men who brought their palsied friend to Jesus is a beautiful example of fellowship in the glad service of bringing others to Christ. But he, too, believed, and so the faith of all five was rewarded.

"Forgiveness! 'twas a joyful sound
　　To guilty sinners doomed to die:
We'd publish it the world around,
　　And gladly shout it through the sky.

'Twas the rich gift of love divine;
　　'Tis full, effacing ev'ry crime;
Unbounded shall its glories shine,
　　And know no change by changing time."

—Gibbons.

"Who can forgive sins but God only? . . . The Son of Man hath power on earth to forgive sins"—Mark 2:7, 10.

NO clearer proof could be given of the deity of our Lord than we find here in His attitude toward this palsied man. His critics were right when they exclaimed, "Who can forgive sins but God only!" What they did not realize was that God incarnate was in their midst. He who had become in grace the Son of Man had all the divine prerogatives still. He had authority, even while sojourning on earth, to forgive sins.

Some time ago a well-known liberal preacher, who denies the Godhead of the Son, said to me, "I am not afraid of Jesus Christ. I can trust Him to deal faithfully with my case." I replied, "Why should you fear Him? Why do you not say, 'I am not afraid of Buddha, or of Mohammed?' If Jesus is only a man, even though the best of men, you do not have to stand before Him for judgment. It is to God all men must give account."

> We may not climb the heavenly steeps
> To bring the Lord Christ down;
> In vain we search the lowest deeps,
> For Him no depths can drown.
>
> But warm, sweet, tender, even yet,
> A present help is He;
> And faith has still its Olivet,
> And love its Galilee.
>
> The healing of the seamless dress
> Is by our beds of pain;
> We touch Him in life's throng and press,
> And we are whole again."

—J. G. Whittier.

"Jesus . . . saith unto them, They that are whole need not a physician but they that are sick. I came not to call the righteous but sinners to repentance"

—**Mark 2:17.**

MEN are not sinners because they sin. They sin because they are sinners. Therefore the sin-question must be settled first of all ere there can be a new order of society which will answer to the mind of God. Nor are men divided by the Lord into classes of little sinners and great sinners, but, "All have sinned, and come short of the glory of God" (Rom. 3:23); therefore all need the same salvation.

Religious forms and ceremonies are powerless to effect the salvation of the soul. The new robe of righteousness is offered in place of the filthy rags of self-righteousness (Isa. 64:6; 61:10). No patching-up process will do. The new wine of the gospel received into the believing heart will give new power in the life. Between salvation by grace and attempted salvation by human effort there can be no compromise.

"I need Thee, precious Jesus!
  For I am full of sin;
My soul is dark and guilty,
  My heart is dead within.
I need the cleansing fountain
  Where I can always flee,
The blood of Christ most precious,
  The sinner's perfect plea.

I need Thee, blessed Jesus!
  For I am very poor;
A stranger and a pilgrim,
  I have no earthly store;
I need the love of Jesus
  To cheer me on my way,
To guide my doubting footsteps,
  To be my strength and stay.

I need Thee, blessed Jesus!
  And hope to see Thee soon,
Encircled with the rainbow,
  And seated on Thy throne:
There, with Thy blood-bought children,
  My joy shall ever be
To sing Thy praise, Lord Jesus,
  To gaze, my Lord, on Thee!"—Frederick Whitfield.

"And He said unto them, The sabbath was made for man, and not man for the sabbath. Therefore the Son of Man is Lord also of the sabbath"—Mark 2: 27, 28.

IT was God who, in the goodness of His heart, designated one day in seven as a season of rest for His people. But the advocates of both license and legality perverted this expression of His loving-kindness to their own spiritual undoing. In the name of liberty the Sabbath was used by the openly ungodly as a day of careless pleasure-seeking or of personal gain (Neh. 13: 15). On the other hand, the self-righteous hedged the holy day about with numberless regulations of their own devising that made the observance of it far more of a burden than a rest. These traditions of the elders, which were fiercely contended for and which made the Word of God of none effect, were looked upon as the very quintessence of orthodoxy. He who dared to set them to one side was branded as a dangerous heretic.

It was inevitable that Jesus must come into conflict with the religious leaders on this question, and in the portion now before us we have two such instances. In each case it was grace clashing with legality. Grace is warm, compassionate, interested more in men than in ordinances, however good and precious in themselves. Legality is cold, exacting, and far more concerned about punctilious obedience to its demands than about the needs of men and their deliverance from bondage and sin.

The same two principles are in active opposition still, and will ever be until we come to the unity of the faith when our Lord returns and gathers all His own around Himself, to enter into that eternal Sabbath-keeping which remains for the people of God (Heb. 4: 9; *see marg. reading*).

> "No curse of law, in Thee was sov'reign grace,
> And now what glory in Thine unvailed face!
> Thou didst attract the wretched and the weak,
> Thy joy the wand'rers and the lost to seek."
>
> —G. W. Frazer.

"There met Him a man . . . with an unclean spirit, who had his dwelling among the tombs; and no man could bind him, no, not with chains"—Mark 5: 2, 3.

HOW often we have heard some poor derelict of a man, overcome by sin and lost to all sense of decency, described as a "good-for-nothing." But it is for such as him, as for all others, that Christ Jesus came into the world. To Him all men, while lost and ruined in themselves, are good for something, because of what His grace can do for them. George Whitefield used to say that "Jesus will take in the Devil's castaways." Lady Huntingdon objected to this expression until one of Whitefield's converts told her of his own redemption from the lowest strata of degraded society. Then she realized the glorious truth embodied in the homely language of the great field-preacher.

Surely, if any man were utterly good for nothing, it was the poor, demon-possessed wretch who had his dwelling among the foul caves of the dead! But he is only a picture of many men as God sees them under Satan's power— "hateful and hating one another." Christ put a new value on men. No matter how wicked and godless, nor how perverted their instincts, they were potential saints for whom He gave Himself. He was able then, as He is able now, to give complete deliverance and to change them by His grace.

> "Sinners Jesus will receive,
>   Sound the word of grace to all
> Who the heavenly pathway leave,
>   All who linger, all who fall.
> Sing it o'er and o'er again,
> Christ receiveth sinful men."

"Jesus said unto them, A prophet is not without honor, but in his own country, and among his own kin, and in his own house. And He could there do no mighty work, save that He laid His hands upon a few sick folk, and healed them"—Mark 6: 4, 5.

HOW strange, it seems, at first, to read that "He *could* there *do no* mighty work," and that because of their unbelief. There is a sense in which man's lack of faith shackles divine omnipotence. God has chosen to do for those who believe what, in the very nature of things, He cannot do consistently for those who spurn His Word. The people of Nazareth shut the door of blessing in their own faces by refusing to trust the Carpenter as the Anointed of Jehovah. His very lowliness proved a stumbling-block to their pride. His holiness was a rebuke to their carnality, and by rejecting His testimony they put up a barrier between Paradise and themselves.

"With the lowly is wisdom" (Prov. 11: 2). Had they been humble enough to sit at His feet as learners, what lessons of grace and power would have been unfolded to them, and what mighty works would have been wrought in their midst! But they were so self-contented and self-satisfied that His message found no response in their unbelieving hearts, and so they lost the greatest opportunity that they would ever know.

> "What will it profit, when life here is o'er
>   Though earth's fleeting love has been mine,
> If, seeking its gifts—I fail to secure
>   The riches of God's love divine?
>
> What will it profit? My soul, stop and think!
>   What balance that day will declare!
> Life's record laid bare, will gain turn to loss,
>   And leave me at last to despair!"

—Grace E. Troy.

"When He had taken the five loaves and the two fishes, He looked up to heaven, and blessed, and brake the loaves, and gave them to His disciples to set before them; and the two fishes divided He among them all. And they did all eat, and were filled"—Mark 6:41, 42.

WHEN God brought His people of old out of Egypt, He sustained them in the wilderness during their forty years' sojourn, providing bread from Heaven. It was therefore quite in keeping with His character as Jehovah's Servant that our Lord should minister to the physical needs of men while here on earth. To question the reality of the miracle and to seek to account for it on merely natural grounds is to discount or even deny His divine power and authority. If we accept the truth of the divinity of Christ and acknowledge His true Deity, we need not be concerned about explaining the supernaturalness of His works. In multiplying the loaves and fishes He was but doing in a few moments of time what He is constantly doing in the seas and the grain-fields of the world. This miracle was no more difficult for Him than the daily wonder of propagation of vegetable and animal life from infinitesimal seed. When the Creator and Sustainer of this diversified universe walked among men, it was to be expected that mighty works would be manifested in Him (see Matt. 14:2). It was in keeping, too, with His Messiahship that He should satisfy the poor with bread (Ps. 132:15).

> "I look to Thee in ev'ry need,
>   And never look in vain;
> I feel Thy strong and tender love,
>   And all is well again;
> The thought of Thee is mightier far
> Than sin and pain and sorrow are.
>
> Discouraged in the work of life,
>   Disheartened by its load,
> Shamed by its failures or its fears,
>   I sink beside the road;
> But let me only think of Thee,
> And then new heart springs up in me."
>
> —Samuel Longfellow.

JUNE 30

"In vain do they worship Me teaching for doctrines the commandments of men . . . making the Word of God of none effect through your tradition"
—Mark 7: 7, 13.

MAN is ever prone to suppose that formal religious observances will be acceptable to God as a means of procuring the divine favor. But religion as such has no saving value. If forms and ceremonies could purchase a place in Heaven, there would have been no need for Christ's redemptive work. And even on the part of those already regenerated, the only thing that gives value to outward observances is a right state of heart before God, who desires truth in the inward parts (Ps. 51: 6). He has said, "To this man will I look, even to him that is poor and of a contrite spirit, and trembleth at My Word" (Isa. 66: 2). Again and again He sought to impress upon Israel the importance of *reality* in their approach to Him (Deut. 10: 12; Isa. 57: 15; Micah 6: 28). Yet they were persistently substituting the outward for the inward, supposing that God would be propitiated by sacramental observances, when all the time He was calling for repentance from dead works and a living faith in His promises.

Many today make the same mistake, a mistake fraught with sad and fearful consequences, for it involves the rejection of the only way of life and salvation and the substitution of a "way which seemeth right unto a man, but the end thereof are the ways of death" (Prov. 14: 12).

> "One Priest alone can pardon me,
> Or bid me 'Go in peace;'
> Can breathe that word 'Absolvo te,'*
> And make these heart-throbs cease:
> My soul has heard His priestly voice;
> It said, 'I bore thy sins—Rejoice!' "

* **"Absolvo te"** (I absolve thee) are the words used by the Romish priest when he assumes the Divine prerogative of forgiving sins.

"Jesus said unto her, Let the children first be fed, for it is not meet to take the children's bread and cast it to the dogs"—Mark 7: 27.

SHALLOW critics have dared to charge Jesus Christ with harshness in dealing as He did with the Syrophenician woman. It only shows how little they understand His mission and the need of probing human souls in order to produce repentance and faith. The woman was not of the chosen people. She was not in covenant relationship with God. She had no claim on the Son of David as such (Matt. 15: 22). The searching words of the Lord Jesus as to the impropriety of casting the children's bread to the dogs gave her to see her true condition. She exclaimed, "Yes, Lord," thus owning Him as Master of Jew and Gentile alike, and so humbly pleaded for some crumbs of blessing, which He gladly gave. It was all dispensed dispensationally perfect. Now the middle wall of partition has been broken down and "there is no difference between the Jew and the Greek: for the same Lord over all is rich unto all that call upon Him" (Rom. 10: 12).

"Now in the fulness of His grace,
God puts me in the children's place,
Where I may gaze upon His face,
O Lamb of God, in Thee!

Not half His love can I express,
Yet, Lord, with joy my lips confess,
This blessed portion I possess,
O Lamb of God, in Thee!

Thy precious name it is I bear,
In Thee I am to God brought near,
And all the Father's love I share,
O Lamb of God, in Thee!"

—Jane Deck Walker.

"And when He had called the people unto Him with His disciples also, He said unto them, Whosoever will come after Me, let him deny himself, and take up his cross, and follow Me. For whosoever will save his life shall lose it; but whosoever shall lose his life for My sake and the gospel's, the same shall save it"—Mark 8:34, 35.

SELF-ABNEGATION is the law of the kingdom of God. It is the meek who inherit the earth, the poor in spirit who are infinitely wealthy. In the service of Christ we gain by losing, live by dying, and receive by giving. Does this seem utterly opposed to what the world regards as sound wisdom? It is because the wisdom of this world is foolishness with God (1 Cor. 1:20), and the principles of action which natural men approve are absolutely opposed to those of Heaven.

The Bible abounds with instances of men who triumphed by seeming defeat. Consider Joseph, Moses, David, Daniel, Jeremiah, Paul, and pre-eminently our blessed Lord Himself.

On the other hand, how many there are whose sad failures illustrate the truth that "those that walk in pride He is able to abase" (Dan. 4:37). The names of Cain, Pharaoh, Ahab, Nebuchadnezzar, Herod, and Pilate are only a few that might be cited.

It is the part of those who profess to be followers of Christ to share His rejection. Why should they expect recognition from a world that gave their Saviour a cross of shame? To faith there is no greater luxury than identification with Him in suffering and sorrow, that the life given up may prove to be a life preserved unto eternal glory.

> * The cross on which our Lord expired
>   Has won the crown for us!
> In thankful fellowship with Him
>   We bear our daily cross.
>
> Set free in grace—He vanquished him
>   Who held us in his chains—
> But more than this, He shares with us
>   The fruit of all His pains."

—W. Trotter.

JULY 3

"Verily I say unto you, That there be some of them that stand here, which shall not taste of death, till they have seen the kingdom of God come with power"

—Mark 9: 1.

AFTER six days, or as Luke puts it, "about an eight days after" (Luke 9: 28), that is, on the night of the eighth day, which began according to Jewish reckoning at sunset, and therefore followed the seventh day, including that on which the Lord Jesus Christ gave this prediction, the transfiguration took place.

Peter, who was present on that memorable occasion, tells us that it was then "the power and coming of our Lord Jesus Christ" was portrayed. In other words, it was the manifestation of the kingdom of God in embryo (2 Pet. 1: 10-21).

The King Himself was there in His glory and majesty. The Father's voice acclaimed His perfections and called on all men to "hear Him." There appeared with Him in the same glory two archetypal men: one who had passed through death, the other who had been caught up alive into Heaven. These pictured the heavenly side of the kingdom. The disciples in their natural bodies pictured those on earth, basking in the sunlight of Messiah's presence. It was a momentary glimpse of the kingdom to be set up when Christ returns in power to reign.

With such a vision before their souls, the disciples could well afford to count all things else but loss that they might have part wtih Him in that day.

"Though darker, rougher, grows the way,
And cares press harder day by day,
    And nothing satisfies,
The promise sure before me lies
Of that blest place beyond the skies
    Where Jesus waits for me.
With sight too dim to visualize
The scene, though spread before my eyes,
    I know it will be fair;
Eye hath not seen, ear hath not heard,
The things that are for us prepared,
    But Jesus will be there."

—Robert R. Pentecost.

"This kind can come forth by nothing but by prayer and fasting"—Mark 9: 29.

BACK of all effective service there must ever be a life of prayer. It is only as we ourselves are in touch with God that we can be channels through which divine power and blessing will flow forth to others.

No amount of activity, nor of sincere desire to help, can make up for lack of communion with God. Of old the Levites, who represented ministry, waited on the priesthood, which speaks of worship (Num. 3: 9, 10). "This kind goeth not out but by prayer." Prayer is the recognition of our own helplessness and our appropriation of divine energy, which works in and through the self-judged, obedient believer to the glory and praise of God. This, too, is true fasting—the denial of self and ceasing from all fleshly confidence.

"When you pray at morn or sundown,
  By yourself or with your own;
When you pray at rush of noontide,
  Just make sure you touch the Throne.

When you pray in hours of leisure,
  Praying long and all alone;
Pour not out mere words as water,
  But make sure you touch the Throne.

When you pray in busy moments,
  Oft to restless hurry prone;
Brevity will matter little,
  If you really touch the Throne."

"And John answered Him, saying, Master, we saw one casting out devils in Thy name, and he followeth not us; and we forbade him, because he followeth not us. But Jesus said, Forbid him not: for there is no man which shall do a miracle in My name, that can lightly speak evil of Me. For he that is not against us is on our part"
—Mark 9: 38-40.

IT IS a great thing to learn that each servant of Christ must act individually as before the Lord, and yet, on the other hand, that he is responsible to co-operate with his fellow-servants so far as possible, without seeking to control or dictate to them.

We are always prone to forget that we are not to judge one another, but to remember that each one stands or falls to his own master (Rom. 14: 4). But this should not make us self-centered and disinterested in the work of others. The trials of our fellow-servants should move us to prayer on their behalf, and their victories should cause us to rejoice. We cannot properly appraise even our work now, let alone that of our brethren, but all will come out "in that day" (1 Cor. 4: 1-5).

It seemed hard for our Lord's disciples to learn these things, and it is evident that few of us have learned them today. We are so apt to over-estimate the importance of our own ministry and to under-value the work of our fellow-servants. This is a subtle form of pride which is most hateful to God, and most harmful to the work of the Lord.

"Ah, the judgment-seat was not for thee—
    These servants, they were not thine:
And the Eye which adjudges the praise and the blame,
    Sees further far than thine.

Wait till the evening falls, my child,
    Wait till the evening falls;
The Master is near, and knoweth it all—
    Wait till the Master calls."

"And he was sad at that saying, and went away grieved, for he had great possessions"—Mark 10: 22.

NO more searching incident than this is found in the four Gospels, unless it be the Lord's interview with Nicodemus, as recorded in John 3. Surely, no honest person can contemplate it without facing the question, On what do I base my hope of eternal life? If on self-effort, I build on sinking sand. If on Christ alone, my confidence is founded upon an unshakeable rock.

But I must be sure that my professed faith in Him is not a mere intellectual acceptance of certain historic facts. To believe in Him is to commit myself to Him. This necessarily involves my recognition of His Lordship. He who died to save me is now to have authority over my life.

Anything short of this is but an empty profession. Let me then face the matter honestly and never be satisfied until I know beyond a doubt that I have yielded to the claims of the Lord Jesus.

The rich young man was of charming disposition and pleasant personality, but he was devoid of divine life, which is the result of new birth (John 3:3). There is a vast difference between the attractiveness of what is merely natural and the beauty of character that is spiritual in its origin. No human effort can ever change flesh into spirit. Therefore the need of the impartation of life from above, which comes through faith in Christ (John 3:6, 7, 14-16).

> "What will you do without Him
>   When the great White Throne is set,
> And the Judge, who never can mistake
>   And never will forget,—
> The Judge whom you have never here
>   As Friend and Saviour sought,
> Shall summon you to give account
>   Of word and deed and thought?"

—F. R. Havergal.

"Ye know that they which are accounted to rule over the Gentiles exercise lordship over them . . . but so shall it not be among you; but whosoever will be great among you shall be your minister"—**Mark 10: 42, 43.**

I N WORDLY politics we are accustomed to the selfish saying, "To the victors belong the spoils." Even in a democratic country like our own we have become inured to the idea that when a particular party gets into power, its adherents may expect to be rewarded with public offices at the behest of senators and other officials. And while civil service reform was intended to put a stop to such practices, there is very little activity of conscience regarding this method of recognizing faithful party-henchmen.

But it is far otherwise in the kingdom of God. There self-seeking has no place, and he who serves with self-interest in view will lose out at last. When our Lord sits on the judgment-seat every man's work will be manifested "of what sort it is." Quality will count in that day. The one who will be given the chief place at last is the one who abases himself to serve all.

"Cleave to the poor, Christ's image in them is;
    Count it great honor, if they love thee well;
  Naught can repay thee after losing this.
    Though with the wise and wealthy thou shouldst dwell,
  Thy Master oftentimes would pass thy door,
  To hold communion with His much-loved poor."

—J. J. P.

"Render to Cæsar the things that are Cæsar's, and to God the things that are God's"—Mark 12: 17.

THERE is no conflict of ·duties as between the spiritual life and one's temporal responsibilities. The more truly we love God, the more sincerely will we seek the good of mankind. We express our faith in God by our love for our fellow-men (1 John 3: 23). The Christian should be an example in his community of devotion to everything that is good and for the well-being of his neighbors. But this does not involve a recognition of the present world order as the fulfilment of the divine ideal. So long as earth's rightful Ruler, the Lord Jesus Christ, is rejected, there will never be perfect government in this scene. Nevertheless, "the powers that be are ordained of God," in the sense that they exist only by His permissive will, hence the importance of subjection to the existing authority in any given country.

If human edicts be positively opposed to the expressed will of God, the Christian is to obey God rather than man (Acts 4: 19). Where conditions are such that he can with good conscience cooperate with the government, he is to do so. Any other course would be contrary to the spirit of Him who said, "Render to Cæsar the things that are Cæsar's, and to God the things that are God's."

"Children of a free-born race,
 Happy in your dwelling-place,
 As your blessings ye retrace,
   Think from whence they flow.
 Think of that creative Hand,
 Author of the sea and land,
 By whose power the nations stand,
   In their weal or woe."

"And when ye stand praying, forgive, if ye have ought against any: that your Father also which is in heaven may forgive you your trespasses. But if ye do not forgive, neither will your Father which is in heaven forgive your trespasses"—Mark 12: 25, 26.

THOSE who have entered into the kingdom by new birth (John 3: 5) are all forgiven sinners who stand before God on the ground of pure grace. Nevertheless, as children in the family of God, they are subject to the Father's discipline and are under His government. The moment our responsibility as sinners, having to do with the God of judgment, ended, our responsibility as children, having to do with our Father, began. In this new relationship we are to display the activities of the divine nature and therefore are called upon to act in grace toward any who may offend us. If we fail to do this, we will be sternly disciplined in order that the government of God may be maintained.

It is the Father who deals with the members of His own family, and who will not overlook harshness or lack of compassion on the part of His children toward their erring brethren.

> "How sweet, how heavenly, is the sight,
>   When those that love the Lord
> In one another's peace delight,
>   And thus fulfil His word!
>
> When free from envy, scorn, and pride,
>   Our wishes all above,
> Each can his brother's failings hide
>   And show a brother's love."

"My soul is exceeding sorrowful unto death"
—Mark 14:34.

THE Gethsemane experience of our adorable Lord, incomprehensible as it is to our finite minds, emphasizes, as perhaps nothing else could, the reality of His humanity and His utter abhorrence of sin. Although He had become incarnate for the very purpose of becoming the propitiation for our sins, yet as the solemn hour drew nigh when the weight of a world's iniquity must be heaped upon Him, His holy soul shrank from the fearful ordeal. Hence the impassioned prayer, "O My Father, if it be possible, let this cup pass from Me." But His human will was absolutely subordinated to the divine will, as evidenced by the further words, "If this cup may not pass . . . except I drink it, Thy will be done."

In that garden was settled forever the question as to whether there was any other possible way of salvation for lost men, except through the pouring out of His soul unto death and the draining of the bitter cup of divine wrath against sin.

The *hour* and the *cup* are synonymous. That hour had been before Him ever since He came into the world. It was the hour when He should give Himself a ransom for many. We need to realize that it was not easy for the humanity of Jesus to make this supreme sacrifice. It involved circumstances and conditions that the Holy One could only contemplate with horror. Let us learn from His agony in the garden something at least of what it will mean for impenitent sinners to fall into the hands of the living God (Heb. 10:31).

> "Death and the curse were in that cup,
>   O Christ, 'twas full for Thee,
> But Thou hast drained the last dark drop,
>   Left but the love for me.
> That bitter cup, love drank it up,
>   Now blessing's draught for me."
>   —Mrs. Cousins.

"Be not affrighted: ye seek Jesus of Nazareth, which was crucified. He is risen; He is not here. Behold the place where they laid Him"—Mark 16: 6.

APART from the physical resurrection of the Lord Jesus we could have no proof that God had accepted the sacrifice He offered as a propitiation for our sins. He "was delivered for our offences, and was raised again for our justification" (Rom. 4: 25).

By "many infallible proofs" witness has been borne to this great event. Think of any other outstanding incident which occurred any time within some centuries before or after the days of our Lord and ask yourself, "How many witnesses can be cited to prove that this really took place?" You will be astonished as you realize how slender is the evidence that can be adduced. But we have the sober records of the four Evangelists, the added testimony of St. Paul, who saw Christ in the glory, the definite words of James and Jude, the Lord's brothers, who did not believe during the Lord's lifetime but were converted when they saw and conversed with Him in resurrection, and the witness of Peter—all of these giving their independent accounts, in which they positively declared that they knew Him as the Risen One. And these are not fanatical emotionalists, but serious-minded men who did not expect Him to rise, and at first could not believe He had done so. Then we have the many eyewitnesses cited by the four Evangelists and by the apostle Paul (1 Cor. 15:5-8). Added to all these, we have the proof that He is the living Christ in the mighty works of the early Church, and His continued manifestations of saving power throughout the centuries since.

> "Death's dread power is o'er
> Since Christ rose once more,
>   Turning deepest grief and sadness
>   Into wondrous joy and gladness.
> With Christ's own now say,
> 'He is risen today.'
>   —Anon.

"So then after the Lord had spoken unto them, He was received up into heaven, and sat on the right hand of God. And they went forth, and preached everywhere, the Lord working with them, and confirming the Word with signs following. Amen"—Mark 16:19, 20.

THE Risen Christ is serving still. Though ascended and glorified, the Saviour will never give up the servant character which He assumed in grace when He came from the glory that He had with the Father to this poor world of woe. Throughout all the present age He is "working with" His own as they go forth in His name, and when He brings us into the Father's house He will gird Himself and serve us. He delights to minister with, in, and to those He loves.

He is the servant still! In obedience to His word, His representatives went forth unto all the world, and everywhere He wrought in and through them, confirming the Word with the promised signs, as we read in the Book of Acts.

> "Thou from the dead wast raised—
>   And from all condemnation
> Thy saints are free, as risen in Thee,
>   Head of the new creation!
> On high Thou hast ascended,
>   To God's right hand in heaven,
> The Lamb once slain, alive again,—
>   To Thee all pow'r is given.
>
> Thou hast bestowed the earnest
>   Of that we shall inherit;
> Till Thou shalt come to take us home,
>   We're sealed by God the Spirit.
> We wait for Thine appearing,
>   When we shall know more fully
> The grace divine that made us Thine,
>   Thou Lamb of God most holy!"
>
> —Tregelles.

"And Mary said, My soul doth magnify the Lord, and my spirit hath rejoiced in God my Saviour"
—Luke 1: 46, 47.

IT has often been remarked that Luke's Gospel "opens with a burst of melody." The angels, Mary, Elisabeth, Zacharias, Simeon, Anna, and the shepherds, are all found praising and adoring the God of all grace who has raised up in the house of David, a Redeemer for His people. Mary's song, that which we commonly call, "The Magnificat," is a wondrous expression of her sense of the goodness of God, in providing, through her, a Saviour not only for the race, but for herself. She sings as one who recognizes her own sinfulness by nature, but who rejoices in the divine provision for her salvation; she knew nothing of the Romish doctrine of her own immaculate conception. She gloried in being saved by grace.

"Let sinners saved give thanks and sing,
Salvation's theirs and of the Lord;
They draw from heaven's eternal spring,
The living God, their great reward.

Let sinners saved give thanks and sing,
Whom grace has kept in dangers past,
And oh, sweet truth! the Lord will bring
His people safe to heaven at last."

—T. Kelly.

"And the angel said unto them, Fear not: for, behold, I bring you good tidings of great joy, which shall be to all people. For unto you is born this day in the city of David a Saviour, which is Christ the Lord"
—Luke 2: 10, 11.

THE angel's message was one of joy and gladness, designed to banish fear and fill the heart with hope and peace. But, alas, there were few indeed who responded to it. And although their glad message has been sounding through all the centuries since, this world is still a scene of strife, and often of terror, and the great majority of earth's inhabitants are strangers to that peace which Jesus came to give. Men are so slow to learn that it is only as they receive Him and own Him as Saviour and Lord, that they can appropriate and enjoy the blessings He delights to give. From Bethlehem His path led to the cross where He made peace by His own blood, and now all who believe have peace with God.

"Christ by prophets long-predicted,
    Joy of Israel's chosen race,
Light to Gentiles long afflicted,
    Lost in error's darkest maze,
Bright the star of your salvation,
    Pointing to His rude abode,
Rapturous news for every nation,
    Mortals, now behold your God!"

"Bring forth therefore fruits worthy of repentance, and begin not to say within yourselves, We have Abraham to our father: for I say unto you, That God is able of these stones to raise up children unto Abraham"—Luke 3: 8.

THE searching ministry of John the Baptist was a clarion call to reality. Formalism in religion apart from true heart-exercise is an abomination in the sight of God. He is not served by the work of men's hands or glorified by the declarations of their lips if the inward attitude is not right. All men are called to abase themselves before Him, and take the place of confessed sinfulness, seeking divine grace for deliverance through the Saviour He has provided. Jesus Himself must be the object of faith. It is He alone whose work could meet the claims of God's righteousness. In Him the Father is fully satisfied, and all men everywhere are called to put their trust in Him. While it was not given to John to unfold the gospel in all its blessed detail, he nevertheless directed the people to that One whose mission it is to save all who believe in Him.

"It is not thy tears of repentance nor prayers,
    But the blood that atones for the soul;
On Him then who shed it, thou mayest at once
    Thy weight of iniquities roll.

Then take with rejoicing from Jesus at once
    The life everlasting He gives,
And know with assurance thou never canst die
    While Jesus thy righteousness lives."

—A. M. Hull.

"And many lepers were in Israel in the time of Eliseus the prophet; and none of them was cleansed, saving Naaman the Syrian"—Luke 4: 27.

THE grace of God is abundant and free, all-sufficient to meet the need of the vilest sinner, but no man will receive the benefits who is not simple enough and humble enough to take God at His word, acting in like faith upon the message given. There was complete cleansing and healing for Naaman, without money or price, but only in God's appointed way, and that was summed up in the prophet's message, "Wash, and be clean." So today, there is salvation from sin's guilt and cleansing from its uncleanness for all who will take the place of the needy sinner, and giving up all pretension to human merit will avail themselves of the grace mediated through our Lord Jesus Christ, in whose precious atoning blood we may wash and be clean (Acts 4: 12; Rev. 1: 5, 6).

"Call them in"—the poor, the wretched,
   Sin-stained wand'rers from the fold;
Peace and pardon freely offer;
   Can you weigh their worth with gold?
"Call them in"—the weak, the weary,
   Laden with the doom of sin;
Bid them come and rest in Jesus;
   He is waiting—"call them in."

"Call them in"—the broken-hearted,
   Cow'ring 'neath the brand of shame;
Speak love's message low and tender,
   'Twas for sinners Jesus came.
See, the shadows lengthen round us,
   Soon the day-dawn will begin;
Can you leave them lost and lonely?
   Christ is coming—"call them in."

—Anna Shipton.

"When Simon Peter saw it, he fell down at Jesus'
knees, saying, Depart from me; for I am a sinful man,
O Lord"—Luke 5: 8.

THE miraculous draught of fishes told Peter that he was
in the presence of the Creator. This at once manifested
his own sinful state and led to his taking the place of
repentance at the Saviour's feet. Though he cried, "Depart
from me," it was grace drawing him to the only One who
could meet his need. Instead of departing Jesus met him
in loving-kindness and compassion, and gave him the word
of assurance, " Fear not." It is those who own their sinfulness who find mercy. Peter had joined the goodly fellowship of Job, David and Isaiah, all of whom, when consciously in the presence of God, took the place of self-judgment and found forgiveness and cleansing. The place of
confession is the place of blessing.

"God could not pass the sinner by,
His sin demands that he must die;
But in the cross of Christ we see
How God can save, yet righteous be.

The sin alights on Jesus' head,
'Tis in His blood sin's debt is paid;
And Mercy can dispense her store.
Stern Justice can demand no more,

The sinner who believes is free,
Can say, 'The Saviour died for me;'
Can point to the atoning blood,
And say, 'This made my peace with God.' "

—A. Midlane.

"**A good man out of the good treasure of his heart bringeth forth that which is good; and an evil man out of the evil treasure of his heart bringeth forth that which is evil: for of the abundance of the heart his mouth speaketh**"—Luke 6: 45.

ACTUALLY, until renewed by divine power working in grace, "there is none good, not, not one." But the truly good man relatively speaking, is the one in whose heart the Lord Jesus has found a dwelling-place. He subdues the evil of the natural heart and fills the inward being with the riches of His own love, goodness and grace, so that from within comes what will glorify Him and bring blessing to mankind. The words that flow from the lips express what fills the heart. Where Christ Himself is known and loved, the mouth will be filled with His perfections and others will be blessed and edified. When the heart is filled with worldliness and carnality, the lips will speak of those things which the natural man revels in, as swine in the filth of the sty.

"Our hearts are full of Christ, and long
  Their glorious matter to declare!
Of Him we make our loftier song,—
  We cannot from His praise forbear:
Our ready tongues make haste to sing
The glories of the heavenly King.

Fairer than all the earth-born race,
  Perfect in comeliness Thou art;
Replenished are Thy lips with grace,
  And full of love Thy tender heart.
God ever-blest! we bow the knee,
And own all fulness dwells in Thee."

—C. Wesley.

"When Jesus heard these things He marvelled at him, and turned Him about, and said unto the people that followed Him, I say unto you, I have not found so great faith, no, not in Israel"—Luke 7: 9.

IT HAS pleased God to honor our faith because faith is that which honors Him. Faith takes Him at His word and counts the things which are not as though they were (Rom. 4: 17). But it is not faith that does the work. It is but the means which God uses to unloose His unlimited power. Faith is the hand which lays hold of Omnipotence. As Man on earth, our Lord was the pattern man of faith and He taught faith to others. He chose, in this scene of His humiliation, to live in daily dependence upon the living Father (John 6: 57). Thus the works of power He wrought were those which the Father gave Him to do (John 14: 10). In rebuking disease and death, and in saving from sin those who sought His grace, He was manifesting the heart of God toward a needy world. His concern for the life and health of mankind was but the expressed desire of God the Father, that all men who believe in Him might be at last delivered from the effects of sin. It is not always His will to grant perfect health now, but faith can firmly trust Him in every circumstance.

"More lonely grows the journey as it nears the end,
Yet with me walks the one Unchanging Friend.
Though all should leave, yet He will still abide
Till death, and up through death will safely guide;
And well I know, He ne'er will loose His hold
Till He has led me safe within His fold,
Where loved ones, long in glory, watch and wait,
And lengthening shadows lift at Heaven's Gate."

—M. E. Logie-Pirie.

"He said unto them, But whom say ye that I am? Peter answering said, The Christ of God. And He straitly charged them, and commanded them to tell no man that thing; saying, The Son of Man must suffer many things, and be rejected of the elders and chief priests and scribes, and be slain, and be raised the third day"

—Luke 9: 20-22.

UNTIL we know the Lord Jesus as the Christ, the Son of the living God, we do not know Him at all. He is truly the Son of Man, for He has taken our humanity in grace, apart from sin, into union with His Deity. But He is also the Anointed of Jehovah, the Eternal Son of the Father, who became Man without ceasing to be God, in order that He might redeem sinful men from the judgment that their iniquities have righteously deserved. So the second great truth of divine revelation is that "the Son of Man must suffer." Only by His sacrificial death could expiation be made for iniquity. And no one could make propitiation for sinners but one who was Himself sinless Man and absolute God. He had to be who He was in order to do what He did.

"Thou art my Portion, Lord, Thou art my Rock,
Thou the Good Shepherd who loveth the flock.
Thou art the Life, and the Truth, and the Way,
Sun of God's righteousness, turning to day
Night and its shadowing. Thou art the Vine,
Pouring Thy strength into weakness of mine.
Thou art the Comforter, Healer of strife;
Thou art the Lord, and the Giver of life,
Death's Overcomer, and Saviour from sin,
Victory, Peace, and the Dweller within."

—Bertha G. Woods.

"**For whosoever shall be ashamed of Me and of My words, of him shall the Son of Man be ashamed, when He shall come in His own glory, and in the Father's, and of the holy angels**"—Luke 9: 26.

THE claims of Christ are paramount to all others. He asks for a full, unreserved surrender to Himself. None but God is entitled to this. He is God become Man for our redemption. Therefore all authority is His. To yield to Him will mean the recognition that we are not our own, but are to be henceforth at His command. To lay down our lives is to put them absolutely at His disposal. If this ever means literally to die for Him, it will but open the door to eternal bliss. To shrink from suffering, to seek to avoid death by denying Him, will mean the life—the true self—lost. To acknowledge Him openly before men, whatever the consequences, will mean an open acknowledgment of us by Him in the day of His revelation, His glorious appearing. He who died to redeem the soul claims our fullest allegiance.

> "Not my own, but saved by Jesus,
>   Who redeemed me by His blood,
> Gladly I accept the message,
>   I belong to Christ the Lord.
>
> Not my own! My time, my talents,
>   Freely all to Christ I bring;
> To be used in joyful service
>   For the glory of my King."

—D. W. Whittle.

"But a certain Samaritan, as he journeyed, came where he was: and when he saw him, he had compassion on him, and went to him, and bound up his wounds, pouring in oil and wine, and set him on his own beast, and brought him to an inn, and took care of him"
—Luke 10:33, 34.

HE who sees in the parable of the Good Samaritan only a lesson of neighborliness and consideration for the needy has failed utterly to get what Jesus had in mind. That He was teaching the importance of compassion on the needy is clear enough on the surface of the story. But there is something far deeper than this. We are all like the poor man dying on the roadside. We have all been robbed and wounded by sin, and sore bruised by Satan and his emissaries. Our case is hopeless so far as law-keeping is concerned. No works of righteousness can avail to deliver us from our wretched condition (Titus 3:5). Only the mercy of God as revealed in Christ Jesus, the One who was "despised and rejected of men" (Isa. 53:3) can, and will, undertake for us. He is neighbor indeed to all who submit to His grace. Apart from Him there is no deliverance possible. But he who trusts in Him will henceforth be characterized by loving care for others. To profess to love Him, while indifferent to the need of distressed humanity, is but hypocrisy (1 John 3:17).

"In loving-kindness Jesus came,
    My soul in mercy to reclaim,
And from the depths of sin and shame,
    In grace He lifted me.

He called me long before I heard,
Before my sinful heart was stirred,
But when I took Him at His word,
    Forgiven, He lifted me."

—Charlotte Homer.

"And, behold, there was a woman which had a spirit of infirmity eighteen years, and was bowed together, and could in no wise lift up herself"—Luke 13: 11.

THIS afflicted creature was one whose condition pictured that of all men until touched by divine grace. She was helpless and hopeless so far as her own ability to improve her condition was concerned. Therefore she needed the great Physician, who always delights to undertake for those who admit they can do nothing to deliver themselves. He saw her need and immediately met it. His voice of power told of His determination to set her free. He knew her as one who had faith in God and He responded to the unspoken desire of her heart.

As He laid his tender hands upon that deformed body, a thrill of new life went through her whole being, and for the first time in eighteen years she stood erect, praising God for her remarkable healing. She was made straight. This is most suggestive. The Lord is still engaged in straightening crooked lives to the glory of God.

"I thought I needed many things
    Along life's toilsome way,
When days were long and heavy cares
    Left scarcely time to pray.

I thought I needed many things
    For those I held most dear,
When they were sad and longed for rest
    Or change of portion here.

When it was Thee, I needed, Lord,
    To satisfy my heart.
To fill my days with rest and peace,
    And every grace impart."

—Grace E. Troy.

"Then said he unto him, A certain man made a great supper, and bade many: and sent his servant at supper time to say to them that were bidden, Come; for all things are now ready"—Luke 14: 16, 17.

THE parable of the Great Supper is one of the most delightful, and yet most solemn of all the gospel pictures given us in the New Testament. It is delightful because of the way it sets forth the grace that is in the heart of God, flowing out to the needy and sinful. But it is most solemn because of the manner in which man's response to the message of grace is portrayed. There is a difference between this story as given in Luke and the parable of the Marriage Feast as given in Matthew 22: 1-14. Here in Luke it is the sovereign grace of God that is emphasized. In Matthew, the emphasis is put upon the divine government. This is a great supper to which all are invited. That is a marriage feast intended at first for the select few. There the servants who carry the royal invitation are the ministers of the Word, sent forth to say, "Come; for all things are now ready." Here there is only one Servant in view, the blessed Holy Spirit, and He does what man cannot do: He compels men to come in.

"Why was I made to hear Thy voice
  And enter while there's room,
While thousands make a wretched choice,
  And rather starve than come?

'Twas the same love that spread the feast
  That gently forced me in,
Else I had still refused to taste,
  And perished in my sin."

—Isaac Watts.

"And the son said unto him, Father, I have sinned against heaven, and in thy sight, and am no more worthy to be called thy son. But the father said to his servants, Bring forth the best robe, and put it on him; and put a ring on his hand, and shoes on his feet: and bring hither the fatted calf, and kill it; and let us eat, and be merry: for this my son was dead, and is alive again; he was lost, and is found. And they began to be merry"

—Luke 15: 21-24.

THE three-fold parable of Luke 15 sets forth the joy of heaven over the salvation of sinners who repent. The Lord Jesus is the seeking shepherd; the Holy Spirit is the light that makes manifest the lost coin; the returning prodigal is welcomed to the arms of the Father whose love saw him afar off and led him to run to meet him on the way. Pharisees and haughty scribes could find no joy in the display of grace. But poor sinners revel in its blessedness. The merriment of the Father's house will go on forever.

"As I was my Father loved me,
   Loved me in my sin and shame,
Yet a great way off He saw me,
   Ran to kiss me as I came.
Then in bitter grief I told Him
   Of the evil I had done—
Sinned in scorn of Him, my Father,
   Was not meet to be His son.

But I know not if He listened,—
   For He spake not of my sin—
He within His house would have me,
   Make me meet to enter in;
From the riches of His glory,
   Brought His costliest raiment forth,
Brought the ring that sealed His purpose,
   Shoes to tread His golden court."

—T. P., Trans. by Mrs. F. Bevan.

"And he said unto him, If they hear not Moses and the prophets, neither will they be persuaded, though one rose from the dead"—Luke 16: 31.

THE word of God is His perfect message to men. If that be spurned He has nothing more to say to them until they meet Him in judgment. Wherever that word is proclaimed it puts those who hear it in the place of responsibility, such as they never knew before. The light shines from the word. If they refuse its testimony they prove that they love darkness rather than light. That word contains all that is necessary to show the way of life. It reveals Christ. This was true of the Old Testament. Moses and the prophets all spake of Him. But in the New Testament we have the full-orbed revelation of Him who has come in grace to seek and to save the lost. He who believes finds deliverance. He who turns away will perish in his sins.

"What will it profit, when life here is o'er,
    Though great worldly wisdom I gain,
If, seeking knowledge, I utterly fail
    The wisdom of God to obtain?

What will it profit, when life here is o'er,
    Though gathering riches and fame,
If, gaining the world, I lose my own soul,
    And in Heav'n unknown is my name?

What will it profit, when life here is o'er
    Though earth's farthest corners I see,
If, going my way, and doing my will
    I miss what His love planned for me?"

—Grace E. Troy.

"I tell you, in that night there shall be two men in one bed; the one shall be taken, and the other shall be left. Two women shall be grinding together; the one shall be taken, and the other left. Two men shall be in the field; the one shall be taken, and the other left"

—Luke 17: 24-26.

THE Lord Jesus spoke often of His coming again. He told of His coming in judgment at the end of the age, to deal with unrighteousness and to bring in the long-looked-for kingdom of God upon earth. To His disciples He spoke of His return as something for which they were to watch. It would come suddenly, unexpectedly, to those who were not looking for it. Those counted worthy to stand before the Son of Man will be His own redeemed ones. They will be caught away to Himself, as later revealed through the ministry of the apostle Paul. That blessed event is dateless. It may take place at any time.

"What if, some day when you and I are standing,
　　Watching the fitful lightning in the sky,
Hearing the muttered threat of distant thunder,
　　Knowing humanity's dread hour is nigh,

What if a sudden thrill should quiver through our being,
　　Not the death pang that ends all mortal strife,
But, in a quickening surge of swift ecstatic power,
　　"Mortality be swallowed up of life!"

O Blessed Hope that looks beyond the shadows,
　　That is not troubled by this world's alarms;
That knows The Life and sees a Transformation,
　　That waits the welcome of His outstretched arms!"

—W. C. E.

"And Jesus said unto him, This day is salvation come to this house, forsomuch as he also is a son of Abraham"

—Luke 19: 9.

HOW delightful the incident brought before us! Here was a man under the curse of the law, helpless to deliver himself, yet saved by pure grace and immediately manifesting the fruit of the new life. He was a thief. He had violated not only the eighth commandment, but the tenth, and others too. Hence he was under sentence of death. The law demanded his destruction. But Jesus came to reveal the grace of God and to free repentant sinners from the condemnation of the broken law. That very condemnation Christ was Himself to bear within a few days. In view of it, Zacchæus could be, and was justified before God, regenerated by His divine power and made a new man. How vivid the contrast between the law and the Gospel!

"Out of the distance and darkness so deep,
Out of the settled and perilous sleep;
Out of the region and shadow of death,
Out of its foul and pestilent breath;
Out of the bondage, and wearying chains,
Out of companionship ever with stains;

Into the light and the glory of God,
Into the holiest, made clean by blood;
Into His arms—the embrace and the kiss—
Into the scene of ineffable bliss;
Into the quiet, the infinite calm,
Into the place of the song and the psalm."

—M. T.

"The Son of Man is come to seek and to save that which was lost"—Luke 19: 10.

IT is an interesting and challenging fact that we nowhere find in the Gospels, nor in all the New Testament, for that matter, certain words which are widely used today, and often as though they really provide the key to the ministry of the Lord Jesus. Such terms as "the social order," "social service," "the social gospel" are conspicuous by their absence. Our Lord did not attempt to overturn the social order of His day by some new system of ethical instruction. He did not take into consideration the mass as such. He dealt with the individual. And He showed that personal sin was the root of all the trouble in the world. But He did not merely attempt the reformation of the sinner. He came not to reform, but to save. He did not come to help the race to better its condition. He came to bring in an entirely new creation through the regeneration of individual sinners.

This program adhered to necessarily makes for improved social conditions. If individuals are saved, they will affect in a marked way the environment in which they live. Consequently, the social order has been wonderfully improved through the coming of Christ and the proclamation of His Gospel. But the important thing is to put first things first; preach the gospel to the individual, and when he is saved set him to work seeking the salvation of his neighbors. It was in this way that the Christianity of the first three centuries overturned the paganism of the Roman Empire. To reverse this order is fatal.

"Ye are they which have continued with Me in My temptations, and I appoint unto you a kingdom, as My Father hath appointed unto Me"—Luke 22: 28, 29.

TO be selected by Christ as workers together with Him was a great honor, and the same privilege is ours today (2 Cor. 6: 1). He called, they obeyed, and millions have profited by their service. How different would have been their lives had they planned for themselves instead of heeding His voice! What makes the tragedy of Judas' defection so awful is that he had all the privileges and opportunities of the rest and he threw them all away because of covetousness and worldly ambition.

To do the will of God is to enjoy life at its very best. Jesus said, "I seek not Mine own will, but the will of the Father which hath sent Me" (John 5: 30). The doing of that will meant the cross with all its agony and shame. But only so could He be perfected as Captain of Salvation (Heb. 2: 10). He endured it all for the joy set before Him, and now He sees of the travail of His soul and is satisfied (Heb. 12: 2; Isa. 53: 11). It is given to us not only to believe on Him, but to suffer for His sake (Phil. 1: 29), and to serve with Him for the blessing of a lost world. Then, at His return we shall share His glory.

"And there with Thee we shall rehearse the story,
    Thy faithful love in desert scenes below;
And walking with Thee in that cloudless glory,
    To Thee our endless praise shall ceaseless flow.

Until that day, Lord Jesus, keep us faithful
    To Thy blest Word, and not deny Thy Name!
Oh, shield Thine own from every harm and evil,
    Content to suffer loss and bear Thy shame!"

—J. W. H. Nichols.

"And the Lord said, Simon, Simon, behold Satan hath desired to have you, that he may sift you as wheat: but I have prayed for thee, that thy faith fail not: and when thou art converted, strengthen thy brethren"

—Luke 22: 31, 32.

BACKSLIDING is never a sudden descent from intense spirituality to open sin. Declension is a gradual process, even as growth in grace is that which goes on day by day as one walks with God. The word "backslider" occurs but once in the Bible, and that in Proverbs 14:14, but we frequently find the term "backsliding," though only in the books of Jeremiah and Hosea. However, although these words are not found in the New Testament, we have many warnings against drifting from experiences once attained, and Peter's case is a solemn example of backsliding, and shows us how one wrong state or attitude leads to another, until at last one may fall into grave evil-doing and so bring great dishonor upon the name of the Lord whom we profess to love. Peter's backsliding seems to have begun when he ventured to rebuke Jesus, who had just declared the necessity of going to the cross (Matt. 16:21-23). It was evidently the result of spiritual pride following the Saviour's commendation because of Peter's great declaration as to the true nature of His glorious Person. Though so sternly rebuked, we do not read of any confession on Peter's part, and sin unjudged leads inevitably to something worse as time goes on.

"Thou lovest me! And yet Thy child
Is wayward, foolish, oft defiled;
Is slow to learn and dull to hold,
Quick to forget what Thou hast told;
In service feeble, seeking ease
Ofttimes, instead of Thee to please;
Thus poor my record e'er will be,
And yet, O God, Thou lovest me!"

AUGUST 1

"Thus it is written, and thus it behoved Christ to suffer, and to rise from the dead the third day, and that repentance and remission of sins should be preached in His name among all nations, beginning at Jerusalem"
—Luke 24: 47.

CHRIST in His humiliation confined His ministry almost entirely to the people of Israel. Now in resurrection, all national restrictions are done away and His gospel is to go forth among all nations, for God desires to have all men come to repentance and to the acknowledgment of the truth, that they might be saved. Everywhere the gospel of the risen Saviour is to be proclaimed. To stop at the cross is to preach but a half gospel. It is the truth of the resurrection that completes it. "If Christ be not raised, . . . ye are yet in your sins" (1 Cor. 15: 17). The resurrection is the proof that His work has been accepted, and so God can now offer a full and complete salvation to all who trust in Him. To profess Christianity while denying the physical resurrection of the Founder is to be self-deceived. There can be no salvation apart from the raising up of the Son of God from the dead.

> "They knew that their Redeemer lived,
>   His friends of long ago,
> They saw Him die, and mourned for Him
>   In hopelessness and woe;
> And then they saw Him, touched His hand,
>   Heard His familiar voice;
> And they, in wonder and in awe,
>   Believing, did rejoice.
>
> We know that our Redeemer lives,
>   Though hidden from our view;
> For in His life we have found life,
>   Life full and rich and new;
> Our hearts have felt His touch, our ears
>   Have heard His blessed voice;
> We have the witness in our hearts;
>   Believing, we rejoice."

—M. B. Smith.

"In the beginning was the Word, and the Word was with God, and the Word was God. The same was in the beginning with God. All things were made by Him; and without Him was not anything made that was made"
—John 1: 1-3.

IT is well known that the term "Word" translates the Greek word "*Logos*." This was an expression already well-known to thinking people when our Lord appeared on earth. Everywhere in the Greek-speaking world the writings of Plato were circulated. He had spoken of the insolubility of many mysteries, but had expressed the hope that some day there would come forth a "Word" (*Logos*) from God that would make everything clear. John might even have had this in mind when, directed by the Holy Spirit, he penned the wonderful sentences with which this Gospel begins. It is as though God is saying: "The 'Word' has now been spoken. In Christ the mind of God is fully revealed. He who hears Him hears God, for in Him 'are hid all the treasures of wisdom and knowledge'." The Word never had a beginning. The Son is as truly eternal as the Father is. To teach otherwise is to deny the very foundations of our faith. He could not have a beginning, for He Himself is the beginning and the end (Rev. 22: 13).

> "Thou art the everlasting Word—
>   The Father's only Son,
> God manifest, God seen and heard,
>   The Heaven's beloved One;
>
> In Thee most perfectly expressed
>   The Father's self doth shine;
> Fullness of Godhead, too: the blest,—
>   Eternally divine.
>
> Image of th' Infinite Unseen,
>   Whose being none can know;
> Brightness of light no eye hath seen,
>   God's Love revealed below.
> Worthy, O Lamb of God art Thou
> That ev'ry knee to Thee should bow."
>
> —J. Conder.

"This is He of whom I said, After me cometh a Man which is preferred before me: for He was before me"
—John 1: 30.

FEW preachers have equalled John the Baptist in self-depreciation and Christ-exaltation. He sought to turn the attention of his hearers from himself to Jesus, and if he made disciples, it was only that they might be persuaded to leave him and follow Christ, the One who was preferred before him (John 1:15), because pre-existent. John was happy and content to be esteemed the Bridegroom's friend, and rejoiced as he entered into His joy (John 3: 29).

"Not I, but Christ, be honored, loved, exalted;
Not I, but Christ, be seen, be known, be loved;
Not I, but Christ, in every look and action;
Not I, but Christ, in every thought and word.

Not I, but Christ, in lowly, silent labor;
Not I, but Christ, in humble, earnest toil;
Christ, only Christ, no show, no ostentation;
Christ, none but Christ, the Gatherer of the spoil."

—A. A. F.

"For God so loved the world, that He gave His only begotten Son, that whosoever believeth in Him should not perish, but have everlasting life"—John 3: 16.

LUTHER called this verse, "The Miniature Bible." Others have designated it, "The Gospel in a nutshell." It tells of the infinite love of God to a ruined world, manifested by the supreme gift of His Only Begotten Son, who in grace became Man and gave Himself for our sins upon the cross in order that He might make expiation for our iniquities, that thus God might be able in righteousness to bestow the gift of life eternal on those who deserved eternal death. It is when we believe the message that we receive the benefits of the gospel. To believe is to trust. He who trusts alone in Christ Jesus for salvation shall never perish, but even now is the possessor of eternal life—a life that can never be forfeited.

"FOR GOD, the Lord of earth and Heaven,
SO LOVED, and longed to see forgiven,
THE WORLD in sin and pleasure mad,
THAT HE GAVE the greatest gift He had—
HIS ONLY SON—to take our place,
THAT WHOSOEVER—Oh, what grace!—
BELIEVETH, placing simple trust
IN HIM, the righteous and the just,
SHOULD NOT PERISH, lost in sin,
BUT HAVE ETERNAL LIFE IN HIM."

—Barbara C. Ryberg.

"Jesus answered and said unto her, Whosoever drinketh of this water shall thirst again: but whosoever drinketh of the water that I shall give him shall never thirst; but the water that I shall give him shall be in him a well of water springing up into everlasting life"
—John 4: 13, 14.

WHAT Jesus said of the water of Jacob's well is true of everything that earth can offer. There is nothing in this scene that can effectually quench the thirst of a human soul. Man is made for Eternity, and the things of Time can never satisfy. Augustine spoke truly when he cried, "O God, Thou hast made us for Thyself, and our souls can never find rest until they rest in Thee." But he who drinks the living water of the gospel finds that which quenches his thirst forever. Christ fully satisfies the heart that learns to confide in Him. The word received in the power of the Holy Spirit produces the new birth, thus giving everlasting life. This is the present possession of all who put their trust in the Lord Jesus.

"I heard the voice of Jesus say,
     'Behold, I freely give
The living water; thirsty one,
     Stoop down, and drink and live.'
I came to Jesus, and I drank
     Of that life-giving stream,
My thirst was quenched, my soul revived,
     And now I live in Him."

—H. Bonar.

"God is a Spirit, and they that worship Him must worship Him in spirit and in truth"—John 4: 24.

IN considering the subject of Worship, the highest exercise of which the spirit of man is capable, it is important to remember that there is a great difference between the way it is presented in the two Testaments. In former dispensations God was hidden in large measure. His wisdom and His providence were displayed in creation. His love was seen in His care of those who confided in Him. His grace was declared by the prophets as something yet to be manifested. Consequently there was no immediate access into the presence of God. The veil was unrent. His Word to Israel was, "Draw not nigh hither" (Exod. 3:5); "Worship ye afar off" (24:1). But since the advent of Christ, all is changed. Grace and truth are now revealed. The veil is rent. The way into the holiest is now made manifest. In spirit every believer is invited to "draw near . . . in full assurance of faith" (Heb. 10:19-22). The worship of the new creation is based upon the finished work of our blessed Lord. In spirit we enter the immediate presence of the Father in full consciousness of our sonship. Worship is far more than prayer, or the enjoyment of helpful ministry. It is the spirit's adoring occupation with God Himself, not merely in gratitude for His gifts, but because of what He is. It is this that the Father seeks. Worship is lowered as we become occupied with the externals even of Christianity. It reaches its highest point as our spirits are absorbed in contemplation of the matchless perfections of the eternal God, in the light of the cross and the empty tomb.

> "Father, we Thy children, bless Thee
> For Thy love on us bestowed;
> Source of blessing, we confess Thee
> Now, our Father and our God.
> Wondrous was Thy love in giving
> Jesus for our sins to die!
> Wondrous was His grace in leaving,
> For our sakes, the heavens on high!"

—Tregelles.

"Verily, verily, I say unto you, He that heareth My word, and believeth on Him that sent Me, hath everlasting life, and shall not come into condemnation; but is passed from death unto life"—John 5: 24.

THERE is perhaps no clearer word in all the Bible than this as to how one may know he has eternal life. Note the five great pillars on which assurance rests. First, "He that heareth My Word." Have you heard God's Voice in the Word? Has it spoken to your inner ear—the ear of your soul? Second, "And believeth on Him that sent Me." To believe on Him is to trust in Him. Do you confide in God as the One who sent His Son to die for you? Third, "Hath everlasting life." Note there is no peradventure here. All who believe *have* God's great gift of life eternal. Fourth, "Shall not come into condemnation." That is, "judgment" for all that our sins deserved was borne by Jesus, so no believer will ever have to meet God in judgment about the guilt of the past. Fifth, "Is passed from death unto life." All who have thus come to God as revealed in Christ are born again:

"Verily, verily, I say unto you,
    Verily, verily, message ever new,
    He that believeth on the Son, 'tis true,
        Hath everlasting life."

"I am the living bread which came down from heaven: if any man eat of this bread, he shall live for ever: and the bread that I will give is My flesh, which I will give for the life of the world"—John 6: 51.

JUST as physical life is sustained by bread, so we live spiritually as we feed upon the Lord Jesus Christ. This involves personal faith in Him and daily meditation upon what God has revealed concerning Him. In this way the soul feeds on the Living Bread. The manna of old typified Him who came down from heaven and took the lowest place on earth that He might give life and strength to all who would receive and feed upon Him. But it is not only Christ in incarnation who is thus presented. He had to die in order that He might give His flesh for the life of the world. When He is appropriated by faith the believer receives divine life and stands before God justified from all things. Henceforth the new nature delights in Him, and finds its highest occupation in the contemplation of His perfections.

"Jesus, of Thee we ne'er would tire;
  The new and living food
Can satisfy our heart's desire,
  And life is in Thy blood.

If such the happy midnight song
  Our prisoned spirits raise,
What are the joys that cause, ere long,
  Eternal bursts of praise!"

—Mary Bowley.

"In the last day, that great day of the feast, Jesus stood and cried, saying, If any man thirst, let him come unto Me, and drink. He that believeth on Me, as the scripture hath said, out of his belly shall flow rivers of living water. (But this spake He of the Spirit, which they that believe on Him should receive: for the Holy Ghost was not yet given; because that Jesus was not yet glorified)"—John 7: 37-39.

THE gift of the Holy Spirit, indwelling each believer, was dependent upon the glorification of the Lord Jesus, following His sacrificial death and His triumph and resurrection. The Spirit has come to witness to these great truths. He has taken up His abode in all who have believed the gospel, and henceforth He is the power of the new life and the One who leads us out in testimony to the world. On our part we need to be very careful to deal with anything that would grieve Him or dishonor the Lord Jesus whom He delights to glorify. For it is only when He is unhindered by hidden or overt sin that He is free to do the work in which He delights—revealing the precious things of Christ to the soul that they may be shared with others.

"How changed is life since now I see—
O blessed truth—Christ lives in me!
His Spirit fills me day by day,
And, as I yield, directs my way.
I need not cry in times of strife
For Him to come into my life,
For He is there since I believed
And Christ's atoning work received;

Yea, even when my coolness grieves,
God's Holy Spirit never leaves.
A God Omnipotent and Great,
The Bless'd and Only Potentate,
The Lord of lords and King of kings,
Creator of all living things—
What humbling on my Saviour's part
That He should dwell within my heart!"

—Barbara E. Cornet.

"I am the Good Shepherd"—John 10: 11, 14.

THE shepherd-character of our Lord Jesus Christ is delightful to contemplate. We were all as sheep going astray, until through grace we returned to the Shepherd and Overseer of our souls (1 Pet. 2: 25). But we would never have returned at all unless He in His love had sought and found us (Luke 15: 4-7). Now having made us His own He undertakes to carry us safely home. He makes Himself responsible to supply all our needs; to guide us through this desert scene and to see that we have everything our souls require in order that we may grow in grace and glorify Him in all our ways. Surely the least we can do is to rely upon His love and wisdom and thus be able to say with happy confidence, "I shall not want."

"O Thou great all-gracious Shepherd,
    Shedding for us Thy life's blood,
Unto shame and death delivered,
    All to bring us nigh to God!
Now our willing hearts adore Thee,
    Now we taste Thy dying love,
While by faith we come before Thee,
    Faith which lifts our souls above."

—Mrs. Wellesley.

"Jesus said unto her, I am the resurrection, and the life: he that believeth in Me, though he were dead, yet shall he live: and whosoever liveth and believeth in Me shall never die. Believest thou this?"—John 11: 25, 26.

TWO very precious truths are unfolded in these words of our Lord to Martha, the sister of Lazarus. Death does not end all. When Jesus returns as the Resurrection and the Life all who have died in Christ will live again, raised up from the dead in the likeness of Him who died for them and rose again and all who still abide in the body in that day shall never die, but will be changed in a moment and caught up to meet the descending Saviour in company with all the risen saints. This is our blessed Hope. Do we believe it? When faith lays hold of this glorious revelation all things become new.

"TODAY? Perhaps! Perhaps today
The Lord may come and catch away
His ransomed Church, His blood-bought Bride,
To take her place at His blest side;
When dead and living saints shall share
One trumpet summons to the air.

Perhaps today! Yes! He may come
And call us to our Heavenly Home—
That wondrous place beyond compare
Which He, in love, doth now prepare.
Our Father's house! How sweet, how blest,
To be for evermore at rest!"

"Then took Mary a pound of ointment of spikenard, very costly, and anointed the feet of Jesus, and wiped His feet with her hair: and the house was filled with the odor of the ointment"—John 12: 3.

THE highest exercise of which the human spirit, touched by divine grace and regenerated by omnipotent power, is capable is that of worship, which involves adoration, praise, and implicit devotion. Men may attempt to exalt love of mankind above love to God. But actually the second table of the law finds its basis in the first. He who loves God supremely will love his neighbor unselfishly. The breaking of the alabaster box released the pungent spikenard whose ravishing odor filled all the house. When the best is lavished on the Lord Jesus, forces are freed which make fragrant every department of human life.

The natural heart cannot understand the apparent prodigality of love for Christ. It was Judas who began complaining and so infected the other disciples with the same spirit of faultfinding (John 12: 4). But the Lord Jesus understood the love that prompted Mary's act and He valued it accordingly. He delights in a heart wholly devoted to Himself.

"Lord, as we bless Thee for Thy love
    So world-embracing!—So divine!
May our hearts burn within us, till
    The fire within shall burn and shine,
Consuming all the dross of self,
    All thought of ease; all lesser love;
Until on earth we do Thy will
    E'en as the seraphs do above."

—Margaret E. Barber.

"If any man serve Me, let him follow Me; and where I am there shall also My servant be: if any man serve Me, him will My Father honor"—John 12:26.

PREFERMENT in the kingdom of Christ depends not on self-seeking, nor is it achieved by worldly methods. He who would be honored of God in the day when His Son will be acknowledged as King of kings and Lord of lords must be willing to follow Him in His lowly path of unrequited service for the blessing of a needy world. Following Jesus is not following Him *into* His heavenly Home. It is following Him, if one may so say, *out* of His Heaven, down into a world of sin and wretchedness, taking the path of self-abnegation and readiness to be rejected by men, in order to manifest the spirit of Christ to those who know Him not. It is only thus we can represent our Master, the Servant-Prophet, aright. And in order to do this we must first yield ourselves to Him. We cannot live a Christian life until we have a Christian life to live. There is a life by which we live. And there is a life we are called upon to live. We obtain life only by faith in Him who gave Himself a ransom for all. We manifest that life as we yield ourselves to Him as Lord.

"Christ never asks of us such busy labor
    As leaves no time for resting at His feet;
The waiting attitude of expectation
    He oft-times counts a service most complete.

And yet He does love service, where 'tis given
    By grateful love that clothes itself in deed;
But work that's done beneath the scourge of duty,
    Be sure, He gives to such but little heed.

Then seek to please Him, whatsoe'er He bids thee,
    Whether to do, to suffer, or lie still;
'Twill matter little by what path He led us,
    If in it all we sought to do His will."

"**Jesus saith to him, He that is washed needeth not save to wash his feet, but is clean every whit: and ye are clean, but not all. For He knew who should betray Him; therefore said He, Ye are not all clean**"

—John 13: 10, 11.

THE washing of the disciples' feet by the Lord was more than a lesson in humility, though it was that. It was a wondrous picture of what He has been doing for His own ever since He went back to heaven. It was written of Him, "He will keep the feet of His saints." His present service is just that. He is keeping our feet clean by "the washing of water by the Word" (Eph. 5: 26), while we are exposed to the defiling things of this world. We have been bathed once for all by the washing of regeneration. We need daily to be cleansed as to our ways that we may enjoy fellowship with Him who has redeemed us to Himself. As the girded Servant He undertakes to do this for us. Let us not seek to thwart Him by saying, as Peter did in his ignorance "Thou shalt never wash my feet."

> "Girded with the golden girdle,
>   Shining as the mighty sun,
> Still His pierced hands will finish
>   All His work of love begun
> On the night of His betrayal,
>   In the glory of the throne,
> Still with faithful patience washing
>   All defilement from His own."

"A new commandment I give unto you, That ye love one another; as I have loved you, that ye also love one another. By this shall all men know that ye are My disciples, if ye have love one to another"

—John 13: 34, 35.

THE new commandment, "That ye love one another," is all-embracive. "Love," we are told, "is the fulfilling of the law" (Rom. 13: 10). No one who truly loves his neighbor will ever be guilty of wilfully breaking any of the commandments that set forth man's duty to his fellow. We do not disobey parents when love is in exercise. We will not steal from those we love, nor will we lie about or defame them. To kill or corrupt by uncleanness would be unthinkable, and covetousness, too, is ruled out, for if I love my brother I do not want his goods, but rather rejoice in his possessions. But such love is not human. It is divine, and is only imparted by the Holy Spirit; so it is as we love God, the unseen, that we love our brothers also (1 John 4: 20). Therefore where love rules, we are not under the law. We do not love in order to obtain merit, or to win the divine favor, but because the love of God is shed abroad in our hearts by the indwelling Spirit, after we are justified by faith (Rom. 5: 1-5) and regenerated by the Word of the gospel (1 Pet. 1: 23-25). God is love. It is His very nature, and the man who is born again has become a partaker of that nature (2 Pet. 1: 4). Hence love is as characteristic of the real Christian as apples are characteristic of an apple-tree.

> "Blest be the tie that binds
> Our hearts in Christian love,
> The fellowship of kindred minds
> Is like to that above." . . . .

—J. Fawcett.

"And if I go and prepare a place for you, I will come again, and receive you unto Myself; that where I am, there ye may be also"—John 14: 3.

THIS is the Lord's word to His own redeemed ones. Such are destined to share with Him the joy and gladness of the Father's house which is the eternal Home of all the heavenly saints. He who has gone to prepare this place of rest and unbroken fellowship is coming again in person to receive those purchased by His blood to Himself. Centuries have elapsed since the promise was given, "I will come again," but He has not forgotten. Soon He will descend from heaven with an awakening shout and we who know Him as our Saviour and Lord shall be caught up to meet Him in the air.

"So I am watching quietly
          Every day.
Whenever the sun shines brightly
          I rise and say,
Surely it is the shining of His face,
And look unto the gate of His high place
          Beyond the sea,
For I know He is coming shortly
          To summon me.

And when a shadow falls across the window
          Of my room,
Where I am working my appointed task,
I lift my head to watch the door and ask,
          If He is come?
And the Spirit answers softly
          In my home,
'Only a few more shadows,
          And He will come.'"

—B. M.

"I am the Way, the Truth and the Life. No man cometh unto the Father but by Me"—John 14: 6.

IT is all-important that we recognize in Jesus not simply a great teacher or a religious leader who, having found God for himself, could now point out the right way to others. He was far more than a Wayshower. He is Himself the Way, the Truth, the Life. The authority with which He spoke was the very voice of God, who had become incarnate in Jesus. He who subsisted in the form of God from eternity had divested Himself of His glory and taken the Servant's form that He might become the propitiation for our sins and that we might live through Him (1 John 4: 9, 10). He spoke with authority because He had come to reveal the mind of God; and though in humiliation He chose to be subject in all things to the Father's will, the very words He uttered were those the Father gave Him. All His works, too, were in the power of the Holy Spirit, to whom He yielded Himself for service, choosing to learn obedience by the things which He suffered. He who had always commanded became the obedient Servant in order to carry out the counsels of the Godhead in all perfection.

> "By Thee, O God, invited,
>   We look unto the Son,
> In whom Thy soul delighted,
>   Who all Thy will hath done;
> And by the one chief treasure
>   Thy bosom freely gave,
> Thine own pure love we measure,
>   Thy willing mind to save.
>
> O God of mercy—Father,
>   The one unchanging claim,
> The brightest hopes, we gather
>   From Christ's most precious name;
> What always sounds so sweetly
>   In Thine unwearied ear,
> Has freed our souls completely
>   From all our sinful fear."

—Mary Bowley.

"Ye have not chosen Me, but I have chosen you, and ordained you, that ye should go and bring forth fruit, and that your fruit should remain"—John 15: 16.

MEN talk of choosing a career, selecting a profession, or deciding what gainful trade to follow; and often the ministry of the Word is put on the same level as what are commonly called the learned professions. But actually, it is not the servant of God who chooses his path. It is Christ who calls by His grace and who fits His servants by divinely-bestowed gifts for the work of ministering His truth to others.

Jesus selected and called the twelve. Why Judas was included must remain, in large part, a mystery beyond human ken, though we know it was that Scripture might be fulfilled (John 6: 70; 17: 12).

It has often been said that the disciples were not college or seminary trained men, but what school could offer so rich a curriculum today as these men enjoyed during three-and-a-half years of intimate association and holy fellowship with Him who was both Jehovah's Servant and their Lord?

A disciple is a learner: an apostle is a sent one, a missionary. The twelve were both. They learned of Jesus. They were sent forth by Him to carry the message to others. During the days of His flesh, that ministry was confined to the lost sheep of the house of Israel, the chosen nation. In resurrection our Lord extended its scope to embrace "all the world."

> "Go, labor on; spend and be spent,
> Thy joy to do the Father's will;
> It is the way the Master went;
> Should not the servant tread it still?
>
> Go, labor on; enough, while here,
> If He shall praise thee, if He deign
> Thy willing heart to mark and cheer:
> No toil for Him shall be in vain.
>
> Toil on, and in thy toil rejoice;
> For toil comes rest, for exile home;
> Soon shalt thou hear the Bridegroom's voice,
> The midnight peal: 'Behold, I come!' "

—H. Bonar.

"At that day ye shall ask in My name: and I say not unto you, that I will pray the Father for you: for the Father Himself loveth you, because ye have loved Me, and have believed that I came out from God"

—John 16: 26, 27.

HOW terribly do they dishonor God who tell us that angels, apostles, the mother of Jesus, or other eminent saints, are necessary as go-betweens in order that we may receive of the Father! Even our Lord Jesus Himself tells us the Father gives out of the love of His own heart. It is not necessary to have some one as a special pleader on our behalf. "The Father Himself loveth you." How blessed to realize this, and so to go to Him with implicit confidence, assured that He delights to do for us everything that is consistent with His holy purpose and therefore which will be for our good.

"If you had been living when Christ was on earth,
　And had met the Saviour kind,
What would you have asked Him to do for you,
　Supposing you were stone blind?

The child considered, and then replied,—
　"I expect that, without doubt,
I'd have asked for a dog, with a collar and chain,
　To lead me daily about."

And how often thus, in our faithless prayers,
　We acknowledge with shamed surprise,
We have only asked for a dog and a chain,
　When we might have had—opened eyes."

—M. Colley.

"Sanctify them through Thy truth: Thy word is truth. As Thou hast sent Me into the world, even so have I also sent them into the world. And for their sakes I sanctify Myself, that they also might be sanctified through the truth"—John 17: 17-19.

SANCTIFICATION is two-fold, positional and practical. All believers are sanctified (that is, set apart to God) by the one Offering of our Lord Jesus Christ, and in this sense, "perfected forever" (Heb. 10: 10, 14). But we are called to walk in conformity with our place in Christ. This is practical sanctification and by the Word of truth ministered to the heart in the power of the Holy Spirit. In our Lord's high-priestly prayer in John 17 He stresses the importance of this. He set Himself apart to go to the cross and to the throne that our hearts might be occupied with Him where He now is, in order that we might be separated from all that is of the world.

> "There amidst the joy eternal
> Is the Man who went above,
> Bearing marks of all the hatred
> Of the world He sought in love.
> He has sent us here to tell
> That His love is changeless still.
>
> He has sent us, that in sorrow
> And in suffering, toil and loss,
> We may learn the wondrous sweetness,
> The deep mystery of His cross—
> Learn the depth of love that traced
> That blest path across the waste."

"**Jesus answered, My kingdom is not of this world: if My kingdom were of this world, then would My servants fight, that I should not be delivered to the Jews: but now is My kingdom not from hence**"—John 18: 36.

JESUS did not deny that He would have a kingdom in this world. The prophets from of old predicted the triumph of the kingdom of God, administered by the Son of Man (Dan. 7: 13, 14) in this lower universe. But when that day dawns it will not be a dominion of the present world order. It will be a heavenly kingdom set up on earth. Not by man's power, as through armies and carnal weapons, will His authority be set up and maintained. God the Father will give Him the throne of David when the appointed hour shall strike. Then He will rule the nations with the inflexible rod of righteousness, and His saints will reign with Him, thus sharing His glory.

"Lo! He comes, from heaven descending,
  Once for favored sinners slain!
Thousand thousand saints attending
  Swell the triumph of His train!
    Hallelujah!
  Jesus comes, and comes to reign!

See the Saviour, long expected,
  Now in solemn pomp appear!
And His saints, by man rejected,
  All His heavenly glory share.
    Hallelujah!
  See the Son of God appear!"

—C. Wesley.

"When Jesus therefore had received the vinegar, He said, It is finished: and He bowed His head, and gave up the ghost"—John 19:30.

"IT is finished!" It was only one word of the Greek that Jesus uttered but it told of a completed work to which nothing now can be added. There on the cross He bore the full penalty for sin. He paid the utmost farthing. The anxious sinner seeking salvation has nothing to do but believe the message in order to enter into peace. Nothing can be added to a finished work. To attempt to add to it is but to spoil it. The debt is paid, sin is atoned for. The guilty soul is instantly cleansed from every stain, and justified freely by His grace, when he puts his trust in Jesus, and rests upon that finished work.

"Nothing to **pay**?—no, not a whit:
Nothing to **do**?—no, not a bit;
All that was needed to do or to pay,
Jesus has done in His own blessed way.

Nothing to do?—no, not a stroke;
Gone is the captor, gone is the yoke:
Jesus at Calvary severed the chain,
And none can imprison His freeman again.

Nothing to settle?—all has been paid;
Nothing of anger?—peace has been made:
Jesus alone is the sinner's resource,
Peace He has made by the blood of His cross."

"Then went in also that other disciple, which came first to the sepulchre, and he saw, and believed"

—John 20: 8.

NEITHER John nor Peter knew that Jesus was to rise from the dead. Although He had told His disciples very definitely that He would thus be brought back to life on the third day, their minds were unable to grasp it. But the evidence of the grave-cloths (not "clothes," as in our version) was too convincing to be doubted. They lay in that crypt not folded up, as many have thought, but "wrapped together," just as they had enswathed His body, but like a cocoon from which the butterfly had emerged. The disciples knew that no power on earth could have removed that body and left its cerements undisturbed. It was the resurrection power of God which alone had wrought this stupendous miracle. So they could not but believe.

"O joyful day! O glorious hour!
When Jesus, by almighty power,
  Revived and left the grave;
In all His works behold Him great,—
Before, almighty to create,
  Almighty now to save.

The first-begotten from the dead,
He's risen now, His people's Head,
  And thus their life's secure;
And if, like Him, they yield their breath,
Like Him they'll burst the bonds of death,
  Their resurrection sure."

—T. Kelly.

**"So when they had dined, Jesus saith to Simon Peter,
Simon, son of Jonas, lovest thou Me more than these?
He saith unto Him, Yea, Lord; Thou knowest that I love
Thee. He saith unto him, Feed My lambs"—John 21: 15.**

SOMETIME on the day of the resurrection the Lord had
a private interview with Peter. He sent him a special
message by the women early in the morning (Mark 16: 7),
but He appeared personally to him later (Luke 24:34). A
veil has been drawn over the scene of that sacred interview,
but we cannot doubt it was the means of restoring his soul
and of reassuring the failing disciple's heart. Now we learn
of his public restoration and his confirmation in the office
of the apostolate. That experience by the lakeside was one
that Peter would never be able to forget in after-years. It
revealed, as nothing else could, the tender consideration of
the Lord whom he had denied thrice, who now led him on
step by step to a three-fold confession of his faith and love,
and assured him that some day he should indeed go, for His
name's sake, both to prison and to death. Never again
would Peter be ashamed to own his connection with the
Lord Jesus. On the contrary, he was yet to drive home with
telling effect the fact that all blessing, for time and eternity,
was to be found in Him (Acts 4:12), and that even the
great sin of denying and crucifying the Holy One and Just
(Acts 3: 14, 15) might be fully forgiven if the guilty
offender would but turn to God in repentance and seek
remission of sins in His name (Acts 2: 38; 3: 19). By this
experience, too, the rest of the apostles would realize that
there was no further reason to treat their erring brother with
any degree of reserve; for if the Christ, whom he had denied,
thus openly expressed His confidence in him, they, too, might
consider him as fully restored to the office he seemed to have
forfeited.

> "My great, my wise, my never-failing Friend,
> Whose love no change can know, nor turn, nor end!
> My Saviour-God! who gavest Thy life for me,
> Let nothing come between my heart and Thee!"

"And while they looked stedfastly toward heaven as He went up, behold, two men stood by them in white apparel; which also said, Ye men of Galilee, why stand ye gazing up into heaven? this same Jesus, which is taken up from you into heaven, shall so come in like manner as ye have seen Him go into heaven"

—Acts 1: 10, 11.

FOUR times in this chapter we read that "He was taken up." God has highly exalted Him who stooped to the death of the cross for our redemption. Now He sits in highest glory at the Father's right hand, the Man of patience, waiting for the hour when He is to return to the scene of His sufferings, first to claim His chosen bride and then to reign in righteousness over all the world. In that day of His power "He shall see of the travail of His soul and shall be satisfied." The time draws nigh. Let us labor on in faith while we await His return. The very fact that the hour of the second advent is not revealed should keep us on the alert, ever expecting to hear His shout, and to be called to meet Him in the air.

"But whether it be noontide, or whether it be night,
Or whether at the morning's dawn or in the evening's light,
When we shall see His blessed face and clasp those pierced feet,
And mount with Him above the sky, then is our joy complete.
Yes, "satisfied," thrice "satisfied," to in His likeness wake,
To dwell with Him thro' countless years when that glad morn shall break—
When He will come again."

—M. E. Rae.

"When the day of Pentecost was fully come, they were all with one accord in one place"—Acts 2: 1.

IT is all important to understand aright what took place at Pentecost. There had been many Pentecosts in Israel's history, for it was an annual feast celebrating the beginning of the harvest, but all these were types. The Pentecost of Acts 2 was the fulfilment of the type. On that day God began a new work of taking out a special people to Himself, from Jews and Gentiles, to form the Body of Christ. The Holy Spirit came that day as a divine Person to indwell believers and to baptize them into one Body. He came, too, to empower them for service as a redeemed and cleansed people that the message of the gospel might be carried to the ends of the earth. Strictly speaking, there can never be another Pentecost, any more than there can be another Passover owned by God since Christ our Passover has been sacrificed for us. But it is necessary for each believer to recognize and yield to the Spirit who came at Pentecost if he would be a witness in power to a lost world.

Before the coming of the Spirit the apostles were so many individuals as yet unfilled for the great task allotted to them. After that momentous event they were members of the Body of Christ, endued with power from on high to go forth to proclaim the gospel message to the ends of the earth.

> "The Comforter, now present,
>   Assures us of Thy love;
> He is the blessed earnest
>   Of glory there above:
> The river of Thy pleasure
>   Is what sustains us now,
> Till Thy new name's imprinted
>   On ev'ry sinless brow."

—Mary Bowley.

"The promise is unto you and to your children"
—Acts 2: 39.

IT is a recognized principle, running through all dispensations, that God desires to save the households of His people. Noah prepared an ark for the saving of his house (Heb. 11:7), and God said to him, "Come thou and all thy house into the ark; for thee have I seen righteous before Me in this generation" (Gen. 7:1). Of Abraham the Lord declared, "I know him, that he will command his children and his household after him, and they shall keep the way of the Lord, to do justice and judgment" (Gen. 18:19). David said, "Thou hast spoken also of thy servant's house for a great while to come" (2 Sam. 7:19). The promise to the Philippian jailer was, "Believe on the Lord Jesus Christ, and thou shalt be saved, and thy house" (Acts 16:31).

"O Thou who gave them, guard them—those wayward little feet,
The wilderness before them, the ills of life to meet.
My mother-love is helpless, I trust them to Thy care!
Beneath the blood-stained lintel, oh, keep me ever there!

The faith I rest upon Thee Thou wilt not disappoint;
With wisdom, Lord, to train them my shrinking heart anoint.
Without my children, Father, I cannot see Thy face;
I plead the blood-stained lintel, Thy covenant of grace.

Oh, wonderful Redeemer, who suffered for our sake,
When o'er the guilty nations the judgment-storm shall break,
With joy from that safe shelter may we then meet Thine eye,
Beneath the blood-stained lintel, my children, Lord, and I."

"Then Peter said, Silver and gold have I none; but such as I have give I thee: In the name of Jesus Christ of Nazareth rise up and walk. And he took him by the right hand, and lifted him up: and immediately his feet and ankle bones received strength. And he leaping up stood, and walked, and entered with them into the temple, walking, and leaping, and praising God"

—Acts 3: 6-8.

THE "signs of an apostle" (2 Cor. 12: 12), that is, the ability to work miracles in the name of the risen Christ, followed close upon the Pentecostal endowment in order to accredit the apostles as the direct, authorized representatives of the glorified Lord. When He was on earth and His mission confined to the lost sheep of the house of Israel (Matt. 15: 24), He gave them similar powers, but in resurrection these were confirmed and enlarged. Such gifts were not promised to all believers, but to "them that believe" of the apostolic company (Mark 16: 17, 18). And so we see Peter, once cravenly denying his Lord, now not only boldly confessing Him, but doing mighty deeds in His name, thus bearing testimony to the might of the One whom Jew and Gentile had united to crucify, but who had been raised from the dead by the power of God.

All blessing for mankind is bound up in the risen Christ. He sits now exalted at the Father's right hand to dispense riches of grace to all who come in His name, owning their need and confessing their sin. The healing of the man lame from his birth was in order to demonstrate the power and authority of the name of the Lord Jesus.

> "We see Thee, Lord, vacate Thy home—
>   That scene immune from blight,
> To visit man in all his woe,
>   To save him from his plight.
>
> Thy love to us constrained Thee, Lord,
>   To suffer, bleed and die,
> That we redeemed with Thine own blood
>   Might dwell with Thee on high.
>
> Rejected here and put to death
>   By those whom Thou didst love,
> Thou art no more in Person here,
>   But in bright courts above."　　—C. C. Crowston.

AUGUST 29

"And said, Behold, I see the heavens opened, and the Son of Man standing on the right hand of God"

—Acts 7: 56.

IN the seventh chapter of Acts we have Stephen's address when called to witness before the Jewish Council. He traces all Jehovah's ways with His people from Abraham to Christ and leads us in spirit by the God of glory (ver. 2) up to the glory of God (ver. 55). When he falls smitten by the stones hurled by his cruel murderers he exclaims with rapture, "I see the heavens opened and the Son of Man standing on the right hand of God!" Elsewhere, after the ascension of our Lord, He is set forth as seated at the right hand of the Majesty in the heavens. Here He is standing as though bending eagerly forward to welcome His faithful witness and to express His deep sympathy with him in his suffering. Such is ever His attitude toward His persecuted saints. How blessed to know that His love is unfailing and His welcome sure! Meantime His protecting care is over us.

"Safely covered with His feathers—
  Oh, the blest security!—
Sheltered from all kinds and weathers,
  Covert from the enemy.

In all confidence abiding,
  'Neath His strong protecting wings,
Oh, how sweet is such confiding,
  While the trustful spirit sings.

Covered? Yes, as He can cover.
  Sheltered? Who could shelter thus?
O'er His own His love doth hover—
  His, because of Calv'ry's cross.

Covered, trusting, watching ever,
  Knowing there is naught to fear,
Sweet the confident assurance
  While His coming draweth near."

—Helen McDowell.

"Now when the apostles which were at Jerusalem heard that Samaria had received the Word of God, they sent unto them Peter and John: who, when they were come down, prayed for them, that they might receive the Holy Ghost: (For as yet He was fallen upon none of them: only they were baptized in the name of the Lord Jesus.) Then laid they their hands on them, and they received the Holy Ghost"—Acts 8: 14-17.

THE Pentecostal gift of the Spirit was not granted to these Samaritan converts immediately. They came of a schismatic group who were intensely jealous of their own claims to being the chosen people, as were the Jews to the south of them. They must learn definitely that "salvation *is* of the Jews" as our Lord had declared (John 4: 22), so they had to wait until the apostles came from Jerusalem ere they were baptized into the one Body of Christ.

The gift of the Holy Spirit is to be distinguished both from new birth by the Spirit and from the gifts of the Spirit. All believers are born of the Spirit, by the Word of God when they believe the gospel (1 Pet. 1: 23-25). The gifts of the Spirit are the graces or talents He divides "to every man severally as He will" (1 Cor. 12:11), in order that we may work for God in our various spheres. But the gift of the Spirit is the Holy One Himself, who indwells believers and by whose baptism we are made members of Christ and so added to the Lord.

> " 'One spirit with the Lord;'
>   Oh, blessed, wondrous word!
> What heavenly light, what pow'r divine,
>   Doth that sweet word afford!
>
> 'One spirit with the Lord;'
>   Jesus, the glorified,
> Esteems the Church for which He bled,
>   His Body and His Bride.
>
> And though by storms assailed
>   And though by trials pressed,
> Himself our Life, He bears us up,
>   Right onward to the rest."   —Mary Bowley.

"And as he journeyed, he came near Damascus: and suddenly there shined round about him a light from heaven: and he fell to the earth, and heard a voice saying unto him, Saul, Saul, why persecutest thou Me? And he said, Who art Thou, Lord? And the Lord said, I am Jesus whom thou persecutest: it is hard for thee to kick against the pricks"—Acts 9: 3-5.

THE conversion of Saul of Tarsus was, as every true conversion is, a supernatural event. Brought face to face with the risen, exalted Christ, he saw himself a poor, guilty sinner (1 Tim. 1: 15, 16), who had been fighting against his own best interests in resisting the claims of the Lord Jesus. Repentant and subdued, he yielded himself in whole-hearted allegiance to the One he had spurned, henceforth to count all things but loss for Christ (Phil. 3: 7, 8). Some such crisis there must be in the lives of all who are saved, unless, indeed, they had trusted Jesus so early in life that they have never been consciously His enemies. But they, too, are called to a complete surrender to His will when in years of maturity they recognize that He is not only Saviour but Lord.

It is evident that Saul had known considerable exercise as indicated in the expression, "It is hard for thee to kick against the goads" (Acts 26: 14, R. V.). Like a refractory ox he had been injuring himself while resisting the authority of the Lord. Convinced at last of his error in the past, there was instant surrender to the claims of the risen Christ.

> "I was journeying in the noontide,
>   When His light shone o'er my road;
> And I saw Him in that glory—
>   Saw Him—Jesus, Son of God.
> All around, in noonday splendor,
>   Earthly scenes lay fair and bright;
> But my eyes no more behold them,
>   For the glory of that light.
>
> —Frances Bevan.

"Then Peter opened his mouth, and said, Of a truth I perceive that God is no respecter of persons: but in every nation he that feareth Him, and worketh righteousness, is accepted with Him"—Acts 10: 34, 35.

IN the life and ministry of Simon Peter we see how God made an outstanding witness to His truth from most unlikely material. Who would have thought of the rugged impetuous, profane fisherman Simon ever becoming the eloquent, spiritual preacher, whose burning words would be used to the conversion of thousands of souls? But God works with what He brings, not simply with what He finds. Simon the fisherman, regenerated, becomes Peter the apostle, to whose sermons and letters the whole world owes a debt that it can never pay. While his ministry was primarily toward the Jews, yet the "branches run over the wall" (Gen. 49: 22), and he was the one specially chosen of God to open the door of faith to the Gentiles (Acts 15: 7). A man of strong prejudices, his narrow views were superseded by remarkable breadth of vision when taught by the Holy Spirit. Like his brother apostle, Paul, he delighted in "the true grace of God" (1 Pet. 5: 12), which knows no national or racial boundaries. Hence his messages are the delight of believers from among the nations, whom he once despised, as well as among those of Jewry, who have found in the Lord Jesus the promised Messiah.

"Called from above, and heavenly men by birth,
 (Who once were but the citizens of earth)
As pilgrims here, we seek a heavenly home,
 Our portion, in the ages yet to come.

Where all the saints of ev'ry clime shall meet,
And each with all shall all the ransomed greet,
But oh, the height of bliss, my Lord, shall be
To owe it all, and share it all, with Thee!"

—J. G. Deck.

"**God anointed Jesus of Nazareth with the Holy Ghost and with power; who went about doing good and healing all that were oppressed of the devil, for God was with Him**"—Acts 10: 38.

THE miracles wrought by our Lord differ greatly from the wonders generaly ascribed to the founders and holy men of the great pagan religious systems. He never performed a sign simply to astonish credulous people, or to thwart the will of His enemies. Behind all the works of power was human need and His own gracious compassion for suffering and troubled humanity. The cursing of the fig-tree is the only seeming exception that proves the rule. It was an acted parable designed to illustrate Israel's sad condition and her deep need. Jesus never stooped to anything approaching legerdemain or magical incantation. He did not desire to be known as a wonder-worker. He "went about doing good, and healing all that were oppressed of the devil" (Acts 10: 38), and in this way manifesting His Messianic mission. It had been predicted of old that in His days the dumb would sing, the blind see, the lame leap as an hart, and the poor be satisfied with bread (Isa. 35: 5, 6; Ps. 132: 15).

"At even, ere the sun was set,
  The sick, O Lord, around Thee lay;
Oh, in what divers pains they met!
  Oh, with what joy they went away!

Once more 'tis even-tide, and we,
  Oppressed with various ills draw near:
What if Thy form we cannot see?
  We know and feel that Thou art here.

O Saviour Christ, our woes dispel:
  For some are sick, and some are sad,
And some have never loved Thee well,
  And some have lost the love they had.

Thy touch has still its ancient power,
  No word from Thee can fruitless fall;
Hear in this solemn evening hour,
  And in Thy mercy heal us all."
                              —Henry Twells.

"And he showed us how he had seen an angel in his house, which stood and said unto him, Send men to Joppa, and call for Simon, whose surname is Peter; who shall tell thee words, whereby thou and all thy house shall be saved"—Acts 11:13, 14.

CONSIDER the state of Cornelius before Peter preached to him. He was a moral, upright, devout man, God-fearing and generous. But all this in itself could not save (Acts 11:13, 14). Yet it might be a mistake to conclude that there was no work of grace in his soul before he heard the clear gospel message. He seems to have turned to God from idolatry, as a repentant, seeking soul, which would imply that he was quickened by the Spirit, but needing clearer light in order that he might know and enjoy God's salvation.

Where there is a desire for the knowledge of God, He will see that light is given. No man will be finally lost who honestly desired to be saved. The Lord will bring the seeking soul and the messenger of grace together, for He never disappoints those who cry to Him in repentance for his pardoning grace.

"Can it be right for me to go
  On in this dark, uncertain way!
Say 'I believe' and yet not know
  Whether my sins are put away?

How can it be my joy to dwell
  On the rich power of Jesus' blood,
If all the while I cannot tell
  That it has sealed my peace with God?

How can I be like Christ below,
  How like my Lord in witness shine,
Unless with conscious joy I know
  His Father and His God as mine?"

"Peter therefore was kept in prison: but prayer was made without ceasing of the church unto God for him. And when Herod would have brought him forth, the same night Peter was sleeping between two soldiers, bound with two chains: and the keepers before the door kept the prison. And, behold, the angel of the Lord came upon him, and a light shined in the prison: and he smote Peter on the side, and raised him up, saying, Arise up quickly. And his chains fell off from his hands"
—Acts 12: 5-7.

GOD is better than our faith. While it is true that He has said He will do for us "according to your faith," nevertheless He is not restricted in the exercise of His lovingkindness by our failure to lay hold on His promises. The Church in Jerusalem prayed for Peter's deliverance, but they had a very faulty apprehension both of God's power and His readiness to hear and answer. At the best, perhaps, they hoped grace might be given the apostle to endure a long imprisonment with eventual deliverance, or to triumph in the hour of death. But while they prayed, God answered, and did exceeding abundantly above their asking or thinking. And so it often is today. Our faith at the best is a poor feeble thing. His grace is an all-sufficient dynamic energy that refuses to be restrained by the feebleness of our apprehension or the poverty of our expectation.

"There is an eye that never sleeps beneath the wing of night;
There is an ear that never shuts, when sink the beams of light.

There is an arm that never tires when human strength gives way;
There is a love that never fails, when earthly loves decay.

But there's a power which man can wield when mortal aid is vain,
That eye, that arm, that love to reach, that listening ear to gain.

That power is prayer, which soars on high through Jesus to the throne;
And moves the Hand which moves the world, to bring salvation down."

"Be it known unto you therefore, men and brethren, that through this Man is preached unto you the forgiveness of sins: and by Him all that believe are justified from all things, from which ye could not be justified by the law of Moses"—Acts 13: 38, 39.

FORGIVENESS and Justification. Here are two things divinely joined together which man cannot reconcile. We cannot both forgive one and justify him. If he is justified, he does not need forgiveness. If forgiven, he is not justified, but is admittedly guilty. But God not only forgives the repentant sinner, because of the work of Christ on his behalf, but He justifies forever, clears of every charge all who trust in Him. All such are "accepted in the Beloved." The soul that receives God's testimony concerning His Son is seen henceforth as in Christ, and therefore as truly accepted as He is. He is justified in the risen Saviour, for it is written, "As He is, so are we in this world" (1 John 4: 17).

"What about terror!—it hasn't a place
In a heart that is filled with a sense of His grace:
My peace is divine, and it never can cloy,
And that makes my heart over-bubble with joy.

Nothing of guilt?—no, not a stain,
How could the blood let any remain?
My conscience is purged, and my spirit is free—
Precious that blood is to God and to me!

What of the law?—ah, there I rejoice,
Christ answered its claims and silenced its voice:
The law was fulfilled when the work was all done,
And it never can speak to a justified one."

"Known unto God are all His works from the beginning of the world"—Acts 15: 18.

GOD does nothing at haphazard. He is never taken by surprise. He works according to a plan, the purpose or counsel which He has had in His heart from all eternity. From Moses to Christ He was dealing with Israel as His covenant people, while in large measure He overlooked the ignorance of the Gentiles (Acts 17: 30). He taught His earthly people by laws and ceremonies, which prefigured good things to come. Now He is taking out from the Gentiles a people to His name (Acts 15: 14). These saved Gentiles and the believing Jews are thus united in one Body (Eph. 3: 6). When this work is completed, Christ will return and "build again the tabernacle of David, which is fallen down." That will be the time for the fulfilment of all the Old Testament prophecies in regard to Israel, when the Gentiles shall come to their light and be blessed through them. Failure to see this led many of the early Hebrew Christians to look with suspicion on Gentile converts if they did not submit to legal regulations. The gospel of grace frees the soul from all such bondage, when God's orderly plan is clearly understood.

"I'm glad my times are in Thy hand. It is so sweet to know
That everything by Thee is planned for me where'er I go;
The Hand that holds the ocean's depths can hold my small
    affairs,
The Hand that guides the universe can carry all my cares.
I'm glad I cannot shape my way, I'd rather trust Thy skill;
I'm glad the ordering is not mine, I'd rather have Thy will,
I do not know the future, and I would not if I might,
For faith to me is better far than faulty human sight."

"And brought them out, and said, Sirs, what must I do to be saved? And they said, Believe on the Lord Jesus Christ, and thou shalt be saved, and thy house"
—Acts 16: 30, 31.

THE jailer's question implied an exercised conscience and a repentant heart. He saw his need and longed for the knowledge of God's salvation. The reply to his anxious inquiry came quick and plain, "Believe on the Lord Jesus Christ and thou shalt be saved." Nor did the apostle stop there. The same blessed privilege was extended, through matchless grace, to his household. All were invited to put their trust in Christ. There were no other terms, no demands to make restitution first for wrongs done, no insistence on a deeper sense of sinfulness. Just one thing was put before him as the necessary link between his soul and Christ. "Believe on Him." To believe on Jesus is to trust in Him. He has borne all the sin, paid all the debt. Now the believer goes free.

"Nothing to pay! the debt is so great.
What will you do with the awful weight?
How shall the way of escape be made?
Nothing to pay—yet it must be paid!
    Hear the voice of Jesus say,
'Verily thou hast nothing to pay:
All has been put to My account,
I have paid the full amount.'

Nothing to pay; yes, nothing to pay!
Jesus has cleared all the debt away—
Blotted it out with His bleeding hand!
Free and forgiven, and loved, you stand.
    Hear the voice of Jesus say,
'Verily thou hast nothing to pay!
Paid is the debt, and the debtor free!
Now I ask thee, lovest thou Me?' "

—F. R. Havergal.

"And the times of this ignorance God winked at; but now commandeth all men everywhere to repent: because He hath appointed a day, in the which He will judge the world in righteousness by that Man whom He hath ordained; whereof He hath given assurance unto all men, in that He hath raised Him from the dead"

—Acts 17: 30, 31.

TO all men comes the command to repent and believe the gospel. Repentance is a change of mind, a complete turning right about face, an entirely changed attitude toward God, and sin, and self. It is the soul coming to the bar of judgment now that his case may all be settled before the appointed day when the Man who hung on the cross will sit on the throne. God has raised Him from the dead to give repentance and remission of sins to all who yield to His Spirit's entreaty as set forth in the proclamation of the gospel. Those who thus turn to Him now in this day of grace need have no fear of judgment in that last great assize. They stand forever cleared of every charge.

"Jesus, the Lord, our righteousness!
Our beauty Thou, our glorious dress!
Before the throne, in this arrayed,
With joy shall we lift up the head.

Bold shall we stand in that great day,
For who aught to our charge shall lay,
While by Thy blood absolved we are
From sin and guilt, from shame and fear?

Till we behold Thee on Thy throne
In Thee we boast, in Thee alone,
Our beauty this, our glorious dress,
Jesus, the Lord, our righteousness,"

—Zinzendorf.

"And Gallio cared for none of those things"

—Acts 18: 17.

GALLIO the indifferent! History tells us he was the brother of Seneca the philosopher, who exclaims, "O most sweet Gallio! Few men are so agreeable about anything as my brother Gallio is about everything!" Yet this amiable man lost a marvellous opportunity to hear the gospel from the lips of Paul, and perhaps lost his soul at last just because he was so unconcerned about eternal things that he did not consider them worthy of his attention. To him the whole matter was beneath contempt, consisting only, as he supposed, of a quarrel about words and names and Jewish ceremonial observances. So he turned scornfully away without hearing that glad message which God was sending out in grace to a needy world. His attitude stands out as a warning to others not to treat lightly the privileges God gives, lest the day of doom find them still in their sins.

> "Oh, what will you do in the solemn day,
> When earth and sea shall flee away;
> When the rending heavens in fire shall roll,
> And shrivel up like parchment scroll?
>
> Oh, what will you do when the sins of the past
> Shall rise like clouds that gather fast,
> And stand before you in dread array;
> O sinner, tell me, what wilt thou say?"

"But none of these things move me, neither count I my life dear unto myself, so that I might finish my course with joy, and the ministry, which I have received of the Lord Jesus, to testify the gospel of the grace of God"—Acts 20: 21.

PAUL delighted to speak on various occasions of that which he had "received of the Lord Jesus." It was the assurance that his was a ministry given by the risen Christ which enabled him to "endure all things for the elect's sake." He knew Christ and he knew the value of the things of God, and because of this knowledge he was able to "endure as seeing Him who is invisible." It is as heavenly things loom large before the soul that one can hold the things of earth with a loose hand, and endure suffering and persecution with joyfulness knowing that Christ will estimate all aright at His judgment-seat and reward according to the measure of devotedness manifested here.

"Think it not strange, then, pilgrim, neither faint,
Much less indulge in murmuring and complaint,
If what you meet with in your heavenly road
Is hard to bear; since all is planned by God,
His child to train in wisdom's holy ways,
And form a chosen vessel for His praise.
Now we are slow those ways to understand;
But let us bow beneath His mighty hand,
Sure that His wisdom over all presides,
His power controls, and love unerring guides."

—J. G. Deck.

"To open their eyes, and to turn them from darkness to light, and from the power of Satan unto God, that they may receive forgiveness of sins, and inheritance among them which are sanctified by faith that is in Me"
—Acts 26: 18.

THIS was the charge given by the glorified Lord to Paul at his ordination to the Christian ministry, on the Damascus turnpike. There he tells us he was made a minister and a witness of these things. He was commissioned to carry to the nations an offer of forgiveness and of title to a place in the inheritance of those who were set apart to God through faith in Christ. How blessed it is to enter into the reality of all this. God sees each believer as not only pardoned but freed from every possible charge. Ours is an eternal forgiveness. And we share in a sanctification that is perfect and complete. The heart goes out to God in adoring love and worship as one enters into some realization of this grace wherein we stand.

> "Chosen not for good in me,
> Wakened up from wrath to flee;
> Hidden in the Saviour's side,
> By the Spirit sanctified;
> Teach me, Lord, on earth to show
> By my love, how much I owe."

> —R. M. McCheyne.

"For I am not ashamed of the gospel of Christ: for it is the power of God unto salvation to every one that believeth; to the Jew first, and also to the Greek. For therein is the righteousness of God revealed from faith to faith: as it is written, The just shall live by faith"
—Rom. 1: 16, 17.

THE epistle to the Romans gives us the fullest unfolding of the gospel that we have in the Word of God. Of this glad message none need be ashamed. It answers every objection of the most astute reasoner. It satisfies the need of every exercised conscience. In it we see how God can be just and yet justify the guilty sinner who comes to Him in repentance, owning his need and trusting His grace. Socrates exclaimed, "It may be that the Deity can forgive sins, but I don't see how!" The Holy Spirit here shows that God can forgive in righteousness because of the expiatory work of His Son. This is the message which is revealed on the principle of faith to those who believe, whether Jews or Gentiles by nature, according to the oracle given to Habakkuk so long ago, "The just shall live by faith."

"What Thou, my Lord, hast suffered,
    Was all for sinners' gain:
Mine, mine was the transgression,
    But Thine the deadly pain:
Lo, here I fall, my Saviour!
    'Tis I deserved Thy place;
Look on me with Thy favor,
    Vouchsafe to me Thy grace.

What language shall I borrow
    To thank Thee, dearest Friend,
For this, Thy dying sorrow,
    Thy pity without end?
Lord, make me Thine forever,
    Nor let me faithless prove:
Oh, let me never, never,
    Abuse such dying love."

—Bernard of Clairvaux.
Trans. by Jas. W. Alexander.

"But now the righteousness of God without the law is manifested, being witnessed by the law and the prophets"
—Rom. 3: 21.

"BUT NOW"—exclaims the apostle. It marks a decided change of subject. *Now* that man has been fully shown up, God will be revealed. *Now* upon the proven unrighteousness of all mankind "the righteousness of God is manifested." Of old He had declared, "I will bring near My righteousness." This is in no sense a wrought-out, legal righteousness, such as man was unable to produce for God. It is a righteousness "without the law," that is, altogether apart from any principle of human obedience to a divinely-ordained code of morals. It is a righteousness of God for unrighteous men, and is in no wise dependent upon human merit or attainment.

The righteousness of God is a term of wide import. Here it means a righteousness of God's providing — a perfect standing for guilty men for which God makes Himself responsible. If men are saved at all it must be in righteousness. But of this, man is utterly bereft. Therefore God must find a way whereby every claim of His righteous throne shall be met, and yet guilty sinners be justified from all things. His very nature demands that this must not be at the expense of righteousness but in full accord with it. And this is what has been provided in the work of the cross.

> "Father, Thy sov'reign love has sought
>   Captives to sin, gone far from Thee;
> The work that Thine own Son hath wrought
>   Has brought us back in peace and free.
>
> And now as sons before Thy face,
>   With joyful steps the path we tread
> Which leads us on to that blest place
>   Prepared for us by Christ our Head."

—J. N. D.

"For if, when we were enemies, we were reconciled to God by the death of His Son, much more, being reconciled, we shall be saved by His life"—Rom. 5: 10.

THE 5th of Romans is the chapter of the five "much mores," and it is well worth while considering them carefully in order. That of verse 10 is full of hope and encouragement for the timid believer. It assures us that He who loved us enough to give His Son for us will never give us up and allow us to drift beyond His gracious care. We have been reconciled to Him by the sacrificial death of our blessed Lord. Much more, then, having been thus brought into so happy a relationship with Himself, we shall be saved daily and eternally through the resurrection-life of the same precious Saviour who died for us on the cross. It is important to see that it is not His life on earth that is referred to. As to that we are saved—reconciled—by His death. His life had to be given up in order that He might redeem us. But now we who are redeemed are kept by the ever-living One who undertakes to see us safely through all possible circumstances, and bring us, at last, in triumph to the Father's House.

"Thy love we own, Lord Jesus;
    For though Thy toils are ended,
Thy tender heart doth take its part
    With those Thy grace befriended.
Thy sympathy, how precious!
    Thou succourest in sorrow,
And bidst us cheer, while pilgrims here,
    And haste the hopeful morrow."

"Knowing this that our old man is crucified with Him, that the body of sin might be destroyed (or, rendered powerless), that henceforth we should not serve sin, for he that is dead is freed (or justified) from sin"

—Rom. 6: 6, 7.

MY old man is not merely my old nature. It is rather all that I was as a man in the flesh, the "man of old," the unsaved man with all his habits and desires. That man was crucified with Christ. When Jesus died I (as a man after the flesh) died too. I was seen by God on that cross with His blessed Son.

How many people were crucified on Calvary? There were the thieves, there was Christ Himself—three! But are these all? Paul says in Gal. 2: 20, "I am crucified with Christ." He was there too; so that makes four. And each believer can say, "Our old man is crucified with Him." So untold millions were seen by God as hanging there upon that cross with Christ. And this was not merely that our sins were being dealt with, but that we ourselves as sinners, as children of Adam's fallen race, might be removed from under the eye of God and our old standing come to an end forever.

"Death and judgment are behind us,
　　Grace and glory are before;
All the billows rolled o'er Jesus,
　　There they spent their utmost power.

'First-fruits' of the resurrection,
　　He is risen from the tomb;
Now we stand in new creation,
　　Free, because beyond our doom.

Jesus died, and we died with Him.
　　'Buried' in His grave we lay,
One with Him in resurrection,
　　Now 'in Him' in heaven's bright day."

—Mrs. J. A. Trench.

"For I know that in me (that is, in my flesh,) dwelleth no good thing: for to will is present with me; but how to perform that which is good I find not"

—Rom. 7: 18.

EVERY one of us is by nature worse than any thing he has ever done. The natural heart is a den of every kind of evil (Matt. 15: 19). The flesh is incorrigibly corrupt and can never be improved (Gal. 5: 19-21; Rom. 8: 7). It is all-important that this be recognized and judged in the presence of God. When thus dealt with, we cease to look for good in ourselves, and realize that it is from the new heart (Ezek. 36: 26; Matt. 12: 35), given in regeneration, that all good must come. Then we shall find that, as we walk in the Spirit, we shall not fulfil the lust of the flesh (Gal. 5: 16). Our boast will then be only in the Lord (Ps. 34: 2), for we shall realize that all is grace from first to last.

"Less, less of self each day,
    And more, my God of Thee;
Oh, keep me in Thy way,
    However rough it be.

Less of the flesh each day,
    Less of the world and sin;
More of Thy love, I pray,
    More of Thyself within.

Riper and riper now,
    Each hour let me become;
Less fond of things below,
    More fit for such a home.

More moulded to Thy will,
    Lord, let Thy servant be;
Higher and higher still,
    Nearer and nearer Thee."

"There is therefore now no condemnation to them that are in Christ Jesus"—Rom. 8: 1.

IN Romans seven we have a man renewed by the Spirit of God, but struggling under law, hoping thereby to subdue or find deliverance from the power of the old Adamic nature. In chapter eight we have God's way of deliverance through the death and resurrection of Christ, with which the believer is identified before God, and the power of the indwelling Holy Spirit. The chapter begins with "No condemnation" and ends with "no separation." All who are in Christ Jesus are accepted in the Beloved and as free from all charge of guilt as He is Himself. He met all our deserts on the cross. Now we are linked up with Him in resurrection, not under law, but under grace.

> "No condemnation! Blessed is the word!
> No separation! Forever with the Lord.
> By His blood He bought us,
>   Cleansed our every stain;
> With rapture now we'll praise Him,
>   The Lamb for sinners slain."

"That the righteousness of the law might be fulfilled in us, who walk not after the flesh but after the Spirit"
—Rom. 8: 4.

WE must not confound law and grace, which are two opposing systems that never can be confused without doing violence to both. (See Rom. 11: 6.) But in every dispensation right is right and wrong is wrong, and the greatly increased light of the Christian revelation does not invalidate anything of a moral or spiritual character made known in past ages. Under the law there were certain things which were commanded because they were right. Others were right because they were commanded. So, while believers today are not under law, either as a means of justification or as a rule of law, but are justified by grace and are called upon to walk in grace, this does not give liberty to ignore what God made known in past ages, as though all had now been superseded by Christianity. Rather, Christianity takes up and embodies in itself all that was spiritual in every era, and adds much that was not previously known. No dispensational change can transform sin into holiness, or righteousness into unrighteousness. The basis of iniquity is self-will, and that continues always the same.

> "Free from the law, O happy condition!
> Jesus hath died, and there is remission!
> Cursed by the law, and bruised by the fall,
> Christ hath redeemed us once for all."

"Because the carnal mind is enmity against God: for it is not subject to the law of God, neither indeed can be. So then they that are in the flesh cannot please God"—Rom. 8: 7, 8.

WHAT the law forbids, the heart of the unrenewed man produces. It is like a field full of noxious weeds which thrive despite all effort to curb or destroy them. By the new birth men become "partakers of the divine nature" (2 Pet. 1: 4) and so learn to delight in those things which please God, for the new life imparted is heavenly in origin and uncontaminated by lust. Nevertheless, the old nature abides until the day when the returning Christ shall transform these bodies of our humiliation, hence the importance of the exhortations to uprightness, honesty, and integrity that abound in the Epistles, where true Christian life is set forth in all its fulness.

> "The Lord looked down upon the earth,
>   But what did He behold?—
> A groaning, wretched, sinful world
>   By Satan's will controlled.
>
> He saw corruption like a flood
>   Roll o'er His fair domain,
> Rebellion, lust, and wickedness
>   Possessing hill and plain.
>
> He saw man's heart, He knew his will,
>   He saw sin's full extent—
> The whole creation rife with wrong—
>   Man's race on evil bent."
>
> —C. C. Crowston.

"**If thou shalt confess with thy mouth the Lord Jesus, and shalt believe in thine heart that God hath raised Him from the dead, thou shalt be saved. For with the heart man believeth unto righteousness; and with the mouth confession is made unto salvation**"

—**Rom. 10: 9, 10.**

EVERYTHING, for the Christian, centers in the glorious reality that Jesus, who died for our sins upon the cross of shame, has been raised from the tomb and now lives to save eternally all who trust in Him. It is with the recognition of this great truth that we begin, and in the power of it we are enabled to continue in the path of devotedness to the very end, sustained by One whose endless life is the pledge of ours (Heb. 7: 16, 24, 25). To deny the physical resurrection of Jesus is to repudiate the Gospel, which is based upon it (1 Cor. 15: 13-18).

"The Saviour lives, no more to die;
He lives, our Head, enthroned on high;
He lives triumphant o'er the grave;
He lives eternally to save.

The chief of sinners He receives;
His saints He loves and never leaves;
He'll guard us safe from ev'ry ill,
And all His promises fulfill.

Abundant grace will He afford.
Till we are present with the Lord;
And prove what we have sung before,
That Jesus lives for evermore."

—S. Medley.

"I beseech you therefore, brethren, by the mercies of God, that ye present your bodies a living sacrifice, holy, acceptable unto God, which is your reasonable service. And be not conformed to this world: but be ye transformed by the renewing of your mind, that ye may prove what is that good, and acceptable, and perfect, will of God"—Rom. 12: 1, 2.

THE human body is a marvelous testimony to the personality and the wisdom of God. It is inconceivable that anything so wonderful should have come into existence without the guiding hand of a personal Creator. "He that planted the ear, shall He not hear? He that formed the eye, shall He not see?" (Ps. 94: 9.) In creating our bodies He designed them for the highest of all purposes: that they might be used to glorify Him.

When He saves a man He claims all there is of him. Some have thought that if the soul is saved, it is a small matter how the body is used. But the believer's body is the vehicle through which he expresses himself, and it is to be recognized as a sanctuary in which God dwells by His Spirit, as He dwelt, first in the Tabernacle and then in the Temple of old. The spirit of man is the holy of holies, and the body is like the building itself, all of which was to be kept holy to the Lord. All debasing habits, all unlawful appetites, all evil inclinations are to be judged in the presence of God, confessed as sin, and rigidly turned away from, in order that we may rightly represent Him in this world, through whose grace we have been saved.

"Laid on Thine altar, O my Lord divine,
    Accept my will this day, for Jesus' sake.
I have no jewels to adorn Thy shrine,
    Nor any world-proud sacrifice to make;
But here I bring within my trembling hand
    This will of mine—a thing that seemeth small,
And Thou alone, O God, canst understand
    How when I yield Thee this I yield Thee all."

"It is good neither to eat flesh, nor to drink wine, nor any thing whereby thy brother stumbleth, or is offended, or is made weak"—Rom. 14: 21.

TO use God's good gifts without abusing them, to exercise our divinely-given privileges without infringing upon the rights of others, and to avoid all things that are injurious to ourselves or set an evil example to those who are weaker is to live nobly and worthy of our calling as members of Christ. And even though one does not yet have the full assurance of his own acceptance with God, yet life here on earth is richer and sweeter if temperate habits prevail and considerations of decency and unselfishness are characteristic. We should remember that evil once done is evil that will never be undone. One may be forgiven for sins against God, against society, and against one's self, but the sins themselves, once committed, can never become as though they had not been. There are evil effects which go on forever. We may know all the beginnings of sinful behavior, but we can never know the final effects of evil actions or of a bad example. Therefore the importance of self-control and of sober, healthful living, that we may glorify God in our bodies and our spirits, which are His. Paul shows us that life at its best is only enjoyed as we walk in the fear of the Lord and are dominated by His Holy Spirit.

"Live for others while on earth you live
Give for others what you have to give;
Flowers do not hoard their sweet perfume,
Nor withhold the glory of their bloom.

Sunshine helps to melt the winter's snow,
Timely rains compel the grain to grow;
So a smile can banish grief and care,
And a kindly word encourage prayer."

—Wm. Runyan.

"Now I beseech you, brethren, by the name of our Lord Jesus Christ, that ye all speak the same thing, and that there be no divisions among you; but that ye be perfectly joined together in the same mind and in the same judgment"—1 Cor. 1: 10.

THE security and growth of the churches of God depend upon their obedience to His Word. The personnel of these early assemblies was very similar to that found in practically the same circumstances today. In themselves they were weak and unreliable. But their confidence was in the living God. In His Word He has given all necessary instruction for the confirmation and development of His disciples, both as individuals and in their Church relationships. It is all-important to realize that we have in the Scriptures, especially in the Book of the Acts and in the Epistles of Paul, who deals particularly with truth bearing on the privileges and responsibilities of the Church and the churches, all that is needed to guide us aright.

> " 'Mid scenes of confusion and creature-complaints,
> How sweet to the soul is communion with saints;
> To find at the banquet of mercy there's room,
> To feel in communion a foretaste of home.
>
> Sweet bonds, that unite all the children of peace!
> And thrice-blessed Saviour, whose love cannot cease!
> Tho' oft amid trials and dangers we roam,
> With Thine we're united, and hasting toward home."
>
> —D. Denham.

"And I, brethren, when I came to you, came not with excellency of speech or of wisdom, declaring unto you the testimony of God. For I determined not to know any thing among you, save Jesus Christ, and Him crucified"—1 Cor. 2: 1, 2.

IT is the preaching of the cross which is the appointed method of winning souls and building men up in Christ. Paul did not undervalue culture and education, but he dreaded the possibility of the refinements of rhetoric and the cleverness of the orator so occupying the minds of his hearers that they would become occupied with his ability instead of with the Christ he proclaimed. Therefore he studiously avoided anything that would have such a tendency, and in all simplicity he preached the message of the cross in humble dependence on the Holy Spirit to use that proclamation for the salvation of souls. In this he became an example to all other preachers.

> "Yonder, on a cross uplifted,
>   One in ignominy dies;
> Wounded, He, for our transgressions,
>   Bruised for our iniquities;
>   Utmost love is there revealed;
>   By those stripes our wounds are healed.
>
> Not by men was He delivered,
>   Thus to suffer and to die;
> God Himself had preordained it,
>   Had foreknown—eternally;
>   He is pleased to bruise Him thus,
>   To provide release for us.
>
> Lo! the land is whelmed in darkness;—
>   Nature cannot bide the sight;
> But upon His anguished spirit
>   Falls a deeper, denser night,
>   Whence He cries in agony,
>   "Why hast Thou forsaken Me?"
>
> Now His suffering is over;
>   The atonement has been made;
> Stilled, the law's insistent clamors,
>   As in death He bows His head;
>   Now may guilty sinners hide
>   In a Saviour crucified."   —T. O. Chisholm.

"Know ye not that ye are the temple of God, and that the Spirit of God dwelleth in you?"—1 Cor. 3: 16.

INDIVIDUALLY each believer's body is spoken of as a temple of the Holy Spirit, as in 1 Corinthians 6: 19. Collectively, the entire Church is called "the temple of God" (1 Cor. 3: 16). This is the building of living stones (1 Pet. 2: 5), the house of God (Heb. 3: 6; 1 Tim. 3: 15), the habitation in which He dwells and through which He reveals Himself to the world (Eph. 2: 20-22). We read in Ps. 93: 5, "Holiness becometh Thine house, O Lord, for ever." So, whether as individuals or in our collective capacity, we are responsible to walk before God in holiness and righteousness, as controlled by His Spirit who dwells within us.

The Holy Spirit in the believer is grieved by any careless behavior or intemperate indulgences which war against the soul; and so long as He is thus grieved He is not free to carry on His special ministry of taking the things of Christ and making them real to us.

"Created by Omnipotence,
And fashioned by the Only Wise,
Who bade us from the dust arise,
    I bow before unerring love,
And humbly say before His throne,
'Thine am I, Lord, and not my own.'

Created now anew in Christ,
By faith in His atoning death,
And quickened by the Spirit's breath,
    I own God's two-fold in-wrought claim,
And gladly say without reserve,
'Thine am I, Lord, and Thee I serve'."

—W. R. Moore.

"And such were some of you: but ye are washed, but ye are sanctified, but ye are justified in the name of the Lord Jesus, and by the Spirit of our God"—1 Cor. 6: 11.

A HARD field presents a challenge to the man of faith in which he delights. He knows that God works, not with what He finds, but with what He brings. His Spirit is able to break down and save the most indifferent or the most contentious men. Athens was the center of Greek culture—a veneer of learning that covered but did not destroy the wickedness of paganism, which caused and even pretended to sanctify the vilest practices. Corinth was notorious for its vice and corruption. To "Corinthianize" was a synonym for a life given over to shame and sensuality of the most degrading character. The worship of the gods of Greece produced no change in the lives of their devotees. Religion and immorality went hand in hand. The gods themselves were but deifications of lust and ambition. Those who worshipped them were like unto them.

But to these cities Paul came with a message which he knew to be the dynamic of God (Rom. 1:16), mighty to the destruction of Satanic strongholds and powerful in building new and holy lives which would demonstrate the might of the Spirit of God to renew and regenerate the most depraved of mankind, as well as those who gloried in their self-righteousness and fancied superiority. No new message was needed. It was the story of the cross—Jesus Christ and Him crucified—which revolutionized multitudes in Corinth and resulted in the establishment of a strong and highly-gifted church of God in that iniquitous city.

> "O'er this wide waste I loved to roam,
> My back to God and heaven and home,
> Till Jesus met me far astray,
> And beckoned me to come away.
>
> He said on Calv'ry's cross He died,
> A sacrifice for sin was made,
> And all because He loved me so,
> Then how could I do else but go?"

"What? know ye not that your body is the temple of the Holy Ghost which is in you, which ye have of God, and ye are not your own? For ye are bought with a price: therefore glorify God in your body, and in your spirit, which are God's"—1 Cor. 6: 19, 20.

GOD would have us realize that the body, which is such a wonderful evidence of His power and wisdom as our Creator, should be used for the glory of Him who gave us being and died to redeem us. To abuse the body by pernicious habits is to displease the Lord, and is wrong done to ourselves.

The salvation purchased for us by Christ's atoning death is threefold. Spirit and soul and body (1 Thess. 5: 23) have all been bought by the blood of Christ and all are to be devoted to His glory. We cannot grow in grace if we are indulging in sinful and fleshly lusts of any kind. Carnality is the bitter foe of spirituality. The body and its appetites are to be kept in subjection by the power of the indwelling Holy Spirit (1 Cor. 9:27). Only thus can there be success in the Christian race (Heb. 12: 1). The body is to be yielded to Christ (Rom. 12: 1), and not to be polluted by that which would impair its usefulness, under the guise of Christian liberty (Gal. 5: 13).

"I have been 'bought with a price'—
 A price no pen can compute;
The wondrous grace of the Buyer
 Forbids my soul to be mute.
Redemption, the price of my pardon,
 Unties the string of my tongue—
The praise of my gracious Redeemer
 By me shall ever be sung.

I have been 'bought with a price'
 Th' Eternal was willing to die,
That I a poor worm of the dust
 Might share His glory on high.
Oh, wonder of wonders, that He,
 The Creator of heaven and earth,
Should assume the form of a servant—
 Like sinful mortals have birth!"

"Know ye not that they which run in a race run all, but one receiveth the prize? So run, that ye may obtain. And every man that striveth for the mastery is temperate in all things. Now they do it to obtain a corruptible crown; but we an incorruptible"—1 Cor. 9: 24, 25.

SCRIPTURE distinguishes between salvation which is by grace alone, and therefore altogether apart from human merit or works of any kind, and reward which is for service rendered in loving devotion to our rejected Lord, as we seek to glorify Him in this world, our place of testimony. This is the race we are called to run and in order to do so, it is imperative that the servant of Christ exercise godly self-control over all physical appetites. The incorruptible crown is the reward which we hope to receive at the hand of our Lord when we stand at His judgment-seat. To miss this token of His approval will be loss indeed!

"Not at death I shrink or falter,
    For my Saviour saves me now,
But to meet Him empty-handed,
    Thought of that now clouds my brow."

"There hath no temptation taken you but such as is common to man: but God is faithful, who will not suffer you to be tempted above that ye are able; but will with the temptation also make a way to escape, that ye may be able to bear it"—1 Cor. 10: 13.

TEMPTATION is used here in the sense of trial. Christians are exposed to the same trying circumstances that men of the world have to face. But they do not have to meet them alone. The Lord whom they serve is guarding His own and will never permit the furnace to be over-heated, nor allow His people to face conditions which will not work out for blessing, if gone through in fellowship with Himself. To know that "God is faithful" is as a sheet-anchor to the soul no matter how the storms may rage and the tempests blow. He will not forsake those who put their trust in Him. He will either deliver from the trial or give grace to bear it.

"I would not ask Thee why
  My path should be
Through strange and stony ways—
  Thou leadest me!

I would not ask Thee how
  Loss worketh gain,
Knowing that some day soon—
  All shall be plain.

My heart would never doubt
  Thy love and care,
However heavy seems
  The cross I bear.

Nor would I, Father, ask
  My lot to choose,
Lest seeking selfish ease
  Thy best I lose."

—Grace E. Troy.

"For as the body is one, and hath many members, and all the members of that one body, being many are one body: so also is Christ. For by one Spirit are we baptized into one body, whether we be Jews or Gentiles, whether we be bond or free; and have been all made to drink into one Spirit"—1 Cor. 12: 12, 13.

THE unity of the body is not merely a doctrinal tenet. It is a blessed and precious reality. Through the baptism of the Holy Spirit all believers are united to the Risen Lord, the Church's Head, in heaven, and to one another. This is an indissoluble relationship, and because of it, "the members should have the same care one for another," rejoicing when a member is honored, feeling for one who suffers, and standing loyally by those who have to endure persecution. This is to hold the truth of the one Body. It is quite another thing to acknowledge it as an article of faith. Many do this who show little or no concern for their fellow-members and the trying experiences many of them are called to pass through.

> "Oh, how we thirst the chains to burst
> That weight our spirits downward;
> And there to flow, in love's full glow,
> With hearts like Thine surrounded!
>
> No more to view Thy chosen few
> In selfish strife divided,
> But drink in peace the living grace
> That gave them hearts united!
>
> Lord, haste that day of cloudless ray,
> That prospect bright, unfailing;
> Where God shall shine in light divine,
> In glory never fading."
>
> —F. Whitfield.

"Though I speak with the tongues of men and of angels and have not charity (love, R.V.), I am become as sounding brass or a tinkling cymbal"—1 Cor. 13: 1.

THERE is a great difference between the love of God shed abroad in our hearts by the Holy Spirit, given unto us, and mere natural affection, precious as that is. The love of 1 Cor. 13 is the expression of the new life communicated to believers in regeneration. It is the manifestation of the divine nature. It was seen in all its perfection in our Lord Jesus Christ as Man on earth. In the measure in which we live and walk in communion with Him the same love will be seen in us. If we were to change "love" into "Christ," in verses 4 to 7 of this chapter, we would have a perfect pen-picture of our blessed Lord Himself. It is as we manifest this love that our witness really counts for God, even among those who spurn our message.

> "Faith and hope and love we see,
>   Joining hand in hand agree,
>   But the greatest of the three
>   And the best is love.
>   Faith will vanish into sight,
>   Hope be emptied in delight;
>   Love in heaven will shine more bright;
>   Therefore give us love."
>
> —Bishop Christopher Wordsworth.

"Then shall I know even as also I am known"

—1 Cor. 13: 12.

LIFE is full of mysteries. Again and again the bewildered spirit asks "Why?" And to many of our questions there is no answer. It has not pleased God to explain all His ways with us here and now. Elihu said to Job, "He giveth not account of His matters" (Job 33: 13). But faith counts on His infinite love and wisdom, and knows that some day all will be made plain, and in the light of His presence we shall get the answers to all the questions that have perplexed us. Then we shall know the hidden reasons for every trial, every sorrow, and we shall see that there was a "needs be" for all of His dealings with us. We may be sure that, when we see everything from the divine standpoint we shall be able to praise Him for all that now seems so bewildering.

"My life is but a weaving
   Between my Lord and me;
I cannot choose the colors,
   He worketh steadily.
Ofttimes He weaveth sorrow,
   And I, in foolish pride,
Forget He sees the upper,
   And I, the under side.

Not till the loom is silent
   And the shuttles cease to fly,
Shall God unroll the canvas
   And explain the reason why
The dark threads are as needful
   In the Weaver's skillful hand,
As the threads of gold and silver
   In the pattern He has planned."

"But now is Christ risen from the dead, and become the firstfruits of them that slept. For since by man came death, by Man came also the resurrection of the dead. For as in Adam all die, even so in Christ shall all be made alive"—1 Cor. 15: 20-22.

APART from the fact of the resurrection of the Lord Jesus Christ from the dead, Christianity would be just another religious system, or philosophical speculation. It is because of His triumph over death that our great High Priest is able to save to the uttermost all those who come unto God by Him (Heb. 7: 25). That which converted Saul of Tarsus and changed him to Paul the apostle was the revelation that Jesus, who had been crucified, is now alive in highest glory. He had seen Him and heard His voice, and he never doubted afterward (1 Cor. 15: 8). Everywhere he went he preached Jesus and the resurrection (Acts 17: 18). A message that sees in the cross simply a martyr's death is not the Gospel. The good news revealed from Heaven is that Christ died for our sins (1 Cor. 15: 3) and that He has been raised again for our justification (Rom. 4: 25). The same gospel is today the power of God unto salvation when proclaimed with no uncertain sound in the energy of the Holy Spirit.

> "Once we stood in condemnation,
>   Waiting thus the sinner's doom,
> Christ in death has wrought salvation,
>   God has raised Him from the tomb.
>
> Now we see in Christ's acceptance
>   But the measure of our own;
> Him who lay beneath our sentence
>   Seated high upon the throne.
>
> Quickened, raised, and in Him seated,
>   We a full deliv'rance know,
> Ev'ry foe has been defeated,
>   Ev'ry enemy laid low.
>
> Now we have a life in union
>   Now the risen life above,
> Now we drink in sweet communion
>   Some rich foretaste of His love."
>   —G. W. Frazer.

"Blessed be God, even the Father of our Lord Jesus Christ, the Father of mercies, and the God of all comfort; who comforteth us in all our tribulation, that we may be able to comfort them which are in any trouble, by the comfort wherewith we ourselves are comforted of God"—2 Cor. 1: 3, 4.

THE God of all comfort! How our troubled hearts respond to such words as these. He who has manifested Himself in the cross as the God of all grace meeting every need of our souls when distressed by a sense of guilt, now makes Himself known as the source of all consolation when we are troubled by the sorrows of the way and in danger of being cast down because of burdens that seem too heavy to bear. It is noteworthy that every person of the Holy Trinity is engaged in this gracious ministry. Here it is the Father who is the God of all comfort. Both the Son and the Spirit are designated as Comforters. The word for "Advocate" in 1 John 2: 1 is the same as that which the Lord uses in John, chapters 14 to 16, when speaking of the Holy Spirit, who is "another Comforter." It is for God's tried saints to find their solace in Him and so to share with others the comfort He gives.

> "Be comforted! In God thy comfort lies!
>   If He doth pain, He also would console;
> The anodyne which soothes—just He supplies;
>   He, He alone, the wounded can make whole.
>
> The word is His! Nor will it mock nor fail!
>   Be comforted! Let Him thy comfort be;
> Balm for all pain, and light for loneliest vale,
>   Himself the peace, the joy, the company."

—J. Danson Smith.

"Now thanks be unto God, which always causeth us to triumph in Christ, and maketh manifest the savor of His knowledge by us in every place"—2 Cor. 2: 14.

ANOTHER translation reads, "God which always leadeth us in Christ's triumph." He, the mighty conqueror, has come forth from the battle with Satan at the cross, leading His foes in chains at His chariot-wheels. He has spoiled principalities and powers and annulled him that had the power of death, that He might deliver us, and now we who have been delivered from captivity to sin and Satan march with Him in His triumphal procession sweeping onwards to the glory of God which we are destined to share in all the ages to come. But as we journey on we are privileged to tell abroad the gospel of His grace which rises up to God as fragrant incense, to His praise and honor. Whether men heed the message or reject it, God is glorified as we proclaim the story and tell out His love to a ruined world.

> "O Jesus, Lord, 'tis joy to know
> Thy path is o'er of shame and woe,
>   For us so meekly trod:
> All finished is Thy work of toil,
> Thou reapest now the fruit and spoil,
>   Exalted by our God.
>
> We triumph in Thy triumphs, Lord;
> Thy joys our deepest joys afford,
>   The fruit of love divine.
> While sorrow'ng, suff'ring, toiling here,
> How does the thought our spirits cheer,
>   The throne of glory's Thine."

—J. G. Deck.

"But we all, with open face beholding as in a glass the glory of the Lord, are changed into the same image from glory to glory, even as by the Spirit of the Lord"
—2 Cor. 3: 18.

THE secret of Christian holiness is heart-occupation with Christ Himself. As we gaze upon Him we become like Him. Do you want to be holy? Spend much time in His presence. Let the loveliness of the Risen Lord so fill the vision of your soul that all else is shut out. Then the things of the flesh will shrivel up and disappear and the things of the Spirit will become supreme in your life. We do not become holy by looking into our own hearts. There we only find corruption. But as we look away from self altogether, "looking off unto Jesus," as He is the object in which we delight, as we contemplate His holiness, purity, love, and compassion, His devotion to the Father's will, we shall be transformed, imperceptibly to ourselves, perhaps, but none the less surely, into His blessed image. There is no other way whereby we may become practically holy, and be delivered from the power of the flesh and of the principles of the world.

"Fix your eyes upon Jesus,
Look full in His wonderful face,
And the things of earth will grow strangely dim
In the light of His glory and grace."

OCTOBER 7

"For God, who commanded the light to shine out of darkness, hath shined in our hearts, to give the light of the knowledge of the glory of God in the face of Jesus Christ. But we have this treasure in earthen vessels, that the excellency of the power may be of God, and not of us"—2 Cor. 4: 6, 7.

OUR minds are carried back in these verses to the time when God said, "Let there be light," and dispelled the darkness of the primeval chaotic world, and then to that incident related in the book of Judges where Gideon's army went to battle against the Midianites with a sword in one hand and a lamp hidden in a pitcher in the other. At Gideon's command they broke the earthen vessels and the lights shone out striking terror to the hearts of the enemy who could not account for the crash and the blaze of light in the midnight hour. So we who are saved, having been turned from darkness to light, now have the responsibility of shining for God in this world. But in order that this may be, these earthen vessels of our humanity must be broken. Then others can behold the light.

"Our earthen vessels break;
  The world itself grows old;
But Christ our precious dust will take
  And freshly mould:
He'll give these bodies vile
  A fashion like His own;
He'll bid the whole creation smile,
  And hush its groan.

To Him our weakness clings
  Through tribulation sore,
And seeks the covert of His wings
  Till all be o'er.
And when we've run the race,
  And fought the faithful fight,
We then shall see Him face to face,
  With saints in light."

—Mary Bowley.

"Now then we are ambassadors for Christ, as though God did beseech you by us: we pray you in Christ's stead, be ye reconciled to God"—2 Cor. 5:20.

"AMBASSADORS for Christ." This is the title Paul gives to those who seek to carry out our Lord's instruction as to evangelizing the nations. While our Saviour Himself is personally in Heaven, seated on the right hand of the divine Majesty (Heb. 1:3), we are called to represent Him in this world, going to rebels against the authority of the God of Heaven and earth, and pleading with them to be reconciled to Him who sent His Son in grace that all men might through Him have life and peace. We are unfaithful representatives indeed if we fail to respond to the command laid upon us, and allow our fellowmen to perish in their sins unwarned and knowing not the way of life.

This is the first great business of every member of the Church of the living God. All are called to be witnesses, according to their measure. It is ours to "go" (ver. 19), to "pray" (Matt. 9:38), and to help send forth (Acts 13:3) and sustain those who are able to leave home and friends as they hasten forth into distant lands to carry the gospel to the regions beyond (3 John 6-8).

> "From the glory and the gladness,
>   From His secret place;
> From the rapture of His Presence
>   From the radiance of His face—
> Christ the Son of God hath sent me
>   Through the midnight lands;
> Mine, the mighty ordination
>   Of the pierced Hands."

"Having therefore these promises, dearly beloved, let us cleanse ourselves from all filthiness of the flesh and spirit, perfecting holiness in the fear of God"

—2 Cor. 7: 1.

CARELESS habits and unholy ways are inconsistent with the truth of the new creation. God has given us exceeding great and precious promises, and because of His goodness we owe it to Him to judge in ourselves every tendency to unholiness, whether in body or mind. Once we walked according to the lust of the flesh and of the mind. Now we are called to walk in the Spirit that we may not fulfil these unclean desires. "Perfecting holiness" suggests growth, which should be continuous. As we are daily occupied with Christ and walk in the Spirit, reckoning ourselves dead indeed unto sin but alive unto God through Jesus Christ, we shall detect the least beginnings of evil. If these are judged and confessed immediately, we shall be kept from sin's power, and as we go on in faith we shall enjoy unclouded fellowship with God.

"There is a faith unmixed with doubt,
    A love all free from fear;
A walk with Jesus, where is felt
    His presence always near.
There is a rest that God bestows,
    Transcending pardon's peace,
A lowly, sweet simplicity,
    Where inward conflicts cease."

"For ye know the grace of our Lord Jesus Christ, that, though He was rich, yet for your sakes He became poor, that ye through His poverty might be rich"—2 Cor. 8: 9.

A CHRISTIAN, challenged by a Unitarian to produce a solitary passage of Scripture to prove that Jesus had any existence before He was born of Mary, quoted this verse. The other objected that it had no bearing on the question at issue. The Christian replied, "But the text says, 'He was rich.' Was He ever rich on earth? When was He rich?" The position is unanswerable if one believes the Bible to be the Word of God. Jesus was never rich on earth. But He was rich in the glory that He had with the Father before the world was. What riches were His! And He gave all up and became poor in order that bankrupt sinners might be made wealthy for Eternity. He who trusts in Him is made heir to all the riches of glory which the Father delights to share with all who come to Him and accept His grace.

He came from the light and the gladness
To the darkness and woe where I lay,
He touched me and healed the foul leper,
My debt in His love stooped to pay.

For a stranger becoming the Surety
He smarted on Calvary's tree;
Though rich became poor as the poorest,
To lavish His wealth upon me.

—H. A. I.

"Now He that ministereth seed to the sower both minister bread for your food, and multiply your seed sown, and increase the fruits of your righteousness"

—2 Cor. 9: 10.

THE seed, we are told, is the Word. Sown in faith, the results may not be seen immediately but the harvest is sure, for God has declared His word shall not return unto Him void. Many a tender gospel message has seemed to fall upon deaf ears, but in afterdays there has come back to some who heard words that seemed to have been completely ignored or utterly forgotten. So the laborer is to work on, sowing in hope, trusting that God will give the seed to germinate and to bear fruit for His glory in time to come. To a discouraged evangelist an aged brother exclaimed, "Many a one will die easier for what he has heard tonight!"

"It was only a tiny seed at the first,
  And its power I little knew;
But 'twas sown, and the germ from its prison burst,
  And was nourished by sunshine and dew.
The grain of the past was a blessing at last,
  In the bountiful harvest that grew.

Go hopefully on in the work of the day,
  Scatter broadcast the seed of the Word;
Sing thy song, though unseen; drop the word by the way,
  And leave the results with the Lord.
Though but little at most—and with nothing to boast,
  'What she could' will insure a reward!"

—W. J. H. Brealey.

"And He said unto me, My grace is sufficient for thee: for My strength is made perfect in weakness. Most gladly therefore will I rather glory in my infirmities, that the power of Christ may rest upon me"—2 Cor. 12: 9.

PAUL pleaded thrice for deliverance from the sharp thorn that caused such suffering. But at last the answer came in a way he had not looked for. The Lord said, as it were, "No, Paul; I will not remove the thorn, but I will give you grace to endure." And this moved the apostle to glory in his very infirmities that the power of Christ might rest upon him. Happy the soul that has learned the folly of striving against the permissive will of God, and can receive all at His hand and look to Him for strength to endure. It was this that enabled Job to triumph as he cried, "Shall we receive good at the hand of God, and shall we not also receive evil?"

"With eager heart and will on fire
I fought to win my great desire:
'Peace shall be mine,' I said, but life
Grew bitter in the endless strife.

My soul was weary, and my pride
Was wounded deep. To heav'n I cried,
'God grant me peace, or I must die!'
The dumb stars glittered no reply.

Broken at last, I bowed my head,
Forgetting all myself, and said,
'Whatever comes His will be done.'
And in that moment, peace was won."

OCTOBER 13

"Grace be to you and peace from God the Father, and from our Lord Jesus Christ, who gave Himself for our sins, that He might deliver us from this present evil world, according to the will of God and our Father: to whom be glory for ever and ever. Amen"

—Gal. 1: 3-5.

CHRIST did not die merely to save us from eternal doom, blessed as that aspect of salvation is; but "He gave Himself for our sins that He might deliver (or save) us from this present age of evil," as the expression "this present evil world," really means. The age is evil because Christ has been rejected and men are living in independence of God. From this the believer is delivered as he recognizes his identification with Christ in His death. Because of the fact that He died in our place, as our representative, we too have died. We have died to the law, died to sin, died to self, and died to the world that has no place for Christ.

"Farewell! Henceforth my place
　Is with the Lamb who died.
My Sovereign! While I have Thy love,
　What can I want beside?
Thyself, dear Lord, art now
　My free and loving choice,
'In whom, though now I see Thee not,
　Believing, I rejoice!'

Shame on me that I sought
　Another joy than this,
Or dreamt a heart at rest with Thee
　Could crave for earthly bliss!
These vain and worthless things,
　I put them all aside;
His goodness fills my longing soul,
　And I am satisfied.

Lord Jesus! let me dwell
　'Outside the camp,' with Thee.
Since Thou art there, then there alone
　Is peace and home for me.
Thy dear reproach to bear
　I'll count my highest gain,
Till Thou return, my banished King,
　To take Thy power, and reign!"

—Margaret Mauro.

"I am crucified with Christ: nevertheless I live; yet not I, but Christ liveth in me: and the life which I now live in the flesh, I live by the faith of the Son of God"
—Gal. 2:20.

CRUCIFIXION with Christ is judicial. When He died God saw the end of man in the flesh. All believers therefore can look back to the cross and say in faith, "It was there I died, in the Person of my Substitute." Therefore I am no longer viewed as in Adam. I am now in Christ. In the power of this truth I am called to walk. I live in Him. He lives in me. My life here in the body is to be the manifestation of Christ in me. This is true experimentally as I reckon myself dead indeed unto sin but alive unto God in Christ Jesus. It is not that I am to try to die to the old order. I have died, and I take that place in relation to everything that is of the flesh, mortifying the deeds of the body. Practically, I die daily, as earth-claims are refused. Thus I live unto God.

> Now I will glory in the cross,
> For this I count the world but dross.
> There I with Christ was crucified,
> His death is mine; with Him I died;
> And while I live my song shall be,
> No longer I, but Christ in me.

—H. A. I.

"Christ hath redeemed us from the curse of the law, being made a curse for us: for it is written, Cursed is every one that hangeth on a tree: that the blessing of Abraham might come on the Gentiles through Jesus Christ; that we might receive the promise of the Spirit through faith"—Gal. 3: 13, 14.

TO redeem is to buy back. Because of his sins the Jew was sold under the curse of the law. The same applies in principle to Gentiles, who now have the knowledge of the law, which the Galatians to whom Paul wrote had not, in their unconverted days. But Christ died not only to free believing Jews from the curse, but that the blessing of Abraham, that is, of justification by faith, might come to the Gentiles also. All who believe are delivered from the law's condemnation, Christ having taken our place in judgment and borne what our sins deserved, in His own body on the tree. He became a curse for us. He was made sin for us. In the fullest possible sense He answered for us before God. Now we go free.

> "He bore on the tree
>   The sentence for me,
> And now both the Surety and sinner are free;
>   And this I shall find,
>   For such is His mind,
> He'll not be in glory and leave me behind."

"But when the fulness of the time was come, God sent forth His Son, made of a woman, made under the law, to redeem them that were under the law, that we might receive the adoption of sons. And because ye are sons, God hath sent forth the Spirit of His Son into your hearts, crying, Abba, Father"—Gal. 4: 4-6.

SONSHIP is more than new birth. Through that we become children of God. This was true of believers in all dispensations. But now by the reception of the Holy Spirit, who is the Spirit of adoption, we become sons. This is the distinctive blessing of the present dispensation of grace. Old Testament saints were as children in their nonage. New Testament Christians are sons who have attained their majority and are joint heirs with Christ. We are all children of God by the second birth and sons of God by adoption. This is what is unfolded here in Galatians, as also in Romans 8: 14-17. In Roman law all born in the family were children, but only those legally adopted were reckoned as sons.

> "Abba," Father—thus we call Thee,
>   (Hallowed name!) from day to day;—
> 'Tis Thy children's right to know Thee,
>   None but children "Abba" say.
> This high honor we inherit,
>   Thy free gift, through Jesus' blood;
> God the Spirit, with our spirit,
>   Witnesseth we're sons of God."

"This I say then, Walk in the Spirit, and ye shall not fulfil the lust of the flesh. For the flesh lusteth against the Spirit, and the Spirit against the flesh: and these are contrary the one to the other: so that ye cannot do the things that ye would"—Gal. 5: 16, 17.

THE inward conflict between flesh and spirit disturbs and bewilders many believers, often leading to the anguished cry, like that of Rebecca of old, "If it be so, why am I thus?" (Gen. 25: 22). The struggle seems to cast doubt on the reality of conversion. It is rather an evidence of it, for the two natures are in every child of God, and this produces a condition unknown in days before the new birth took place. The way of victory is not to fight the flesh and endeavor by our own power to suppress its activities. It is to yield to the control of the Spirit of God and as we walk in the Spirit whose delight it is to occupy our hearts with, and conform us to Christ, we find practical deliverance from the power of fleshly lusts. In place of "cannot" in the last clause we should read "may not." It is only as we are Spirit-led we are enabled to do the things that we would, and should.

"O may Thy Spirit guide our souls,
  And mould them to Thy will,
That from Thy paths we ne'er may stray,
  But keep Thy precepts still.

That to the Saviour's stature full
  We nearer still may rise,
And all we think, and all we do,
  Be pleasing in Thine eyes."

—Doddridge.

"Be not deceived; God is not mocked: for whatsoever a man soweth, that shall he also reap. For he that soweth to his flesh shall of the flesh reap corruption; but he that soweth to the Spirit shall of the Spirit reap life everlasting. And let us not be weary in well doing: for in due season we shall reap, if we faint not"

—Gal. 6: 7-9.

THEY who, in youth, sow wild oats will have a terrible crop to reap in older days (Prov. 22: 8). No wonder the world has so many disillusioned and disappointed old men and aged women. They frittered away the golden hours of youth in careless living and selfish indulgence, and as a result their wrecked constitutions, and in some cases impaired minds, make their later years most distressing and unhappy. It is quite otherwise with men and women who, in the days of their youth, lived in an orderly manner, walking before God in self-control, refusing to become the slaves of sensuality and voluptuousness. For them, the hoary head is indeed a crown of glory, because found in the way of righteousness (Prov. 16: 31). Someone has well said, "The Devil has no happy old men." But how different it is with those who have known and loved the Lord through the long years! When they reach the eventide of life, theirs is a peace and a serenity which is found only in the service of God. Of them it can be said, "At eventide it shall be light."

> "Sowing the seed of a ling'ring pain,
> Sowing the seed of a maddened brain,
> Sowing the seed of a tarnished name,
> Sowing the seed of eternal shame,
> Oh, what shall the harvest be?"

"He hath chosen us in Him before the foundation of the world, that we should be holy and without blame before Him in love"—Eph. 1: 4.

IT is a striking fact, often overlooked by zealous controversialists that, in Scripture, no one is ever said to be elected or predestinated to go to heaven. Nor of course, are people ever said to be predestinated to be lost, or reprobated before birth to eternal ruin. On the contrary we who are saved are said to be chosen beforehand unto holiness and blamelessness before God, and predestinated to become like Christ the first-born of many brethren. This is blessed indeed. It should be a comfort and an encouragement, when conscious of weakness and failure, to know that I am yet to be wholly conformed to the image of God's Son. No power on earth or in hell can hinder the completion of God's purpose of grace.

> "O Lamb of God, we thank Thee,
>   We bless Thy holy name!
> Thy love once made Thee willing
>   To bear our sin and shame.
> And now Thy love is waiting
>   Thy saints like Thee to raise;
> Firstborn of many brethren,
>   To Thee be all the praise."

"We are His workmanship, created in Christ Jesus unto good works, which God hath before ordained that we should walk in them"—Eph. 2: 10.

TWICE this word, here translated "workmanship" is used in the epistles of Paul. In Romans 1: 20 it is translated "things that are made." It is the Greek word *poima*, from which we get our English word "poem." A poem is a well-constructed literary piece, the work of a master mind. In Romans 1 we see the creation as God's great epic poem. In Ephesians 2 we have the poem of redemption.

> " 'Twas great to call a world from naught,
>
> 'Twas greater to redeem."

Each saved one is, so to speak, a syllable in this great masterpiece, this marvellous poem, that tells out, as nothing else could, the wondrous wisdom and grace of God. How lyrical should be our lives as we enter into and appreciate this!

> "No good in creatures can be found,
>   All, all is found in Thee;
> We must have all things and abound,
>   Through Thy sufficiency.
>
> Thou that hast made our heaven secure
>   Wilt here all good provide;
> While Christ is rich, can we be poor—
>   Christ who for us has died?
>
> O Lord, we cast each care on Thee,
>   And triumph and adore;
> Oh that our great concern may be
>   To love and praise Thee more!"
>
> —Ryland.

"For He is our peace, who hath made both one, and hath broken down the middle wall of partition between us"—Eph. 2: 14.

CHRIST Himself, crucified, risen, now exalted to God's right hand in glory, is our peace. On the cross He made peace by the shedding of His blood. Ere returning to heaven He said "Peace be unto you." Now, "being justified by faith we have peace with God through our Lord Jesus Christ" (Rom. 5: 1). He undertook to settle the sin-question by making expiation for iniquity. God is satisfied with His finished work. When the Father raised His Son from the dead He bore witness to the perfection of His work. Now the troubled soul looks up to the Throne, by the eye of faith, and sees the Man who was once on the tree, forsaken of God, crowned with honor and glory. He could not be there if the sin-question had not been disposed of. So the believer can exultingly say, "He is my peace."

> "I hear the words of love,
> I gaze upon the blood,
> I see the mighty sacrifice,
> And I have peace with God.
>
> 'Tis everlasting peace!
> Sure as Jehovah's name;
> 'Tis stable as His steadfast throne,
> For evermore the same.
>
> My love is ofttimes low,
> My joy still ebbs and flows;
> But peace with Him remains the same,
> No change Jehovah knows."

—H. Bonar.

"For this cause I bow my knees unto the Father of our Lord Jesus Christ, of whom the whole family in heaven and earth is named"—Eph. 3: 14, 15.

PAUL locates the whole redeemed family in two places. They are either in heaven or on earth. This is the death-blow to the Romish idea of purgatory—a third state between heaven and hell. And it is also the perfect answer to soul-sleep theories of every kind. Paul does not say, "The whole family in the grave and on earth." He declares they are either in heaven or on earth. This agrees with many other Scriptures. Our loved ones in Christ, when they leave this scene are, at once, "absent from the body, present with the Lord" (2 Cor. 5). They depart to be with Christ, as Paul says in Phil. 1. It is only the tired, weary bodies of the saints that sleep until the resurrection morn when the dead will be raised and the living changed.

> "Our Father's home on high,
> Home to our souls how dear!
> E'en now, to faith's transpiercing eye
> Thy golden gates appear.
>
> Our thirsty spirits faint
> To reach the home we love,
> The bright inheritance of saints—
> Jerusalem above.
>
> And though there intervene
> Rough seas and stormy skies,
> Though by no mortal vision seen,
> Thy glory fills our eyes.
>
> There shall all clouds depart,
> The wilderness shall cease,
> And sweetly shall each gladdened heart
> Enjoy eternal peace."

—J. Montgomery.

"Let him that stole steal no more: but rather let him labor, working with his hands the thing which is good, that he may have to give to him that needeth"

—Eph. 4: 28.

HE who fails to distinguish between "thine" and "mine" has not learned the first principle of integrity in human relations. There is no communism sanctioned by the Bible except that voluntary sharing which at the beginning of the Christian era was practised for a time by the persecuted believers in Christ, who said not that ought they possessed was their own, but distributed as every man had need. Such a system was never obligatory, nor is it practical at all times. Respect for the rights of the individual and the recognition of the sacredness of property lie at the base of all reputable government. These fundamentals were insisted on in the law given at Sinai and confirmed by our Lord Jesus Christ during His earthly ministry as well as by the Holy Spirit afterward. To ignore them is fatal and means the downfall of ordered society. The intelligent Christian will stand firmly against the atheistic and ruinous systems of Marxian socialism and communism, not because of selfishness, but because of conscience toward God and respect for the rights of his fellow-men.

"I'd rather see a sermon than hear one any day,
 I'd rather one should walk with me than merely show the way;
 I can soon learn how to do it if you'll let me see it done,
 I can watch your hands in action, but your tongue too fast may run;
 And the lectures you deliver may be very wise and true,
 But I'd rather get my lesson by observing what you do.
 For I may not understand you and the high advice you give,
 But there's no misunderstanding how you act and how you live."

"Giving thanks always for all things unto God and the
Father in the name of our Lord Jesus Christ"
—Eph. 5: 20.

THE redeemed of the Lord should ever be praising Him
who has saved us in His rich grace and who lavishes
upon us evidence after evidence of His Fatherly love and
care. An unthankful child of God is a strange anomaly.
Praise should ever be welling up in the hearts of those who
recognize their constant indebtedness to the divine mercy
and compassion. We should worry less if we praised more.
Thanksgiving is the enemy of discontent and dissatisfaction.
When tempted to doubt and fear, begin to praise God for
past mercies, and faith will be increased.

"We thank Thee Thou hast spared the lives
   Of those we love, that peaceful rest
Succeeding days of work well done
   Have made our lives serene and blest.

But more we thank Thee that we know,
   That come what may of grief or pain,
Thy power will not, cannot, fail;
   Thy love will still our hearts sustain.

We thank Thee that though hills be moved,
   And though earth reel beneath the shock
Of tumult, we have naught to fear
   Who stand upon the ageless Rock."

"For this cause shall a man leave his father and mother, and shall be joined unto his wife, and they two shall be one flesh. This is a great mystery: but I speak concerning Christ and the Church"—Eph. 5: 31, 32.

THE union of one man and one woman and the faithfulness of each to the other for life is the Christian ideal of the marriage relationship. Whether human laws accord with this or whether they legalize its violation, the divine principle remains. Yet it is appalling how lightly even professed Christians and members of evangelical churches often look upon wedlock. We need not be surprised to find that selfish worldlings flout the sacredness of the home and make and break conjugal ties to suit their whims and desires. But it is pitiable when those who know that God Himself has chosen the married state to picture the union of Christ and His redeemed ones, seek the aid of the world's courts to dissolve a relationship which, once entered into, can only be broken by disobedience to the Word of God. The violation of the Seventh Commandment is the only ground given by our Lord for one to "put away his wife, . . . and . . . marry another" (Matt. 19: 9). Divorce and re-marriage, apart from this, is to incur the condemnation of the Lord, and such a union is denominated adultery. Of course, where this took place before conversion, all is wiped out by the blood of Christ, and if saved in this condition each party is to "abide in the same calling wherein he was called" (1 Cor. 7: 20). Every marriage union is intended to portray the relationship between Christ and His own.

"And soon the months will roll away,
  And quickly come the nuptial day,
  When Thou, the Lamb, shalt take Thy throne
  And fully there Thy Church shalt own."

—I. Watts.

"**Children, obey your parents in the Lord: for this is right. Honor thy father and mother; which is the first commandment with promise; that it may be well with thee, and thou mayest live long on the earth**"
—Eph. 6: 1-3.

RESPECT for and obedience to parents is the foundation of all society. Children who are rebellious and unsubject in the home will be impatient of control and enemies of orderly government when they grow older. More than that, if they do not obey their parents in early days, they will not obey God in later years. This is why some consider that the Fifth Commandment really belongs to the first table of the Law rather than to the second. The first table sets forth man's responsibility to God, the second his responsibility to his neighbor. In childhood our parents stand in the place of God. We learn His mind through them, if they themselves are subject to His Word. In this our blessed Lord is, as in all other things, our great Exemplar. He who brought all things into existence by the word of His power voluntarily took the place of a child in a Jewish home and honored the Law by being subject to Mary His mother, and to Joseph His foster father. Young Christians need to remember that they honor God by honoring their parents.

"Give of your best to the Master,
Give Him the strength of your youth,
Clad in salvation's full armor,
Join in the battle for truth."

"For me to live is Christ, and to die is gain"
—Phil. 1:21.

THESE words express, as none others could, the secret of Paul's wonderful missionary activity and his deep devotion to the will of the Lord. From the moment when divine grace arrested him on the Damascus turnpike to his last hour on earth, he had yielded his heart wholly to the Blessed One who had saved him. Life meant only one thing for him, and that, the opportunity to become better acquainted with the Lord Jesus Christ and to serve Him wholeheartedly. Nothing else seemed worth while. All that earth could offer was but as filth and dross compared to this (Phil. 3:7-9). He had learned to look at everything below the skies in the light of the cross of Christ (Gal. 6:14). Now he looked forward eagerly to the end of the way, when he should be with Christ and receive at His hand the recognition of His approval of his service.

> "Though absent, I have known His love,
> And by His mercies daily prove
>   The wonders of His grace,
> He, whom, not having seen, I love,
> Will call, and in His home above
>   I'll see Him face to face.
>
> With patience, in His love I'll rest,
> And whisper that He knoweth best,
>   And I am satisfied.
> Then, clinging to that guiding hand,
> A weakling, in His strength I'll stand,
>   Though I be sorely tried.
>
> Though burdened with a load of care,
> He's promised me the strength to bear
>   The trials that appal;
> So, hiding pain away from sight,
> I'll let my life be fair and bright,
>   While waiting for His call."

—Robert R. Pentecost.

"Let this mind be in you, which was also in Christ Jesus: who, being in the form of God, thought it not robbery to be equal with God: but made Himself of no reputation, and took upon Him the form of a servant, and was made in the likeness of men: and being found in fashion as a man, He humbled Himself, and became obedient unto death, even the death of the cross"

—Phil. 2: 5-8.

THE mind that was in Christ Jesus is the lowly mind. He ever sought the glory of His Father and the blessing of others. In His gracious condescension He who had every right to command became servant of all. Though in the form of God from Eternity He did not consider equality with God the Father something to be retained, but He divested Himself of the outward semblance of Deity, the glory that He had with the Father before the world was, and took a bondman's form. Having become Man He humbled Himself yet farther, stooping to death, and such a death, that of the cross. This is the One whose example the Spirit brings before us, that our ways may be conformed to His.

"Thou would'st like wretched man be made
    In everything but sin;
That we as like Thee might become
    As we unlike had been."

"Brethren, I count not myself to have apprehended: but this one thing I do, forgetting those things which are behind, and reaching forth unto those things which are before, I press toward the mark for the prize of the high calling of God in Christ Jesus"—Phil. 3: 13, 14.

PAUL was no "sinless perfectionist." After he had walked with God and served his Lord for a generation, he did not yet consider that he had laid hold in all its fulness, of that for which God had laid hold of him. One thing only he had laid hold of, and that covered all his experience — namely, that he was ever to press on, forgetting past experiences and reaching forth to new appreciation of what God had for him in Christ. The prize of the high calling was to be fully conformed to his Lord. This would not be until he met Him and stood face to face. Then he would be transformed into His image.

> "I'm pressing on the upward way;
> New heights I'm reaching day by day,
> Still singing as I onward bound,
> Lord, plant my feet on higher ground."

"But my God shall supply all your need according to His riches in glory by Christ Jesus"—Phil. 4: 19.

SOME one has called this verse a blank check on the Bank of Faith to be filled in by the believer as need arises. The Bank's credit is infinite. There are assets in abundance, riches of grace, riches of love, riches of mercy, and riches of glory. Whatever the circumstances in which the child of God is found there is sufficient for every need, whether temporal or spiritual. We are to be anxious about nothing, but prayerful for everything as we come to God in a spirit of thanksgiving to appropriate in faith what He delights to give. We are so prone to doubt and worry when we should trust and enjoy the goodness of our Father's mercies. A motto we have often seen says, "If you worry you do not trust. If you trust you do not worry." Commit all to Him. Claim His promise and He will meet every need.

"Friend, dost thou in thine inmost heart believe this word?
Then trust—yea, wholly trust thy loving Lord.
Trust Him each day, each hour, and thou shalt see
Each need supplied, Christ's riches used for thee."

"Who now rejoice in my sufferings for you, and fill up that which is behind of the afflictions of Christ in my flesh for His body's sake, which is the Church: whereof I am made a minister, according to the dispensation of God which is given to me for you, to fulfil the Word of God"—Col. 1: 24, 25.

A DISPENSATION is a stewardship or economy in God's ways with men, in which He is dealing with them in a different way from that in which He has dealt with them before. Some people decry what is called "dispensational truth," yet all Bible students believe in it to some degree. No one seriously contends that God is dealing with men today in the same manner as He dealt with them under law from Moses to Christ. And it is clear from Scripture that when the Church age is ended and the kingdom age has dawned, man's responsibility will be different from what it is now. The word "dispensation" is found four times in the Authorized Version and five times in the Revision. It is a translation of the Greek word *oikonomia*, from which we get our word "economy," and is translated also "order," "administration," and "stewardship." It refers to the ordering of God's ways with men.

"Head of the Church, Thy body,
  O Christ, the great Salvation!
Sweet to the saints it is to think
  Of all Thine exaltation!
All power's to Thee committed,
  All power on earth, in heaven;
To Thee a name of widest fame
  Above all glory's given.

With Thee believers raised,
  In Thee on high are seated;
All guilty once, but cleared by Thee:
  Redemption-toil's completed.
And when Thou, Lord and Saviour,
  Shalt come again in glory,
There, by Thy side, Thy spotless Bride
  Shall crown the wondrous story."

—Gilpin.

"And ye are complete in Him, which is the head of all principality and power: in whom also ye are circumcised with the circumcision made without hands, in putting off the body of the sins of the flesh by the circumcision of Christ: buried with Him in baptism, wherein also ye are risen with Him through the faith of the operation of God, who hath raised Him from the dead"

—Col. 2: 10-12.

THE believer is looked upon by God as so completely identified with Christ that His death is viewed as ours, and we are seen as buried in His grave and alive in His resurrection. But there is more than this. It is not only that our standing before God is perfect because of our identification with Christ; but as to our new state or condition we are so intimately linked up with Christ that we partake of His fulness and His life has been imparted to us, so that now as we live by faith, that new life is operative in us, enabling us to glorify God in all our ways. From our glorified Head in heaven grace flows down to every member of His Body on earth, sufficing for every emergency.

"A fulness resides in Jesus our Head,
A fulness abides to answer all need.
The Father's good pleasure has laid up a store,
A plentiful treasure, to give to the poor.

Whatever distress awaits us below,
Such plentiful grace the Lord will bestow,
As still shall support us and silence our fear,
And nothing can hurt us while Jesus is near."

—Fawcett.

"If ye then be risen with Christ, seek those things which are above, where Christ sitteth on the right hand of God. Set your affection on things above, not on things on the earth. For ye are dead, and your life is hid with Christ in God"—Col. 3: 1-3.

IT is not as though Paul cast any doubt on our having been raised with Christ, and our identification with Him as He sits at God's right hand. But it is as though he said, "Since these things are true, now set your mind on things above." We belong to the scene where Christ our Head has gone. We have died to the old life and all that belonged to it. We are now associated with Christ in new creation. Our real life is that divinely imparted eternal life which we received in regeneration. Nothing on earth can satisfy its desires or meet its demands. We must look up to where our Saviour sits exalted. As we are occupied with Him the things of this lower realm will lose their power over our souls, and heavenly things become more real.

"Whom have we, Lord, but Thee,
Soul-thirst to satisfy?
Exhaustless spring! The waters free!
All other streams are dry.

Our hearts by Thee are set
On brighter things above;
Strange that we ever should forget
Thine own most faithful love."

—Mary Bowley.

"Lie not one to another, seeing that ye have put off the old man with his deeds; and have put on the new man, which is renewed in knowledge after the image of Him that created him: where there is neither Greek nor Jew, circumcision nor uncircumcision, Barbarian, Scythian, bond nor free: but Christ is all, and in all"
—Col. 3: 9-11.

GOD is called the "God of truth" (Isa. 65:16). The Holy Spirit is the "Spirit of truth" (John 16: 13). Christ said, "I am . . . the Truth" (John 14:6). No one can have fellowship with the Holy Trinity who does not walk in the truth (2 John 4; 3 John 4). God desires truth in the inward parts (Ps. 51: 6). Falsehood of every kind is hateful to Him. There is nothing that so manifests the alienation of the natural man from God as his tendency to falsehood. Of the wicked we are told that they go astray from their very birth speaking lies (Ps. 58:3). Satan himself is the father of lies (John 8:44). It is he who injects the venom of untruthfulness into the heart of man (Acts 5:3). Only by the new birth can this lying spirit be overcome. It is as the regenerated man yields himself to God as one alive from the dead that he learns to delight in the truth objectively revealed and to walk in the truth subjectively.

"O Jesus Christ, grow Thou in me,
  And all things else recede;
My heart be daily nearer Thee;
  From sin be daily freed.

In Thy bright beams which on me fall,
  Fade every evil thought;
That I am nothing, Thou art all,
  I would be daily taught."

"Continue in prayer, and watch in the same with thanksgiving; withal praying also for us, that God would open unto us a door of utterance, to speak the mystery of Christ, for which I am also in bonds"—Col. 4: 2, 3.

PRAYER is talking with God. He invites us to come in all simplicity and to tell Him our needs (which He promises to supply) and to intercede on behalf of others. Paul, the very chiefest of all the apostles, felt the need of the prayers of others. Again and again he pleads with the believers in various places to speak to God concerning him and his ministry. How much do we pray for Christ's servants? And, for ourselves, do we pray for God to endorse our programs, or do we ask that He will reveal His mind to us and give us grace to act accordingly?

"Once I prayed—
(I knew not what I said)
'Show me myself, O Lord!'
Alas, I did not dread
　　The hideous sight
(Which now I shudder to behold),
Because I knew not self aright.

　　And I was led
In answer to my prayer,
As step by step, to see
My wretched heart laid bare;
　　Then I prayed,
'Stay, Lord, I cannot bear the sight!'
And pityingly His hand was stayed.

　　Now I pray
(I know the prayer is right),
'Show me Thyself, O Lord,
Be to my soul the Bright
　　And Morning Star,
To shine upon the grave of self,
And lead my heart from earth afar!' "

—Helen McDowell.

"For our gospel came not unto you in word only, but also in power, and in the Holy Ghost, and in much assurance; as ye know what manner of men we were among you for your sake. And ye became followers of us, and of the Lord, having received the word in much affliction, with joy of the Holy Ghost"—1 Thess. 1: 5, 6.

THE faithful preaching of the Word of God, backed by a consecrated life, is bound to bring results. A holy minister of Christ is a tremendously effective weapon in the hand of God. Paul believed the gospel. He knew what it had done in his own life, and he proclaimed it with absolute confidence to others. He never sought simply to amuse or astonish his audiences, but he stood before them in all the holy authority of an ambassador for Christ, representing the high court of Heaven. Consequently, his word was with power. We may well follow his example today and, renouncing all the fripperies and fropperies of the present age of sham, as Carlyle called it, preach the gospel, assured that "it is the power of God unto salvation to every one that believeth."

"Still in a land of drought and dearth
    Our longing spirits cry
To Thee, the Lord of heaven and earth,
    Our thirst to satisfy.

O Thou with love more strong than death,
    Unquenched by deepest waves,
We need throughout the walk of faith
    The same free grace that saves.

We would not take from falsehood's fire,
    Though glitt'ring be the spark;
Thou only art our heart's desire,
    Art light where all is dark."

—Mary Bowley.

"For this cause also thank we God without ceasing, because, when ye received the word of God which ye heard of us, ye received it not as the word of men, but as it is in truth, the word of God, which effectually worketh also in you that believe"—1 Thess. 2: 13.

THERE is a science known as Comparative Religions. It has much in it that is worthy of our attention and consideration so long as we do not include Christianity among the "religions" to be compared. All forms of pagan systems have much in common. But the gospel of God is diverse from all of these. They are but the speculations of men's minds, and often give evidence of Satanic origin. The Christian message is a revelation from heaven. The gospel is an inspired announcement given by God Himself to be proclaimed to all men everywhere, as the only remedy for sin. It proves its divine origin by what it does. It works miraculously in the lives of those who believe it, giving new life, in the energy of the Holy Spirit, and delivering from the power of evil.

> "He breaks the power of cancelled sin;
>   He sets the prisoner free;
> His blood can make the vilest clean,
>   His blood avails for me."

"For what is our hope, or joy, or crown of rejoicing?
Are not even ye in the presence of our Lord Jesus Christ
at His coming? For ye are our glory and joy"
—1 Thess. 2: 19, 20.

THE Thessalonian Christians were the fruit of Paul's
labor in the Lord. He looked forward to the day of
manifestation when every one's works shall be manifested,
and he was sure that those whom he had led to Christ
would be to him a crown of rejoicing in that day. Every
soul we are privileged to bring to the Saviour will shine as
a star in our crown when we give an account of our service.
"They that turn many to righteousness" shall shine "as the
stars forever and ever." Are we keeping this in view or do
we live selfishly, seldom telling others of Christ and so
rarely, if ever, winning them for Himself? If saved ourselves we owe the gospel to those still in their sins, for it
is the only way out of the darkness in which they live.

"See, o'er the world wide open doors inviting;
   Soldiers of Christ, arise, and enter in!
Christians, awake! Your forces all uniting,
   Send forth the gospel, break the chains of sin."

"This is the will of God, even your sanctification, that ye should abstain from fornication"—1 Thess. 4: 3.

THAT which God's Word would impress upon us, above all else, in this connection, is the sinfulness of unchastity in all its forms. We live in the days of a revolting revival of paganism. Men would fain excuse every sort of impurity as "natural," and not to be held in check. Scripture well describes such as behaving like "natural brute beasts" (2 Pet. 2: 12), and solemnly declares that such "shall receive the reward of unrighteousness." It becomes the Christian to shun every approach to uncleanness, and to remember that "the body is not for fornication, but for the Lord; and the Lord for the body" (1 Cor. 6: 13). It has been purchased by the precious blood of Christ and is not to be used selfishly or made the victim of evil appetites and unholy passions.

> "Yield not to temptation,
>   For yielding is sin;
> Each victory will help you
>   Some other to win;
> Fight manfully onward,
>   Dark passions subdue;
> Look ever to Jesus,
>   He'll carry you through.
>
> To him that o'ercometh
>   God giveth a crown;
> Through faith we shall conquer,
>   Though often cast down;
> He who is our Saviour
>   Our strength will renew;
> Look ever to Jesus,
>   He'll carry you through."

—H. R. Palmer.

"**For the Lord Himself shall descend from heaven with a shout, with the voice of the archangel, and with the trump of God: and the dead in Christ shall rise first: then we which are alive and remain shall be caught up together with them in the clouds, to meet the Lord in the air: and so shall we ever be with the Lord. Wherefore comfort one another with these words**"

—**1 Thess. 4: 16-18.**

IN these verses the Holy Spirit tells us what will transpire when the Lord returns for His own, to fulfil the promise made in the upper room, "I will come again, and receive you unto Myself." It tells of His personal bodily descent from heaven, of the resurrection of the dead in Christ and the rapture of the living who will be caught up without passing through death to meet the Lord in the air. This glorious event may take place at any moment. No prophecy awaits fulfilment ere it can take place. It should be our constant expectation and comfort.

"Quite suddenly—it may at the turning of a lane,
Where I stand to watch a skylark soar from out the swelling grain,
That the trump of God shall thrill me, with its call so loud and clear,
And I'm called away to meet Him, whom of all I hold most dear.

Quite suddenly—it may be in His house I bend my knee,
When the Kingly voice, long-hoped-for, comes at last to summon me,
And the fellowship of earth-life that has seemed so passing sweet,
Proves nothing but the shadow of our meeting round His feet.

Quite suddenly—it may be as I tread the busy street,
Strong to endure life's stress and strain, its every call to meet,
That through the roar of traffic, a trumpet, silvery clear,
Shall stir my startled senses and proclaim His coming near.

Quite suddenly—it may be as I lie in dreamless sleep,
God's gift to many a sorrowing heart, with no more tears to weep,
That a call shall break my slumber and a Voice sound in my ear;
'Rise up, My love, and come away! Behold, the Bridegroom's here!'"

"We are bound to thank God always for you, brethren, as it is meet, because that your faith groweth exceedingly, and the charity of every one of you all toward each other aboundeth"—2 Thess. 1: 3.

A GROWING faith tells that one is going on with God and learning to depend upon His Word because of having proven the truth of its promises. Faith is confidence, and confidence is increased as we see the Lord working in accordance with His revealed will, for the blessing of those who walk in obedience to His precepts. When growing faith and abounding love go hand in hand there is true spiritual development. Unbelief dishonors God and lack of love is a reproach upon the Name of Him who prayed for His own, "that they all may be one." The better we know God our Father the more we shall love all the household of faith. To profess to love Him while cold to His children is but hypocrisy.

"We ask not, Lord, for sight: increase our faith,
Unquestioning alike in life or death.
No earthly joys can give to restless hearts
The joy and peace that trust in Thee imparts.

Beyond this earth-bound vista human sight
Could not endure to see heav'n's unveil'd light,
Or read the future, mercifully seal'd,
And day by day in Thy good time reveal'd.

—W. A. Rice.

"But we are bound to give thanks always to God for you, brethren beloved of the Lord, because God hath from the beginning chosen you to salvation through sanctification of the Spirit and belief of the truth: whereunto He called you by our gospel, to the obtaining of the glory of our Lord Jesus Christ"—2 Thess. 2: 13, 14.

NOTICE the order here. Believers were chosen by God from the beginning. He foreknew all who would form part of the Church, the Body and Bride of His Son. In bringing them to the knowledge of salvation He wrought upon their hearts by His Holy Spirit, thus separating them from the godless world around. As a result of the Spirit's working they were led to believe the truth—"the word is the truth of the gospel"—and now they can look forward in faith to the coming glory into which they shall enter at our Lord's return. How every heart should go out to God in thanksgiving, when such grace is known!

"I am not told to labor,
    To put away my sin;
So foolish, weak, and helpless,
    I never could begin.
But blessed truth—I know it!
    Though ruined by the fall,
Christ for my soul hath suffered,
    Yes, Christ has done it all.

And if I now would seek Him,—
    In love He sought for me,
When far from Him I wandered
    In sin and misery;
He oped my ears and gave me
    To listen to His call;
He sought me and He found me—
    Yes, Christ has done it all."

—Eversfield.

"Now the Lord of peace Himself give you peace always by all means. The Lord be with you all"—2 Thess. 2: 16.

PEACE is more than joy, and is far deeper than happiness. It is that restful sense that all is well which comes from confiding in the Word of God. Christ Jesus is called "the Lord of Peace." He is the only Man who ever walked through this world in perfect peace at all times—until in Gethsemane He faced the judgment He was to bear when taking the sinner's place upon the cross. As a result of that work peace has been made between God and the needy sinner, a peace which is entered into by faith alone. But there is not only peace with God which has to do with the sin-question which has been settled forever. Daily the peace of God is poured into the heart that learns to commit all to Him in prayer.

"There is a calm—the calm of sins forgiven—
　Through knowing sin on Christ by God was laid;
Through looking to and resting on His merit,
　And knowing that our debt He fully paid.

And there's a calm about the unknown future;
　The earthly road; the fuller life above;
And things unknown—here, and in life's hereafter—
　Vex not the soul who knows that God is Love."

—J. Danson Smith.

"This is a faithful saying and worthy of all acceptation that Christ Jesus came into the world to save sinners, of whom I am chief"—1 Tim. 1: 15.

NONE can be too bad for Christ. If the enemy of our souls cannot keep us from coming to Christ by deceiving us with the notion that we are good enough for God without Him as our Saviour, he will often attempt to make us believe we are too bad ever to be saved. But this is impossible, for "Christ Jesus came into the world to save sinners; of whom," says Paul, "I am chief." Surely, since the chief of sinners has been saved already, none need despair. "Where sin abounded, grace did much more abound" (Rom. 5: 20). God delights to show His grace to the lowest and the vilest, as well as to those who have fancied themselves to be righteous, but have learned that all their righteousness is but as filthy rags in His sight (Isa. 64: 6).

There is no more successful way to influence others than by the personal testimony of one who has been saved himself. Mere theory, however true it may be, is not enough. There must be a personal experience of saving grace if one would be a winner of souls. To say, "Christ can save sinners," is blessedly true, but it is not enough. To be able to say, "He has saved me," gives power to the message and produces assurance in the hearts of the hearers as they realize that the speaker is bearing witness to what he has himself experienced.

> "Then dawned at last that day of dread,
>   When, desolate, yet undismayed,
> With wearied frame and thorn-crowned head
>   He, now forsaken and betrayed,
> Went up for me to Calvary;
> And, dying there in grief and shame,
> He saved me.—Blessed be His name!"

"For there is one God, and one mediator between God and men, the Man Christ Jesus; who gave Himself a ransom for all, to be testified in due time."—1 Tim. 2: 5, 6.

SINFUL man feels the need of One who can stand for him in the presence of God. The lack of the realization of this troubled Job. He cried, "There is no daysman who can lay his hand upon us both!" (Job 9:33). This is exactly what we find in Christ Jesus, the Mediator whom God has provided. He is both God and Man in one glorious Person, hence He can act for both the offended Majesty of heaven and the guilty sinner. On the cross He gave Himself a ransom. It was for this He came into the world. "Not," He says, "to be ministered unto, but to minister and to give His life a ransom for many." Yea, that ransom is available for all, both Jews and Gentiles, who will venture on Him in faith. If any are lost now, it is because they refuse to avail themselves of the provision made for their salvation. Through the One Mediator all may now draw nigh to God who desire to know His saving grace and power.

> "None like the ransomed host
>   That precious blood have known;
> Redemption gives faith's holy boast
>   To draw so near the throne."

"And without controversy great is the mystery of godliness: God was manifest in the flesh, justified in the Spirit, seen of angels, preached unto the Gentiles, believed on in the world, received up into glory."
—1 Tim. 3:16.

THE mysteries of the New Testament are sacred secrets, long unrevealed, but now made known by the Holy Spirit for the blessing and edification of the children of God. The mystery of godliness, or, as it might be rendered, the secret of piety, is Deity enshrined in Humanity in the Person of our Lord Jesus Christ. He has been manifested in flesh. This refers to His incarnation. Though He took the sinner's place He was justified in the Spirit. His justification proved Him to be the suited One to make expiation for iniquity. Then we have His manifestation. Angels beheld their Creator clothed in the body of the Babe of Bethlehem! His proclamation to the nations in accord with the purpose of God tells of redemption accomplished. By faith He is received, believed on in the world, acceptation; and last of all we have His glorification at the Father's right hand. He is the manifestation of the Father and the Center of all His counsels.

"Of the vast universe of bliss,
  The centre Thou, and Sun;
Th' eternal theme of praise is this,
  To Heaven's beloved One—
Worthy, O Lamb of God, art Thou
That ev'ry knee to Thee should bow."

"For every creature of God is good, and nothing to
be refused, if it be received with thanksgiving: for it is
sanctified by the word of God and prayer"
—1 Tim. 4: 4, 5.

BLESSED it is to recognize in the temporal, creative
mercies of each day, the evidences of a loving Father's
care. "He giveth us richly all things to enjoy." To receive
all as from His own hand, giving thanks in the name of
our Lord Jesus, is to honor the Giver in the use of His
gifts.

There is a golden mean between fleshly asceticism on the
one hand which discounts many of God's gifts and thus
throws discredit on Him who provides them, and carnal
self-indulgence on the other hand which uses the mercies
of God with no regard to Him from whom they come, and
in such a way as to turn even our blessings into curses.
We should ever recognize the bounty of our Father in these
things, and whether we eat or drink do all to His glory, our
hearts going out to Him in adoring gratitude.

"Ten thousand thousand precious gifts
My daily thanks employ;
Nor is the least a cheerful heart,
That tastes those gifts with joy.

Through every period of my life
Thy goodness I'll pursue;
And after death, in distant worlds,
The glorious theme renew.

Through all eternity, to Thee
A joyful song I'll raise;
For oh, eternity's too short
To utter all Thy praise!"

—Joseph Addison.

"Some men's sins are open beforehand, going before to judgment; and some men they follow after. Likewise also the good works of some are manifest beforehand; and they that are otherwise cannot be hid"—1 Tim. 5:24, 25.

THE unsaved do not always manifest all that they are in this life, but in the day of judgment every hidden thing will be brought to light and men will be judged every man according to his works. And so with the children of God. Some who are rich in good works go through life so quietly that few ever dream of all they are doing for the blessing of their fellows. These are the people who let not the right hand know what the left hand doeth. But at the judgment-seat of Christ all shall be made manifest, and there will be a rich reward for every thing that was done in accordance with the Word of God. No one is competent now to judge others. That is the prerogative of the Lord alone.

"Is your place a small place?
Tend it with care!—
He set you there.

Is your place a large place?
Guard it with care!—
He set you there.

What'er your place, it is
Not yours alone, but His
Who set you there."

—J. Oxenham.

"And the servant of the Lord must not strive; but be gentle unto all men, apt to teach, patient, in meekness instructing those that oppose themselves; if God peradventure will give them repentance to the acknowledging of the truth; and that they may recover themselves out of the snare of the devil, who are taken captive by him at his will"—2 Tim. 2: 24-26.

CHRIST was the perfect Servant who came not to do His own will, but the will of the Father who sent Him. He has left us an example that we should follow His steps. There is a new glory shed on the servant's path since He has trodden it before us. Those who now would follow Him as ministers of the Word are called to lowliness and patient grace. Self-assertiveness, emulation of others, striving for recognition by men rather than seeking the honor that comes from God only, are utterly foreign to the spirit of true service. Christ's representatives are to manifest the meekness and gentleness that were seen in all their perfection in Him whom they own as their Master in heaven.

"When I am dying, how glad I shall be
That the lamp of my life has been blazed out for Thee;
I shall not regret one thing that I gave,
Money or time, one sinner to save.
I shall not mind that the way has been rough,
That Thy blest feet led the way for me is enough.
When I am dying, how glad I shall be
That the lamp of my life has been blazed out for Thee."

"All Scripture is given by inspiration of God, and is profitable for doctrine, for reproof, for correction, and for instruction in righteousness, that the man of God may be perfect, throughly furnished unto all good works."
—2 Tim. 3: 16, 17.

IT is of all importance to realize that "to obey is better than sacrifice, and to hearken than the fat of rams" (1 Sam. 15: 22). The only way anyone can know what is acceptable to God is through careful and prayerful consideration of His written Word, which is the revelation of the living Word (Heb. 4: 12, 13). Forms and ceremonies, no matter how impressive, doctrines and traditions, no matter how venerable, are all to be refused if contrary to the mind of the Lord as set forth in the Bible. The supreme test is "What saith the Scripture?" Where the Word speaks, it should be ours to obey. Where Scripture is silent, we may well be silent, too. But a merely mental acceptance of Bible doctrines will not do for God. There must be heart subjection to His truth. When Christ is received by faith, and His Word becomes the rule of our lives, we shall be enabled to glorify God in all our ways (Isa. 59: 21).

"How precious is the Book divine,
  By inspiration giv'n!
Bright as a lamp its doctrines shine,
  To guide our souls to heav'n.

Its light, descending from above,
  Our gloomy world to cheer,
Displays a Saviour's boundless love,
  And brings His glories near.

It shows to man His wand'ring ways,
  And where His feet have trod;
And brings to view the matchless grace
  Of a forgiving God.

This lamp thro' all the dreary night
  Of life shall guide our way,
Till we behold the clearer light
  Of an eternal day."

      —John Fawcett.

"For I am now ready to be offered, and the time of my departure is at hand. I have fought a good fight, I have finished my course, I have kept the faith: henceforth there is laid up for me a crown of righteousness, which the Lord, the righteous judge, shall give me at that day: and not to me only, but unto all them also that love His appearing"—2 Tim. 4: 6-8.

WHAT a word to come from a dungeon death-cell. Bereft of all that ordinary men consider necessary to make life worth-while, Paul the prisoner of Jesus Christ was able to rejoice in the Lord as he looked back over all the way he had come, and looked onward to the glad hour when he should lay his armor down at the Redeemer's feet and receive from His hand the crown of righteousness, that blessed award which is reserved for all who love His appearing. The apostle's wish, expressed some years before (Acts 20: 24), that he might finish his course with joy, had been gloriously fulfilled. He had fought in the good conflict for truth and righteousness. He had kept the faith and now he anticipated his home-call with joyful confidence. To him Christ was all and Christ was enough!

"Ask those who now their palm of victory wave,
 Conquerors through Him, who died the lost to save,
 If now they murmur at their former lot,
 Or wish they had escaped one mournful spot?
 No, you would hear each grateful pilgrim tell,
 That vale of grief was blessing's richest well:
 The pools of trouble, filled with heavenly rain,
 Turned into myrtles every thorn of pain."

—J. G. Deck.

"For the grace of God that bringeth salvation hath appeared to all men, teaching us that, denying ungodliness and worldly lusts, we should live soberly, righteously, and godly, in this present world; looking for that blessed hope, and the glorious appearing of the great God and our Saviour Jesus Christ; who gave Himself for us, that He might redeem us from all iniquity, and purify unto Himself a peculiar people, zealous of good works"
—Titus 2: 11-14.

THE same grace that saves becomes our instructor after we know Christ. In this school we learn important lessons of the unprofitableness of the flesh, and need to turn away from all carnality and worldliness that Christ may be glorified in our lives. To spur us on to earnest endeavor the blessed hope of the Lord's return is put before us. When we behold His face we shall never regret one thing we have suffered for His sake nor think His demands upon us have been too great. Viewed in the light of that cross where He gave Himself for us, our most devoted service seems trivial indeed, and the least we can offer as an expression of our love for the One to whom we owe so much.

"Perhaps today! Then, much-tried saint,
Look up, nor let thy spirit faint;
The stretching road thine eyes may see
May never be traversed by thee—
One moment's space, and then above,
To find thyself in cloudless love!

Perhaps today, afflicted life,
Thou shalt be taken from the strife;
From all that hatred to thy word
Which comes as thou dost please thy Lord!
And then, ah then, how small the pain
Compared with all thou then shalt gain."

—J. Danson Smith.

"Put them in mind to be subject to principalities and powers, to obey magistrates, to be ready to every good work, to speak evil of no man, to be no brawlers, but gentle, shewing all meekness unto all men"
—Titus 3: 1,2.

THE things that are highly esteemed among men are often thoroughly opposed to the mind of God (Luke 16: 15). It is the ambitious, energetic man, who presses to the front, striving to excel his fellows, who has the admiration of men of the world, who suppose that present gain is the great thing to be desired. But Jesus taught us that it is the meek who inherit the earth (Matt. 5: 5). The "terrible meek," one has called them, who are content to be passed over and to be unnoticed by men, but to whom the approval of the Lord means more than all else; these are they who overcome the world by faith (1 John 5: 4). They can afford to relinquish present advantage, for they know they shall find a sure reward at the judgment-seat of Christ.

There is no room for earthly pomp or worldly glory in the circle of Christ's followers. To seek for personal advancement and to endeavor to lord it over one's brethren is thoroughly contrary to the spirit of Him who became Servant of all, though He created the universe. The spirit of a Diotrephes (3 John 9) is far removed from the spirit of Christ and should be avoided by all of His servants, but that of an Epaphroditus (Phil. 2: 25-29) is a worthy example which all may well emulate.

"O worldly pomp and glory,
    Your charms are spread in vain!
I've heard a sweeter story;
    I've found a truer gain.

Where Christ a place prepareth,
    There is my loved abode;
There shall I gaze on Jesus;
    There shall I dwell with God."

"**If thou count me therefore a partner, receive him as myself. If he hath wronged thee, or oweth thee ought, put that on mine account; I Paul have written it with mine own hand, I will repay it: albeit I do not say to thee how thou owest unto me even thine own self besides**"—Philemon 17-19.

WE have a lovely gospel medallion in this short letter to Philemon. A poor thieving runaway slave, Onesimus, who had been saved through contact with the Apostle Paul in prison, was going back to his master and this letter was to be his passport to favor. Paul undertook to stand surety for all the wrong done, even as Jesus has made Himself responsible for our sins and iniquities. Then Paul requested that Philemon receive Onesimus as if he were the apostle himself. He was to be accepted according to his master's estimate of Paul. In this we see how all believers, though once lost sinners, have now been accepted in the Beloved and are treated by the Father according to His thoughts of His own Son.

> "No condemnation now I dread;
>   Jesus, and all in Him, is mine!
> Alive in Him, my living Head,
>   And clothed in righteousness divine,
> Bold I approach the eternal throne,
> And claim the crown, through Christ my own."

"God, who at sundry times and in divers manners spake in time past unto the fathers by the prophets, hath in these last days spoken unto us by His Son, whom He hath appointed heir of all things, by whom also He made the worlds; who being the brightness of His glory, and the express image of His person, and upholding all things by the word of His power, when He had by Himself purged our sins, sat down on the right hand of the Majesty on high"—Heb. 1: 1-3.

HAVE you ever wished you understood God better? Have you wondered just how He viewed many things that you are faced with in this scene of testing? Then all you need to do is to get better acquainted with the Lord Jesus, for in Him God is perfectly told out. He is the effulgence of His glory; the exact expression of His character. So He could say, "He that hath seen Me hath seen the Father." He is God's last word to man. In times past His revelations were fragmentary through inspired prophets. Now He has come out to us in the Person of His Son, His Heir and the Creator of the Ages. This One has made purification for sins, and He has taken His place as Man on the Father's right hand. In Him we see God.

> "Lamb of God, our souls adore Thee,
>   While upon Thy face we gaze!
> There the Father's love and glory
>   Shine in all their brightest rays.
> Thy almighty pow'r and wisdom
>   All creation's works proclaim,
> Heaven and earth alike confess Thee,
>   As the ever-great I AM.
>
> Lamb of God, Thou now art seated
>   High upon Thy Father's throne,
> All Thy gracious work completed,
>   All Thy mighty vict'ry won.
> Ev'ry knee in heaven is bending
>   To the Lamb for sinners slain;
> Ev'ry voice and heart is swelling,
>   'Worthy is the Lamb to reign.' "

—J. G. Deck.

"For in that He Himself hath suffered being tempted, He is able to succour them that are tempted"
—Heb. 2:18.

THE perfection of Christ's humanity was demonstrated by His temptation as it could not have been manifested in any other way. Adam, the first, was tested in a garden of beauty surrounded by every blessing, and he fell by yielding to the tempter's voice. Adam, the second, was tried in a wilderness among the wild beasts, with all nature apparently arrayed against Him, yet He stood like a rock —invulnerable and impeccable—because He was God manifest in flesh. His temptation was like exposing the gold to the acid test—not to find out if it is a precious metal, but to prove that it is really gold and not base metal gilded. Yet the temptation was very real to Jesus. "He . . . suffered being tempted" (Heb. 2:18). To be brought into such close contact with sin was so revolting it caused Him keenest suffering, because of the purity of His human nature, undefiled by Adamic corruption. We suffer as we resist temptation and so cease from sin (1 Pet. 4:1). In this we may see the contrast between ourselves and Him. But having thus been exposed to all that has wrought such havoc in our frail humanity, He, our ever faithful High Priest, is touched with the feeling of our infirmities and stands ready to render help in every hour of need. We are not left to fight our battles alone. He lives to be our victory.

> "With joy we meditate the grace
>   Of God's High-Priest above;
> His heart is filled with tenderness,
>   His very name is Love.
>
> Touched with a sympathy within,
>   He knows our feeble frame;
> He knows what sorest trials mean,
>   For He has felt the same.   —Isaac Watts.

"We have not an high priest which cannot be touched with the feeling of our infirmities; but was in all points tempted like as we are, yet without sin"—Heb. 4: 15.

THE temptation of Jesus was not to see whether He would fail. It was rather to prove that He would not. The temptation by Satan but made evident the holiness and strength of the Second Man in contrast to the weakness and failure of the first.

In considering the temptation, it is important to remember that Jesus did not cease to be God when He became Man. He is God and Man in one glorious person. This the temptation was designed to make evident. He could ever say, "The prince of this world cometh, and hath nothing in Me" (John 14: 30). There was no traitor within as there is in us. He was ever the sinless One, as Satan himself proved when he retired, defeated from the conflict.

An old Welsh collier, who taught a Bible class, gave his young men full liberty to discuss all Biblical problems, but often cautioned them with the advice, "Whatever else ye do, lads, keep the character of God clear." So in considering the holy and mysterious theme of our Lord's temptation we may well bear his words in mind, and refer them to the blessed Saviour. Be sure to keep the character of Jesus clear. If He were not the sinless, unblemished Lamb of God, He would have needed a Deliverer Himself and could not have saved us (2 Cor. 5: 21).

"Christ at God's right hand unwearied
   By our tale of shame and sin,
Day by day, and hour by hour,
   Welcoming each wanderer in;
On His heart amidst the glory,
   Bearing all our grief and care;
Every burden, ere we feel it,
   Weighed and measured in His prayer."

"Let us therefore come boldly unto the throne of grace, that we may obtain mercy, and find grace to help in time of need"—Heb. 4: 16.

ABUNDANT provision has been made to meet all our needs, temporal or spiritual, and we are invited to come with boldness to the throne where our great High Priest sits exalted, to make known our requests, not only (nor even primarily) for ourselves alone, but for others in whom we are interested. We little realize the power of earnest believing prayer. God delights to give in answer to our supplications many blessings which we shall miss if we neglect thus to call upon Him. He has chosen to meet our needs in this way because of the sanctifying influence of the hour of prayer upon our own souls and because of the proofs He can thus give that we have to do with a personal God who cares for us and loves to minister to us.

"There is a place where thou canst touch the eyes
    Of blinded men to instant, perfect sight;
There is a place where thou canst say, 'Arise!'
    To dying captives, bound in chains of night;
There is a place where thou canst reach the store
    Of hoarded gold and free it for the Lord;
There is a place—upon some distant shore—
    Where thou canst send the worker or the Word.
There is a place where Heaven's resistless power
    Responsive moves to thine insistent plea;
There is a place—a silent, trusting hour—
    Where God Himself descends and fights for thee.
Where is that blessed place—dost thou ask 'Where?'
    O soul, it is the secret place of prayer."

—Adelaide A. Pollard.

"For God is not unrighteous to forget your work and labor of love, which ye have shewed toward His name, in that ye have ministered to the saints, and do minister"
—Heb. 6: 10.

WHILE works of mercy and care for others are not a procuring cause of salvation, they do manifest the activity of the new nature when carried out in and for the Name of our Lord Jesus Christ. He went about doing good, and in this as in all else He has left us an example that we should follow in His steps. Unselfish service for His glory is an acceptable sacrifice well-pleasing in His sight.

"There are loyal hearts, there are spirits brave,
  There are souls that are pure and true;
Then give to the world the best you have,
  And the best will come back to you.
Give love, and love to your life will flow,
  A strength in your utmost need;
Have faith, and a score of hearts will show
  Their faith in your word and deed."

—Madeline S. Bridges.

"In that He saith, A new covenant, He hath made the first old. Now that which decayeth and waxeth old is ready to vanish away"—Heb. 8: 13.

THE old covenant was the testing of man, through the nation that God had selected from all others as the recipient of His special favor. Their failure proved the incorrigibility of all mankind (Rom. 3: 19). Now all are alike shown to be under sin. Hence, there can be no salvation for any apart from the direct operation of God's Spirit upon the heart of man, acting in sovereign grace. This is the blessing of the new covenant. God is now the Worker —not man. He is the only contracting party. He gives freely, to all who are willing to receive, the riches of His mercy in Christ Jesus. He imparts divine life to the believer, and with this life is linked a new and a divine nature which delights in that which pleases God.

"Rest, my soul, the work is done,
Done by God's almighty Son;
This to faith is now so clear,
There's no place for torturing fear.

Not through works of weary toil,
Comes the sunshine of God's smile;
Won by Christ, if found in Him,
Brightly falls the glorious beam.

With belief in Jesus blest,
We are ent'ring into rest;
He who full salvation brought,
In us all our works hath wrought."

—Mary Bowley.

"For if the blood of bulls and of goats, and the ashes of an heifer sprinkling the unclean, sanctifieth to the purifying of the flesh: how much more shall the blood of Christ, who through the eternal Spirit offered Himself without spot to God, purge your conscience from dead works to serve the living God"—Heb. 9: 13, 14.

THE law knew nothing of a purged conscience. The sacrifices of the Levitical economy were designed to ease the conscience but they could not purify it. Every sin required a new offering, for there was not intrinsic value in the blood of beasts to actually settle the sin-question. Outwardly there was purification, fitting one to enter the earthly sanctuary. Inwardly there was no cleansing such as is ours now in virtue of the precious blood of Christ shed for us upon the cross. Dead works are those performed by dead sinners—from these, as from evil works, the conscience needs to be purged. The blood of Christ alone can avail for this. That blood is sprinkled on the mercy-seat. The veil is rent, and man may now draw nigh to God in full assurance of faith.

"The veil is rent:—our souls draw near
    Unto a throne of grace;
The merits of the Lord appear,
    They fill the holy place.

His precious blood has spoken there,
    Before and on the throne:
And His own wounds in heaven declare,
    Th' atoning work is done.

'Tis finished!—here our souls have rest,
    His work can never fail:
By Him, our Sacrifice and Priest,
    We pass within the veil."

—J. G. Deck

DECEMBER 1

"But this Man, after He had offered one sacrifice for sins for ever, sat down on the right hand of God; from henceforth expecting till His enemies be made His footstool. For by one offering He hath perfected for ever them that are sanctified"—Heb. 10: 12-14.

THERE is no mention of a chair, or seat of any kind, for the priests in the sanctuary of old. Their work was never done, but they were constantly occupied presenting the many sacrifices offered all day long. But when our Lord Jesus had offered His own all-sufficient Sacrifice, never to be repeated, He sat down, in token that His work was done. In virtue of that propitiatory sacrifice all who are set apart to God, through faith in Him, are perfected forever. In view of this how blasphemous is the claim of the Romish priest that in the celebration of the Mass he offers a "continual unbloody sacrifice for the sins of the living and the dead." This is to ignore the perfection of Christ's one offering on the cross which has satisfied every claim of God's righteous throne and never needs to be repeated.

"Settled forever! Sin's tremendous claim!
Glory to Jesus! Blessed be His Name!
No part-way measures doth His grace provide,
Finished the work when Christ the Saviour died."

"But without faith it is impossible to please Him: for
he that cometh to God must believe that He is, and that
He is a rewarder of them that diligently seek Him"

—Heb. 11: 6.

FAITH is taking God at His Word. He who comes to
God in prayer must believe in Him, and must have confidence that He hears the petitions addressed to Him and
rewards those who earnestly seek His face. Skeptics may
sneer when Christians speak of a God who answers prayer,
but all the unbelievers' sneers cannot invalidate the blessed
facts which those have known who trust in Him. He
chooses to give in answer to prayer what He will not give
apart from prayer, in order that His people may have a
positive testimony that they have to do with the living
personal God. Faith honors Him, and He delights to bless
those who thus acknowledge His loving care for His own.
He honors them who glorify His Name.

"Giver of every gift,
    Thy choice is best;
All-wise Eternal Love—
    In Thee I rest.

Yielding to Thy wise hand,
    Safe in Thy will—
Not asking why or how,
    Let me be still.

Looking on things unseen,
    By faith I see
Glory exceeding great
    Worketh for me."

—Grace E. Troy.

"By faith Moses, when he was come to years, refused to be called the son of Pharaoh's daughter, choosing rather to suffer affliction with the people of God, than to enjoy the pleasures of sin for a season; esteeming the reproach of Christ greater riches than the treasures in Egypt: for he had respect unto the recompence of the reward"—Heb. 11: 24-26.

LITTLE did Moses know when he made his choice what amazing consequences hung upon it. He acted for God as his conscience dictated and God gave him far more than he surrendered for His name's sake. He renounced the throne of Egypt where Providence seemed to have placed him, in order to become a desert wanderer. But God made him the leader of a mighty people and gave him such privileges as none had ever known before him. Nor was it a forced choice on Moses' part. That expression "choosing rather" tells how he weighed one thing against another and counted the cost; only to decide for a present path of affliction with the Lord's favor rather than a comparatively easy life in disobedience to the divine voice; may it be ours to emulate him in all this.

"Farewell to this world's fleeting joys
   Our home is not below;
There was no home for Jesus here,
   And 'tis to Him we go.

To Him in yonder home of love,
   Where He has gone before:
The home He changed for Calvary's cross,
   Where all our sins He bore.

He bore our sins, that we might be
   His partners on the throne!
The throne He'll shortly share with those
   For whom He did atone."

—W. Trotter.

"But ye are come unto mount Sion, and unto the city of the living God, the heavenly Jerusalem, and to an innumerable company of angels, to the general assembly and church of the firstborn, which are written in heaven, and to God the Judge of all, and to the spirits of just men made perfect, and to Jesus the mediator of the new covenant, and to the blood of sprinkling, that speaketh better things than that of Abel"—Heb. 12: 22-24.

IN the latter part of this twelfth chapter of Hebrews we have law and grace set before us in vivid contrast as two distinct circles, one centering in Sinai, "the mount that burned with fire," and the other in Mt. Sion, which speaks of God's sovereign grace. Linked with this is the heavenly instead of the earthly Jerusalem, the city of the living God, where dwell an innumerable company, a full gathering of angel hosts, whose delight it is to serve those who belong to the assembly of first-born ones—all heirs of God and joint-heirs with Christ. There God Himself dwells, and there, too, Old Testament saints, now perfected through the work of Jesus, the Mediator of the covenant of grace, whose blood speaks not of vengeance but of mercy. This is the circle of God's favor to which all believers have come.

"The gates of heaven are opened wide,
    At His name all the angels bow;
The Son of Man who was crucified
    Is the King of Glory now.
We love to look up and behold Him there,
    The Lamb for His chosen slain;
And soon shall His saints all His glories share,
    With their Head and their Lord shall reign.

And now we draw near to the throne of grace,
    For His blood and the Priest are there;
And we joyfully seek God's holy face,
    With our censer of praise and prayer.
The burning mount and the mystic veil,
    With our terrors and guilt, are gone;
Our conscience has peace that can never fail,
    'Tis the Lamb on high on the throne."   —J. G. Deck.

DECEMBER 5

"Now the God of peace, that brought again from the dead our Lord Jesus, that great shepherd of the sheep, through the blood of the everlasting covenant, make you perfect in every good work to do His will, working in you that which is wellpleasing in His sight, through Jesus Christ; to whom be glory for ever and ever. Amen"
—Heb. 13: 20, 21.

THE Shepherd character of our Lord Jesus suggests loving care for His own. He is Jehovah Ra'ah, "the Lord my Shepherd," who takes complete charge of His sheep, and undertakes to provide for their every need. He has given us many pictures of His shepherd-service. As the Good Shepherd He died for us (John 10). As the Great Shepherd He is ever watching over us. As the Chief Shepherd He will gather us all about Himself when He comes again (1 Pet. 5). His promises are sufficient for every difficulty. Yet in times of stress we forget them all, and worry and fret as though we had to meet all our problems ourselves, instead of trusting to His love and wisdom to undertake for us. He has promised to see us through.

When the Lord has the supreme place in our hearts—not simply the first place—we will not fear all the power of the enemy, for He to whom we have committed the keeping of our souls is more than a match for all that may rise up against us. In all His ways with us He is the unfailing Shepherd, having our best interests in view. His glory and our blessing are indissolubly linked together.

"O Thou great all-gracious Shepherd,
  Shedding for us Thy life's blood,
Unto shame and death delivered,
  All to bring us nigh to God!
Now our willing hearts adore Thee,
  Now we taste Thy dying love.
While by faith we come before Thee—
  Faith which lifts our souls above."
—Mrs. Wellesley.

DECEMBER 6

"Every good gift and every perfect gift is from above, and cometh down from the Father of lights, with whom is no variableness, neither shadow of turning"
—Jas. 1: 17.

GOD is the Source of all good. Every blessing we enjoy comes down from Him. He is the Father of lights, who is unchanging in His love and grace, and in whose dealings with us there is "no shadow cast by turning," as the last part of this verse has been translated. His face is ever toward us. In all circumstances we may go to Him in perfect confidence assured of a welcome and a sympathetic ear as we tell Him all that troubles and perplexes us. It is His joy to undertake for us. He delights to lavish His good and perfect gifts upon His obedient children. If He seems to withhold it is because He has some better thing for us, or because we need to judge something His holy eye has detected in our ways which makes it necessary to treat us with reserve. When all is right He gives without stint in answer to our prayer.

"God answers prayer! the prayer of His dear children!
   He's sure to answer, if they keep His will.
He answers prayer! Yes—prayer concerning all things!
   There's nothing over-much for His great skill.

God answers prayer! Not always when we ask Him;
   It may seem good to Him that we should wait.
How long? Ah well, 'tis only He that knoweth;
   But sure, His answer will not be too late.

God answers prayer! Not always as we want Him;
   He does not always answer prayer with 'Yes';
He sometimes answers 'No!' because He loves us,
   And sees the thing we ask could never bless.

And God would have us learn to sweetly trust Him—
   To chiefly want His will—not our request;
To know, whate'er may be His settled answer,
   His will is highest, holiest, and best."

                          —J. Danson Smith.

"What doth it profit, my brethren, though a man say
he hath faith, and have not works? Can faith save him?"
—James 2: 14.

EMPTY profession is of no profit. He who speaks of faith
in Christ is responsible to manifest it by his renewed
life. In Romans we learn that we are justified before God
by faith alone, without the deeds of the law. In James 2
we are taught that we are justified before men by works,
works that are the fruit of a living faith, which is manifest
to all. Abraham was justified by faith when he believed
God, who spoke of the coming Seed, our Lord Jesus Christ.
He was justified by works, when in obedience to the voice
of God he offered up his son Isaac upon the altar. Thus
faith wrought with his works and by works was faith made
perfect. So it must be with us. If we believe God we will
yield obedience to His Word, and so our faith will be
manifested.

"All that we are, and all we have,
    Shall be forever Thine;
And all a cheerful heart could give,
    Our willing hands resign.

And could we yet make some reserve,
    And duty did not call,
We love Thee, Lord, with such a love,
    That we would give Thee all."

"But the wisdom that is from above is first pure, then peaceable, gentle, and easy to be intreated, full of mercy and good fruits, without partiality, and without hypocrisy. And the fruit of righteousness is sown in peace of them that make peace"—James 3: 17, 18.

EARTHLY principles will not do as guidance for heavenly men. The wisdom of this world is utterly opposed to the wisdom of heaven which is manifested in all perfection in the Lord Jesus Christ. Human philosophies center in self. The wisdom that comes from above centers in God as revealed in His Son. It is first pure. The pure in heart see Him who is its Source. Impurity blinds the eyes of the heart. "Peaceable, gentle, and easy to be entreated," this divine wisdom is "full of mercy and good fruits." It knows nothing of respect of persons and it is downright honest. There is no two-facedness in it. He who walks according to wisdom walks in righteousness and his life is a testimony to its power to produce all manner of goodness and peace.

> "Wisdom! Jehovah's first delight,
>   The everlasting Son!
> Before the first of all His works,
>   Creation, was begun;
>
> Before the skies and wat'ry clouds,
>   Before the solid land,
> Before the fields, before the floods,
>   Thou wast at His right hand!
>
> When He adorned the arch of heaven,
>   And built it, Thou wast there,
> To order where the sun should rise,
>   And marshal ev'ry star."

—Lady Campbell.

DECEMBER 9

"But He giveth more grace. Wherefore He saith, God resisteth the proud, but giveth grace unto the humble"
—**James 4: 6.**

THERE is nothing to which the human heart is so prone as pride, and that in creatures who have nothing to be proud of! Our manifold sins might well humble us to the lowest depths, yet this evil root persists even in the most devoted saints. A Paul needed a thorn in the flesh lest he be exalted above measure. A David insisted on numbering the people for his own glory. A Peter became lifted up when blessed with special spiritual illumination. By this sin fell Lucifer and carried the third of the angels of heaven with him, and its virus has infected the whole human race since Eve was seduced by it in Eden. Christ is our supreme example of humility. His was a meekness that never exalted Himself but sought alone the glory of God. May we follow His steps in this as in all else.

"He would have us wear beautiful garments—
    Those which we may have through grace—
The robe of a tranquil spirit,
    The calm of a peaceful face;

The charm of a gentle manner,
    The lustre of heaven-lit eyes;
That robe of such sacred splendour,
    The spirit of sacrifice.

These, these, and yet other garments,
    All beautiful, bright and fair,
We may, by His grace, adorn us,
    And unto His glory wear."

—J. Danson Smith.

"Elias was a man subject to like passions as we are, and he prayed earnestly that it might not rain: and it rained not on the earth by the space of three years and six months. And he prayed again, and the heaven gave rain, and the earth brought forth her fruit"
—**James 5:17, 18.**

SALUTARY indeed are the lessons which the Holy Spirit has presented for us in the record of Elijah's life. In some respects, the greatest of all the prophets since Moses, until the advent of John the Baptist (Matt. 11:11), he appears suddenly upon the page of Scripture with his amazing declaration to King Ahab, "As the Lord . . . liveth, before whom I stand, there shall not be dew nor rain these years, but according to my word" (1 Kings 17:1). This was the result of, and confidence derived from, a life of prayer. He had learned how to prevail with God, and his prayer shut and opened the heavens in accordance with the will of the Lord. This is most suggestive. Prayer does not cause God to change His mind. But the man who lives in fellowship with Him is guided to pray in accordance with His will. Such prayer is sure to be answered (1 John 5:14, 15).

We must learn to know God in secret if we would be courageous for Him in public. The three years that Elijah spent in retirement, proving God's faithfulness by the brook Cherith and in the widow's home at Zarephath, gave him a background of practical experience that was of inestimable value when he had to face Ahab and the prophets of Baal. It was because he knew God that he dared to witness for Him so boldly.

"Service is good when He asks it,
  Labor is right in its place,
 But there is one thing better—
  Looking up into His face." —Annie Johnson Flint.

"Wherein ye greatly rejoice, though now for a season, if need be, ye are in heaviness through manifold temptations: that the trial of your faith, being much more precious than of gold that perisheth, though it be tried with fire, might be found unto praise and honor and glory at the appearing of Jesus Christ: whom having not seen, ye love; in whom, though now ye see Him not, yet believing, ye rejoice with joy unspeakable and full of glory"—1 Pet. 1: 6-8.

PONDER that expression, "if need be," and it will throw a flood of light upon God's ways with His people which often seem perplexing and even inexplicable. For every trial which His children are called upon to endure He has a reason which will some day be made plain. He is working out some purpose in our lives of such a nature that it can only be wrought in the crucible of suffering. When all earth's experiences are passed and,

"We stand with Christ in glory,
Looking o'er life's finished story,"

we shall see that there was a need's be for every painful testing and every heart-break we have been called upon to endure. We shall praise Him then for every hard thing as well as for all the joyous experiences, which we have known as we trod the pilgrim way.

"Helpless tonight, and weary,
    Almost too tired to speak,
Now on Faith's downy pillow
    I lay my fevered cheek;
I have a mighty Keeper,
    Loving, compassionate, true;
Only to rest, He tells me,
    Is all I need to do.

Pain has been my companion
    Many a night and day;
Often the gathering shadows
    Seemed to surround my way;
Yet I press on, not fearing,
    My Father knoweth best;
I leave to Him the planning,
    And on Faith's pillow rest."

"**Dearly beloved, I beseech you as strangers and pilgrims, abstain from fleshly lusts, which war against the soul; having your conversation honest among the Gentiles: that, whereas they speak against you as evil-doers, they may by your good works, which they shall behold, glorify God in the day of visitation**"—1 Pet. 2: 11, 12.

THERE are questions which cannot be properly decided if only the rights and liberty of the individual men are emphasized. Each one is part of the group with which his lot is cast. He is responsible for the effect of his actions upon those who are thus linked with him. No one lives or dies, we are told, to himself (Rom. 14: 7). It is therefore gross selfishness to insist on my own liberty if that liberty tends to the detriment and enslavement of my fellows. To claim the right to certain indulgences which affect others adversely is to act contrary to the law of love, which should govern all who profess to follow Christ, and also all who would lay any claim to altruistic living. My evil example may be the ruin of weaker ones who become emboldened to do as they see me do. My selfish indulgence may make me a liability rather than an asset to society. I am most inconsistent if I claim to be a follower of Him who "pleased not Himself" (Rom. 15: 3), while I am insisting on my personal liberty in matters that are stumbling-blocks to my fellow-men, whether Christians or not (1 Cor. 8: 9). While I cannot be governed by the consciences of other people, nevertheless I am called upon to avoid all that would unnecessarily stumble others (1 Cor. 8: 12, 13).

"A pilgrim in a hurried world and flurried,
 Where hearts are aching and where hopes are buried;
 Where bowers of ease and pleasures are enticing,
 Where heedless lives the good are sacrificing;
 A world of turmoil and of strife and danger—
 Yes, I'm a pilgrim here, and I'm a stranger."
　　　　　　　　　　　　　—Wm. M. Runyon.

"For it is better, if the will of God be so, that ye suffer for well doing, than for evil doing. For Christ also hath once suffered for sins, the Just for the unjust, that He might bring us to God, being put to death in the flesh, but quickened by the Spirit"—1 Pet. 3: 17, 18.

MY sins put Christ on the cross, where He suffered in fullest measure, bearing all my desert that I might be freed forever from the suffering I had so richly earned. Now I am called to live and witness for Him in the world that rejected Him and to which I once belonged, but out of which He has saved me. Henceforth, holiness and righteousness are to characterize me. I am now to walk as He walked—in fellowship with Him, as enabled by the power of the Holy Spirit. Nothing else is worthy of one who has been so gloriously redeemed at so great a cost. Nor need I expect worldlings to understand. I know I must encounter their enmity and scorn. But I can conquer through Christ.

"Be patient then; with such a rest in view,
  Blessed are they who Zion's ways pursue;
  Each faithful pilgrim, through His mighty grace,
  Shall there appear, and see Him face to face.
  He is their Sun, to chase the shades of night,
  And cheer their souls with heavenly warmth and light.
  'God of all grace,' each day's march He'll bestow
  The suited grace for all they meet below;
  The 'God of glory,' when their journey's done,
  Will crown with glory what His grace begun,
  Rich in the treasures of eternal love,
  His watchful goodness all His people prove;
  Through time's short day, and through eternity,
  'Blest is the man, O Lord, who trusts in Thee.' "

—J. G. Deck.

DECEMBER 14

"Casting all your care upon Him; for He careth for you"—1 Peter 5: 7.

DO we really believe this? If we do why are we so often fretted by the carking cares of daily life? God our Father has promised that all shall work for good for those who love Him, and we have the assurance that He feels for us in all our trials. He bids us bring everything to Him in prayer, and He has promised to undertake according to each day's need. Let us heed the exhortation to cast (or, literally, roll) our burdens on the Lord. He is all sufficient and "He careth" for us. His love and compassion go out to all His suffering saints. We wrong our own souls when we do not refer all our griefs to Him.

> "Through every moment of the day,
>   Whate'er may meet thee on life's way,
>   This thought shall be thy strength and stay:
>   'He cares.'
>
> When shadows veil the fairest scene,
>   And pleasures fade that might have been,
>   On the unchanging Saviour lean:
>   'He cares.'
>
> He marks thy steps, He goes before,
>   From this time forth, for evermore;
>   Then from thy heart let praise outpour:
>   'He cares.' "

—F. Buckley.

"For we have not followed cunningly devised fables, when we made known unto you the power and coming of our Lord Jesus Christ, but were eyewitnesses of His majesty. For He received from God the Father honour and glory, when there came such a voice to Him from the excellent glory, This is My beloved Son, in whom I am well pleased"—2 Peter 1: 16, 17.

IT is in 2nd Peter 1, vers. 16 to 18, that we learn the true significance of the transfiguration. It was the coming Kingdom in miniature. Christ Himself appearing in glory was the center of that wondrous scene. In Moses we see pictured the state of those who pass through death, but will be raised in glorified bodies. Elijah pictures the living saints who will be changed and caught up to be with Christ at His coming. Then the three disciples in their natural bodies set forth the earthly saints who will enjoy the blessings of the kingdom in this world during the millennial reign of the Lord Jesus, when blessing will flow forth to all mankind from the exalted Saviour reigning in righteousness as King of kings and Lord of lords. All this confirmed the word of prophecy and made clearer to the disciples, in after days, what God has in store for His saints and the world at large when the hour of Christ's glory shall come.

"Nearly now the last stage trodden
          Of the desert way;
All behind us lies the darkness,
          All before—the day.
Wondrous day of glowing promise,
          Dimming all beside,
When the One who died to win us
          Comes to claim His Bride.

And while watching for His coming,
          Waiting here below,
He would have us in the desert
          Find the waters flow.
Streams of sweet and deep refreshment
          Gladdening all the throng,
Giving us, when gathered round Him,
          Blessing and a song."   —A. S. O.

"But there were false prophets also among the people, even as there shall be false teachers among you, who privily shall bring in damnable heresies, even denying the Lord that bought them, and bring upon themselves swift destruction"—2 Peter 2: 1.

THE conflict between truth and error has been going on ever since the effort of Satan, when he successfully misled our first parents in the garden of Eden with his subtle "Hath God said?" thus insinuating doubt and questioning into the mind of Eve. Toleration of false teachers in the Church of God is treachery to Christ. The false prophets in Israel were the bitter opponents of the revelation given through holy men who wrote and spoke as they were moved by the Spirit of God. The same is true today, except that the basis for all true testimony is now the completed volume of Holy Scripture, by which all teaching is to be tested. Against all false prophets we are to oppose the faith once for all delivered to the saints, as declared in the Epistle of Judge.

> "The Christ is in Court today;
>   The World and the Flesh deride Him,
> Mankind is jury and judge,
>   And the right of appeal is denied Him.
> Who are His witnesses? Whom will He call
> To answer for Him in the judgment hall?
>
> The Christ is in Court today,
>   The World and the Flesh will try Him,
> Mankind is jury and judge,
>   Shall those He hath loved deny Him?
> We are His witnesses, ours is the call,
> To speak for our Lord in the judgment hall."

—Annie Johnson Flint.

"If we confess our sins, He is faithful and just to forgive us our sins and to cleanse us from all unrighteousness"—1 John 1: 9.

GOD will never refuse the plea of a seeking soul who comes to Him, in the name of Jesus, confessing his sins and suing for pardon. The sin question has been settled to the divine satisfaction in the work of the cross. Now God can be just and the Justifier of all who believe in Jesus (Rom. 3: 26). To look for something meritorious in ourselves, to endeavor to propitiate God by fancied works of righteousness, is to fail to recognize our utterly lost condition. To acknowledge our sins and to trust His grace gives the happy consciousness of iniquity purged and guilt removed. God's word to Israel of old was, "Only acknowledge thine iniquity" (Jer. 3: 13). This is ever the gateway to blessing (Hos. 5: 15) because "the Lord hath laid on Him the iniquity of us all" (Isa. 53: 6).

> "Wash'd in Thy blood, from all my guilt made clean
> In Thee, my Righteousness, alone I'm seen:
> Thy home my home—Thy God and Father mine!
> Dead to the world—my life is hid with Thine;
> Its highest honors fade before my view—
> Its pleasures, I can trample on them too."

"Again, a new commandment I write unto you, which thing is true in Him and in you: because the darkness is past, and the true light now shineth. He that saith he is in the light, and hateth his brother, is in darkness even until now"—1 John 2: 8, 9.

THE new commandment tests man as nothing else could.

It reveals the latent evil hidden in every heart. Christ's standard and ideals are too high for men of this world, who have their portion in this life. Only he who has received eternal life, through faith in the Lord Jesus (John 5: 24) will be able to exemplify the love here inculcated. He who gave the command to love one another proved His own love for mankind by dying for our sins. When He dwells in the heart by faith, His love is reproduced in others. It is not something that has to be pumped up as from an almost dry well. It is an ever-rising, overflowing stream coming from the renewed hearts of those who have been born of God and whose very nature it is to love as He loved us (1 John 4: 7).

> "Love of God, so pure and changeless;
>   Blood of Christ, so rich and free;
> Grace of God, so strong and boundless,—
>   Magnify it all to me,
>   Even me."

"Behold, what manner of love the Father hath bestowed upon us, that we should be called the sons of God: therefore the world knoweth us not, because it knew Him not. Beloved, now are we the sons of God, and it doth not yet appear what we shall be: but we know that, when He shall appear, we shall be like Him; for we shall see him as He is. And every man that hath this hope in Him purifieth himself, even as He is pure"
—1 John 3: 1-3.

THE manner of love spoken of in these verses, is something more than the general love of John 3:16. There it is love for the world. Here it is the Father's love for His own children. He will never be fully satisfied until He has them all in the glory with Himself. Now, they are living in a scene where failure and temptations abound. When the Lord Jesus returns again they will be translated into His blessed image—to be like Him physically and spiritually and to dwell with Him and all the redeemed in the Father's house forevermore. With such an expectation controlling us we should become more and more like Him as the days of waiting go by.

"Now with this hope to cheer us,
    And with the Spirit's seal,
That all our sins are pardoned,
    By Him whose stripes did heal,
As strangers and as pilgrims,
    No place on earth we own,
But wait and watch as children,
    Until our Lord shall come."

"He that loveth not knoweth not God; for God is love. In this was manifested the love of God toward us, because that God sent His only begotten Son into the world, that we might live through Him"—1 John 4: 8, 9.

THE practical evidence of the new birth is love for the children of God. He has manifested His perfect love toward us in the gift of His only-begotten Son. Now we manifest our love to Him by our care for and interest in His own. Christ was sent that He might give life to those who were dead in trespasses and sins. That life is divine and he who possesses it loves others because God has so loved him. The next verse tells us that Christ also came to be the propitiation for our sins. On the basis of this we are justified freely by His grace. When one is converted to God the two things are true. He is both regenerated and justified. The child of God stands before His Father as free from guilt as if he had never sinned at all. Such is the fulness of God's salvation which calls forth our adoring gratitude manifested in unselfish love.

"Though higher than the highest,
  Most mighty King Thou art,
Thy grace, and not Thy greatness,
  First touched my rebel heart.
Thy sword, it might have slain me;
  Thine arrows drunk my blood,
But 'twas Thy cross subdued me,
  And won my heart to God."

DECEMBER 21

"Look to yourselves, that we lose not those things which we have wrought, but that we receive a full reward"—2 John 8.

WE should be careful to distinguish between reward for service and salvation by grace. All who trust in the Lord Jesus are saved, and this altogether apart from human merit. But all who profess to believe in Him are responsible to serve Him and to use whatever gift, ability, or means they have for His glory and to further His interests in this world. There are those who profess to be servants who are not even born of the Spirit. But God holds men accountable for what they know and profess. It is incumbent on all who believe His Word to serve whole-heartedly in view of the day when every one of us shall give an account. In that solemn hour no one will regret having been too much concerned about living for Him, but many will regret the hours spent in selfishness and folly which might have been used for His glory, and talents wasted or hidden away that if properly invested in the light of eternity would have earned Christ's "Well done." He will reward all that is in accordance with His Word (1 Cor. 3:13).

"A group of boys and girls may be
 My God-appointed task;
Help me to lead each one to Thee—
 What greater could I ask?
I ask no place of prominence
 Where all the world can see,
But in some needy corner, Lord,
 There let me work for Thee.
No task too great, no task too small,
 Sufficient is Thy grace;
The darkened heart, my mission field,
 My light, the Saviour's face."

DECEMBER 22

"I have no greater joy than to hear that my children walk in truth"—3 John 4.

TO walk in truth is to live in accordance with the mind of God as revealed in His inspired Word. In order to do this we need to know our Bibles; not only to have a casual knowledge of the great outstanding facts of Scripture, but to so feed upon the Word that we take it into our very being and thus are formed by the truth. This is practical sanctification and it is this that gives joy to the heart of God. For when we read such words as those quoted above we should think of them not simply as expressing the feelings of the inspired writer, the apostle John, but rather of the One who controlled His servant's pen and guided his thoughts. It is God our Father who finds such joy when His children, those who have been born from above, walk in obedience to His Word.

> "I heard His call, 'Come, follow!'
>   That was all.
>   My gold grew dim,
>   My soul went after Him,
>   I rose and followed:
>   That was all.
>   Who would not follow
>   If they heard Him call?"
>
> —William R. Newell.

"Beloved, follow not that which is evil, but that which is good. He that doeth good is of God: but he that doeth evil hath not seen God"—3 John 11.

THE epistles of John insist upon reality. Mere lip-profession that is not backed by love and righteousness cannot suit the Holy One with whom we have to do. God is good. Both words come from the same root. Those who are born of God will be characterized by goodness. He who takes the name of being Christ's but who practises evil, is a stranger to God. Whatever his profession he has not seen Him. In this short letter the aged apostle denounces scathingly those who would make the Name of Christ to be dishonored by an apparent jealousy for the principles of church fellowship while acting unkindly and unrighteously toward others who came in the same blessed Name. We show how much we love the Lord by the way we treat our brethren.

> "That I am so beloved of God,
> Must form my manners on the road
> I journey, till I meet Thy Son,
> My Lord, who all Thy love has shown;
> Must separate from world and sin,
> From every path that He's not in;
> Incite to toil, bring victory;
> The only power, Thou lovest me!"

"But ye, beloved, building up yourselves on your most holy faith, praying in the Holy Ghost, keep yourselves in the love of God, looking for the mercy of our Lord Jesus Christ unto eternal life"—Jude 20, 21.

FOUR important things are here stressed, which go to make up a consistent Christian life.

First: Building up on the faith. That is finding edification in the careful study of the Word of God. "The faith" here is not faith by which we lay hold of God, but the faith which He has revealed for our acceptance; that faith once for all made known to His saints.

Second: Praying in the Holy Spirit. We can only do this as we walk in the Spirit. Then He who dwells within us indites our prayers and guides us as we present our supplications.

Third: We are to keep ourselves in the conscious enjoyment of God's unchanging love. This is the place of blessing and of spiritual repose.

And, fourth, the hope of our Lord's return must be kept before our souls as the beacon light which leads us on to the Father's house. The Word, prayer, divine love, and the blessed hope sustain all along the way.

> "Everlasting arms uphold thee,
>   Love divine surrounds thy way;
> Why should earthly fears distress thee
>   Or thy trembling heart dismay?"

DECEMBER 25

CHRISTMAS DAY

"And she brought forth her first-born son, and wrapped Him in swaddling clothes, and laid Him in a manger; because there was no room for them in the inn"—Luke 2:7.

EACH recurring Christmastide gives occasion to emphasize anew the wonderful story of the love of God that led Him to send His only begotten Son into the world, that we might live through Him. Christianity rests on three great pillars, the Incarnation, the Crucifixion, and the Resurrection of the Lord Jesus Christ. Incarnation alone could not redeem sinful men. But apart from the Incarnation there could be no propitiatory sacrifice that would avail to put away sin. God became Man in order to die. We cannot, therefore, make too much of the mystery of the union of the human and the divine in Him who was both Son of God and Son of Mary. In Him we have the Daysman for whom the patriarch Job longed, one who can lay His hand upon both God and man (Job 9:33) because He combines the natures of both in one glorious Person. Bethlehem, Calvary, and the empty tomb, all alike should stir our souls and draw our hearts out to God in wonder, love, and praise.

PEACE ON EARTH

"Here Peace alighted once,
　But could not find a home,
To Him who brought it, earth
　Could give no room.

Him and His peace man would not have,
　And in this Child of peace
Man saw no heavenly excellence,
　No grace, no comeliness.

Peace in that cradle lay,
　The Prince of Peace was there;
The fulness of His Peace
　He brought with man to share."

　　　　　　　—Horatius Bonar.

"Unto Him that loved us, and washed us from our sins in His own blood, and hath made us kings and priests unto God and His Father; to Him be glory and dominion for ever and ever. Amen"—Rev. 1: 5, 6.

IT is really the present tense in the first clause—"Him that loveth us." His love is unchanging and eternal. Saints in glory will take up this pæan of praise which will sound through endless ages through the courts of heaven. But they who sing up there must learn to use the words down here. For God has willed that those who believe on His Son should know that their sins have been washed away by the precious blood of Christ and they are even now constituted a Kingdom of priests unto God, His Father, and ours, to be adoring worshippers for all eternity.

"When the heavenly hosts shall gather,
    And the heavenly courts shall ring
With the rapture of the ransomed
    And the new song they shall sing,
Though they come from every nation,
    Every kindred, every race,
None can ever learn that music
    Till he knows God's pardoning grace.

All those vast eternities to come
    Will never be too long
To tell the endless story
    And to sing the endless song:—
'Unto Him who loved us,'
    And who 'loosed us from our sin'—
We shall finish it in heaven,
    But 'tis here the words begin."

—Annie J. Flint.

"I am He that liveth, and was dead; and, behold, I am alive for evermore, Amen; and have the keys of hell and of death"—Rev. 1:18.

THE gospel of Christ (Rom. 1: 16) is the glad tidings of the death and resurrection of the Lord Jesus (1 Cor. 15: 1-4). To believe and proclaim the death of the Son of God is not enough. It is the resurrection that tells us that His propitiation has been accepted, and God can now justify all who put their trust in Him (Rom. 4: 25). Everywhere that the apostles of the new dispensation went, they preached Jesus and the resurrection (Acts 2:24, 32; 17: 18, 31). This implies nothing short of the actual resurrection of the physical body of our Saviour. And so-called spiritual resurrection is a denial of the truth revealed in Scripture. If Christ be not risen, our hope is vain, we are yet in our sins (1 Cor. 15: 17). But thanks be unto God, He has indeed been raised from the dead and become the first-fruits of them that slept.

The witnesses to the resurrection, as given in the Gospels and in 1 Corinthians 15, were many and varied. There was no possibility that so many people were deceived or suffered from hallucinations. Moreover, the change that came over the apostles and the new spirit of boldness infused into the members of the early Church all bore witness to the certainty of the disciples that their Lord had overcome the power of death.

> "If through the darksome vale of death
> We pass, we need not fear;
> Our Saviour, He who gave us breath,
> Brings light and triumph there.
>
> Surely Thy sweet and wondrous love
> Shall measure all our days;
> Thy Father's house, our home above,
> Where dwells eternal praise."

DECEMBER 28

"He that hath an ear, let him hear what the Spirit saith unto the churches"—Rev. 2: 7.

WE need to distinguish between the Church, the Body of Christ, which includes all God's children in this dispensation of grace, and local churches of God, which are responsible groups of believers meeting together for Christian fellowship and testimony. Christ Himself builds what He calls "My Church" (Matt. 16: 18). The building of local churches is committed in large measure to His servants (1 Cor. 3: 10). As Paul went from place to place, when people were saved he was used of God to gather them out from the world and into the fellowship of the churches, or assemblies of God, where they would be nurtured and edified and could maintain a testimony in their respective communities to His saving grace. These churches were directly responsible to Christ Himself, while they maintained communion with each other as representatives of the one glorified Head. (See 1 Thess. 2: 14). In the beginning there was but the one great circle of Christian fellowship. Unhappily, divisions almost innumerable have come in, through human infirmity, throughout the Christian centuries, but the closer the churches keep to the divine pattern laid down in the Book of Acts and in the apostolic letters to the churches, the more we shall have the Lord's approval and blessing. We cannot undo the mistakes of the past, but we can cleave to the Lord and the Word of His grace, and so be kept from much that is unscriptural and divisive.

> "Head of the Church triumphant,
>   We joyfully adore Thee!
> Till Thou appear, Thy members here
>   Would sing like those in glory.
> We lift our hearts and voices,
>   In blest anticipation,
> And cry aloud, and give to God
>   The praise of our salvation."   —C. Wesley.

"And they sung a new song, saying, Thou art worthy to take the book, and to open the seals thereof: for Thou was slain, and hast redeemed us to God by Thy blood out of every kindred, and tongue, and people, and nation; and hast made us unto our God kings and priests: and we shall reign on the earth"—Rev. 5: 9, 10.

THE new song is the song of redemption. When God created the universe it was so beautiful that the morning stars sang together and all the sons of God shouted for joy. But that old song was soon hushed when sin came in to mar God's wondrous handiwork. Now that His own Son has wrought our redemption, we who once were lost ruined sinners take up the new song and praise the Lamb once slain, who has washed us from our sins and made us to be a royal priesthood. Angels cannot sing this song. They have never known what it is to be thus redeemed. It is for the sons of God by faith to lift their voices in this glorious anthem which will fill the courts of heaven with melody. But only those who learn it here can sing it there.

"For Him who washed us in His blood
Let us our sweetest songs prepare;
He sought us wand'ring far from God,
And now preserves us by His care.

One string there is of sweetest tone,
Reserved for sinners saved by grace;
'Tis sacred to one class alone,
And touched by one peculiar race.

Though angels may with rapture see
How mercy flows in Jesu's blood,
It is not theirs to prove, as we,
The cleansing virtue of this flood."

—Thos. Kelly.

"Blessed and holy is he that hath part in the first resurrection: on such the second death hath no power, but they shall be priests of God and of Christ, and shall reign with Him a thousand years"—Rev. 20: 6.

SCRIPTURE distinguishes between the resurrection of life, which will take place at our Saviour's pre-millennial advent (1 Thess. 4: 13-17), and the resurrection of judgment, which takes place at the end of time, just prior to the setting up of the Great White Throne where all the wicked must give account before God. They who participate in the resurrection of the just have been saved by grace. Theirs will be a blessed part indeed. They are holy, set apart to God in Christ. The second death, which is final separation from God, they shall never know, for they are possessors of eternal life received by faith in Christ. For eternity they will have access as priests into the immediate presence of God and the Lamb, and when the Kingdom is set up over this earth they will reign with Him for whom once they suffered in the time of His rejection. Best of all, they shall see and be with Him forever.

"Ah, this is what I'm wanting—
  His lovely face to see,
And, I'm not afraid to say it,
  I know He's wanting me!
He gave His life a ransom
  To make me all His own,
And He can't forget His promise
  To me, His purchased one."

—J. G. Deck.

"He which testifieth these things saith, Surely I come quickly, Amen. Even so, come, Lord Jesus. The grace of our Lord Jesus Christ be with you all. Amen"
—Rev. 22: 20, 21.

THE last word ever heard from heaven, the last that shall be heard until the Lord's return, was the promise of His coming again, and that quickly. God does not count time as we do. Not two days (2 Pet. 3: 8), according to His reckoning, have elapsed since Jesus went away. Soon He will fulfil His promise. The heart that loves Him looks for Him, and responds, "Even so. Come!" Till then there is grace for every moment of the way. The Old Testament closed with "a curse" because of man's failure to keep God's holy law. The New Testament closes with "grace," because of Calvary. On the basis of the work there accomplished grace flows out in abundant fulness.

"Grace is flowing like a river,
    Millions there have been supplied;
Still it flows as fresh as ever,
    From the Saviour's wounded side;
None need perish,
    All may live since Christ has died."